Magic
Power of the
Goddess

INITIATION, WORSHIP, AND RITUAL IN THE WESTERN MYSTERY TRADITION

GARETH KNIGHT

Destiny Books
Rochester, Vermont

Destiny Books
One Park Street
Rochester, Vermont 05767
www.DestinyBooks.com

Destiny Books is a division of Inner Traditions International

Originally published in 1985 by Destiny Books and Aquarian Press in Wellingborough,
    England, under the title *The Rose Cross and the Goddess*
Revised edition published in 1993 by Destiny Books under the title *Evoking the Goddess*
Third edition published in 2008 by Destiny Books under the title *Magic and the Power
    of the Goddess*

Library of Congress Cataloging-in-Publication Data
Knight, Gareth.
  Magic and the power of the goddess : initiation, worship, and ritual in the Western
mystery tradition / Gareth Knight.—3rd ed.
    p. cm.
  Rev. ed. of: Evoking the goddess.
  Includes index.
  ISBN 978-1-59477-235-1 (pbk.)
  1. Goddess religion. 2. Magic. 3. Ritual. 4. Femininity—Religious aspects. I. Knight,
Gareth. Evoking the goddess. II. Title.
  BL473.5.K593 2008
  202'.114—dc22

                                                                      2008006641

Printed and bound in the United States by Lake Book Manufacturing

10 9 8 7 6 5 4 3 2 1

Text design by Priscilla Baker
This book was typeset in Garamond, with Phaistos and Agenda used as display typefaces.

To send correspondence to the author of this book, mail a first-class letter to the author
c/o Inner Traditions • Bear & Company, One Park Street, Rochester, VT 05767, and we
will forward the communication.

To the memory of Margaret Lumley-Brown,
who knew about these ancient things

Contents

Preface to the New Edition   vii

PART ONE

The Magic Circle Maze Dance   1

Working the Circle   2

PART TWO

Evocation of the Goddess and the Planetary Being   47

Evoking the Goddess   48

BRANCH ONE   Ancient Heroes and the Goddess Powers   51

BRANCH TWO   The Mysteries of Isis Revealed   79

BRANCH THREE   The Trembling of the Veil of Orthodoxy   106

BRANCH FOUR   The Lady Venus in Rosicrucian Alchemy   132

BRANCH FIVE   The Faery Queen and the Magic Mountain   165

BRANCH SIX   The Initiation of the Earth   190

Index   205

Preface to the New Edition

A great challenge faces us today. It involves nothing less than realizing the importance of the well-being of Earth. It is commonly expressed in terms of climate change through global warming, but this is simply the most materialistic way of looking at it—entirely from the outside of things.

This is perhaps to be expected as the first hint of this crisis came about through the insight of environmental scientist James Lovelock some thirty years ago. Lovelock began to see the planet as a great super-organism that chemically and atmospherically regulates itself to stay fit to bear life. That is to say, for all intents and purposes, that it behaves like a conscious living being.

He did not go so far as to call Earth the Planetary Being, but, being a scientist, he felt obliged to put it in terms of "a biocybernetic universal system tendency." It was left to the novelist William Golding to come up with the more appropriate name of Gaia, after the Greek Earth goddess, while a broadening awareness of all that this might imply came about largely through realizations of the neo-pagan movement.

Throughout the ages there has always been recognition of the divine feminine principle in all its guises, but the intellectual climate of the past three hundred years or so, a time during which science and technology have made such strides, has tended to drive it underground. Yet now is surely the time to restore the balance, to begin to rediscover the true nature of things and our relationship to them. Then we might find ourselves ready to enter a new age rather than worry about our survival in it!

To do this we need to see ourselves as allies of creation rather than its rulers, to choose to work in harmony with the natural world, to realize Earth as a great elemental being who provides the means for the generation of life within and upon herself. The forms of life that she nurtures and nourishes include us as members of the human race. They also include the animal kingdom in all its forms. Those who have a certain degree of psychic and elemental awareness, along with the breadth of vision to take in the fact, may realize that this also includes the so-called faery realm.

There are many things we can do to bring about this reconnection, including seeing beyond the surface nature of things, whether trees, grass, water, plants, or even stones—indeed all of nature at large. And if we continue far enough and deeply enough in this endeavor we may begin to communicate with the spirit of the forms of consciousness that we are observing. Then we may cease to be mere observers and manipulators and join forces with the natural world about us.

Only when we begin to understand the true nature of things and our relationship to them will we be liberated from the narrow limits we have imposed upon ourselves. With clouded eyes and narrow minds, conditioned by paternalistic and materialistic attitudes, we are much like prisoners, blinkered and bound, confined within stonewalls. Fortunately, even if this is unhappily true for the majority of the human race there remains hope that there are enough of us who have realized that there is something more to life than surface appearances. To this effect it is not enough to confine our interest to purely intellectual speculation or wishful thinking. We must not only believe in the reality of the Goddess and the forms of elemental and spiritual consciousness that make up her being but come to understand and cooperate with them by means of an active and enlightened imagination.

By creative work with traditional imagery we can awaken and realign our energies. We can free up our preconditioned energy patterns and begin to work within a framework of realization that holds great potential for inner transformation. For we literally imagine ourselves into being what we are. And it is only through a culture of organized greed, indifference to others, and materialistic blindness that we have imagined ourselves into a kind of antagonistic isolation, feeling alone and unloved in an alien universe.

Yet if we use our imagination to open ourselves to the hidden glory that surrounds us we can discover this sense of isolation to be an illusion. We may then discover a world of many beings and many realities. And by working with the light and power within Earth, which throughout history has typically been revealed in feminine imagery, we may open ourselves to energies inherent in this Otherworld through which remarkable changes can occur. Not only to ourselves but also to the world at large.

In this book I hope I have given you various indicators to light your way.

GARETH KNIGHT
FEBRUARY 2008

PART ONE

The Magic Circle
Maze Dance

Working the Circle

Our current delusion is an over-valuation of the intellect—that which has given us so much and enabled us to transform the conditions of our being by technological wonders. Our inherent psychic unbalance is projected into our environment, that "vegetable glass" in which we see our own image. Half the world starves; the rich get richer, the poor get poorer. Technology, which does so much to release many from labor and fear and pain, does nothing for others except allow them to be exploited the more efficiently. And this applies not only to humankind itself but to the other units of consciousness that share the planet, in animal and elemental forms. Some of these have been exploited shamelessly—the rape of nature with the machine. To others, the subtle elemental worlds, we do not even acknowledge existence, let alone rights.

Whatever we do to lesser forms of life we do to ourselves. As the balance is tipped more and more askew with technological contrivance, so does the day approach more quickly when our own brain children, the chemical, mechanical, electronic, subatomic monsters, will destroy us.

This dangerous imbalance is part of a wider phenomenon—the repression of the feminine principle. Fortunately, a realization of this state of affairs is beginning to dawn, with consequent movements of the mind to achieve a rebalancing.

Feminism and green politics are a part of this movement and a neo-pagan revival of religious sensibilities—of celebration of the wonders of the earth and the cycles of nature under the provenance of the divine feminine, so long neglected.

And the Goddess, the divine feminine, is no mere product of a trendy fashion in New Age philosophy. She has been with us from the beginning of time, as we will discover in some of the paths of her expression that we intend to follow in this book.

What we shall do first is provide a manual of techniques (magical and mystical, active and contemplative) for contacting the Goddess within, which will also serve as a basis for living harmoniously within the Earth. This is the function of Part One, which is largely concerned with the dynamics of the sacred or magic circle.

Then having set up our sacred or magic circle, our mandala, our holy place of evocation within the heart and home, we will explore how the Goddess has been revealed down the ages by those who sought to evoke her. And we shall find that these ways are equally valid for us today. In the ancient world, the threefold Goddess was a very powerful force, far beyond the subjective sphere of archetypes described by modern psychology.

In Part Two we shall show the kind of reality these feminine powers represent—not only by drawing upon source material from different periods over the past two thousand years, but by active imaginative workings that will demonstrate their ongoing reality and relevance today.

THE MAGIC CIRCLE

The magic circle is a model of all that exists in creation. It therefore holds within itself both masculine and feminine principles. In one sense the center is the masculine, the central point, the seed; and the circumference is the feminine, the womb within which all that occurs can be brought to fruition and new life.

And insofar as all creation is an expression of form, and it is through form that spiritual potential may be expressed, the whole circle is very much an expression of the feminine. This is revealed by the way it responds to the cycles of nature, be they the nodal points of the day and night or the seasons of the year. The dynamics of the circle are the aspects of the Goddess.

The fourfold cycle of the seasons and of the daystar is one way in which the magic circle may be expressed. That is: spring, summer, autumn, and winter; dawn, noon, dusk, and midnight. These stations also mark the elemental cross of air, fire, water, and earth at the cardinal points of east, south, west and north. The symbols of these directional stations of inner space are the sword, the wand, the cup, and the disk.

From these four-fold properties do all the other attributes derive that form a model of the human soul and also of the universe. In the star stations of the zodiac, of what we might call the girdle of the Goddess, are further symbols of this cross. They are the cherubic emblems of the vision of Ezekiel, later adopted for those of the Evangelists: the man, the lion, the eagle, and the bull, or Aquarius, Leo, Scorpio, Taurus— the "fixed" signs of the zodiac.

Thus a great compendium of symbolic lore can be made that may form the alphabet for a mode of communication between the planes. From *use* of the symbolism a language is made. But mark the word *use*. It must be made a part of the fabric of our being, by *meditating* upon the stations. This includes, but is much more than, intellectual speculation. We must read the magic circle with the feet as well as with the heart and mind.

Exercise: Treading the Primal Spiral

Mark out a circle upon the ground. This act is a parallel of the original act of creation. It involves the determination of a center and of a certain area of influence. Take a rod or peg to hold a stable center, and from it extend a cord. Start, if you wish, with the cord wrapped around the rod as if drawing spun thread from around a spindle. Proceed in a clockwise direction, to unwind the cord. You will find that you mark or trace out a spiral dance that culminates in a circle. Thus are you reenacting the primal creation. Do this many times, fully aware of the significance of what you are doing. You will thus learn much of your spiritual origin and the principles of creation.

In treading the primal spiral, you may come to an awareness of primal masculine and feminine principles. As central seed shooting forth into manifestation forms the cosmos from apparent nothingness, one is asserting the masculine. As one unwinds the spiral path, one is partaking increasingly of the feminine until at the outermost circle the feminine principle, as polar complement to the central point, is fully displayed.

(Incidentally, this feminine involvement with the serpentine way is one expression of cosmic truth behind the much misunderstood story of Adam and Eve and the Serpent. In other ancient creation myths, such as the Orphic, the feminine principle danced with a snake to create the worlds. It is a strange twist of Judaic interpretation of the ancient myths that caused this story to be interpreted in terms of original sin and female moral inferiority.)

Merely to read these exercises is to miss the experience. You cannot travel to market without stirring your feet and you cannot experience reality from the pages of a book. The pages can guide your feet, but it is up to your feet to follow. Intellectual curiosity and impatience are no substitute for patient plodding behind the plough. Mental speculation grows and hoes no cabbages. You learn only by doing. If you are not prepared to learn by doing you may as well close this book. It has nothing to teach you.

The first time you perform this exercise you will be preoccupied by physical problems and distractions. With persistence you will find that you can perform it with your inner faculties to the fore, aware of the profound significance of the pattern which you trace.

Early humans spent much time and effort carving spiral symbols on rock. You will be much rewarded by spending a fraction of that time and effort carving these same symbols upon your consciousness.

You may find it worthwhile to construct a pillar as a central pole for your circumambulations—or you might utilize a tree.

These props will not be necessary after a time. You can later tread the spiral and circular path from an imaginary point. It is no less real because it is fixed only in the imagination. But initial grounding in the physical is important.

The dynamics of scale are also important. Scale is a measure of human proportion. Let the circle so traced be relative to the human form—some six to twelve feet in diameter. Certainly no less, probably not much larger. Tracing out spirals and circles on a sheet of paper is no substitute. Expression by treading is of prime importance. How far do you really expect to travel if you will not take the first step? When you have constructed a circle in this manner you can leave the implements of construction behind. Then, whenever you wish, you can tread the spiral and circle dance in meditation, fully aware of the profound significance of the patterns that you tread.

Meditation: The Cosmic Dance

Develop your meditation in the following manner. Spend some time in silent contemplation at the center point, being aware of nothing but stillness and darkness. You are a being of latency, a babe of the abyss, floating in a dark warm sea of interstellar space. You see nothing about you, but you have a warm sense that somehow you are cared for, that you are not entirely alone, but are watched over, encompassed by a love you do not see or comprehend. You are drifting in a warm sea of love, in the cosmic womb of the Goddess, the divine feminine principle.

Then as if from a center in another dimension than your own, become aware of an approaching being—a being of great light and vastness—that approaches singing and in spiral dance—like a great Catherine wheel, or nebula. A great being who by his coming through your space attracts little beings like yourself. You see that there are already others about him in a great whirling spiral of light. You are caught up in a great positive love and attraction for this being who is like an elder brother to you, though an elder brother of vastly greater age and cosmic experience. Feel yourself caught up into his ambit and responding to his invitation to the dance.

At this point commence your own spiral movement outward from the center, and as you do so, be aware of being in the company of a host of others as yourself, all in the joyful train of this Great Being. As you move outward in your spiral be aware that you are proceeding through areas of space that are gradually denser—that there is a different quality of abstraction the further you approach the full extent of your circle, the ring-pass-not of your system. Feel that you are proceeding through different bands of possible life expression until you reach the outer ring of the extent of the radius of your circle.

There continue to pace in a clockwise direction. Be aware that as you revolve, the host of other sparks of divine fire, with whom you are conjoined about the Great Entity, are gradually sorting themselves into concentric bands.

Be aware now of that Great Being of light and love and power being at the center of your circle, and of others like yourself in stately circular movement about him, at various radial distances, some moving more slowly, others more quickly, but all in stately order. See them as colored spheres, or other geometric shapes, and be aware that you are part of a great system of ordered being—like the popular model of a solar system of sun and planets, or of subatomic particles about a nucleus.

As a conclusion to this meditation you may stop, face inward and imagine at the center, in whatever form you choose to use, the presence of God, the center of your creation, the axis of your being. Form a loving rapport with that Being. Then turn and face the outer world across the circumference of your trodden circle and go about your daily duties.

Thus is the initial circle built up from which much else may follow. We are creating a two-dimensional spatial model of the inner universe, a model on one plane of a reality that extends into many dimensions.

Average people never dream of these realities. It is an ignorance that is sad and poignant in individual terms. They are like children who think they are orphans because they do not recognize their own birthright. It is also dangerous to the world at large when this limited view becomes the accepted "reality," and a godless humanity, cut off from its own roots, runs mad in spiritual darkness and blindness. When, like Oedipus it has killed its own parent and rendered itself blind.

To such, humanity seems confined on a planetary penal colony, cut off light years away from its nearest starry neighbors. In truth the universe is a loving and close family. Only loveless illusion makes it seem as it does to the scientific instruments of men: vast and lifeless. Man projects his own inner condition upon the "vegetable" or cosmic glass about him. We hope and pray that he melts with love the confines of his prison; that he will not allow it to remain and become his cosmic condemned cell; that mankind will choose love, and live.

THE CROSS OF THE ELEMENTS

Let us learn the stations of the circle situated at the cardinal points. They are modes of reality and as such they are creatures of the imagination. Yet so, indeed, far more than many realize, is the structure of the universe. This too is the projection of human imagination. Change the imagining and you change the world. The demonstration of this concept demands faith. And if demonstration is sought, then faith is insufficient. This is an instance of divine paradox upon which all fundamental reality is based.

We have already named the four cardinal points. Locate within your room the points of east and south and west and north. Align them with a compass if you will, although this is not of prime importance; we deal with inner directions beyond the confining illusions of space and time.

In general terms, however, if the configuration of your room seems generally to agree with it, it does no harm to consider East to be more or less the direction in which the sun rises. The other directions follow from this.

The following exercises should be performed slowly, with much imagination, and many times. Indeed, as this is done so will they cease to be exercises and become living experiences, as you develop the organs of perception that go beyond the limitation of physical sense.

Yet, all that follows is based upon sensual physical reality and this is of imperative importance. If you have not your ground base of physical experience then all is a shimmering mirage, the flickering of a lantern. Think well: the physical is the end result of spiritual forces. Therefore, to seek the source of those spiritual forces, the Ariadne's thread, to lead you through the psychic astral maze, must be anchored in the forms of earth. These physical forms are reflections of a spiritual reality. They are reflections of the ultimate truth beyond form. Look well into the mirror of nature to see the reflection of the spiritual stars.

Exercise: Becoming One with the Earth

No time is wasted in cultivating the world of sense and communing with nature: rising early to walk out and see the dawn; lying in the noonday sun; walking in contemplation at eventide; and going abroad at midnight, gazing at the moon and the starry sky. Listen to the birds, feel the breeze, smell the scents of nature, lean against the trees and feel their vitality and strength. Walk through the brooks, the dewy grass, the oozing mud, the sharp frost and driven snow, the drifting fallen leaves, the driving rain, the gentle drizzle. Learn the alphabet of nature. It is also the alphabet of the core of your being, by which you can learn to speak the language of God and the gods, of angels, elementals and justified human beings.

With this fund of experience, much of which you gathered as a child, learn to become like a child again, and experience with equal vividness the stations of your circle. This is the sacred dance of life.

INVOCATIONS OF THE QUARTERS

When practice and proficiency are gained, all the four quarters may be built in imagination at one session. To begin with, however, one quarter alone will be more than sufficient. When all quarters are, in course of time, built with some reality in the manner described, they should be worked with in a balanced fashion, rotating from one to another each day, or perhaps over a longer period of a week or, at most, a month. Remember that we are building a cross that is a model of the forces of life in which we live and move and have our being. In the course of time, when you are fully proficient, it can be realized and worked with as a balanced whole.

Invocation of the East

Go to the eastern point and face outward. Be aware of a darkened horizon across a wide plain. In the sky before you is a single light in the darkness of predawn, that of Venus, the morning star. Then see the sky gradually begin to lighten to a light turquoise green. And see a smaller light, just before the sun comes up, of its companion and herald Mercury, the messenger of the gods. Then the tip of the golden disk of the sun itself begins to rise above the horizon and all is slowly bathed in red and gold, and long dark purple shadows gradually give way to increasing light. At the same time be aware of "the voice of the day," the morning chorus of bird song welcoming another dawn. Realize too that it is springtime. See about you on the low bushes and the trees behind you the green buds bursting forth with new life and the spring flowers shooting up sharp shafts of green through the earth at your feet. And then be aware of a gentle but persistent breeze upon your cheeks—for this is the quarter that is dedicated to the air element. Be aware also, with the inner eye, of little winged beings with the appearance of nursery tale fairies, but which have an ancient lordliness that comes from experience since the beginnings of time. Finally, as the sun rises above the horizon, see standing before it a great stag, with branching antlers. If you count them they number twelve and each tine, as it reflects the early morning sunlight, seems to be afire with a point of incandescent light. Imagine you have a great sword before you. See and feel its jeweled, cross-formed hilt. Withdraw it from its scabbard. See its blade shine out brilliantly in the sun's light and with it salute the mighty stag, Cernunnos, and the beings of the dawn and spring. Replace the sword, and take a longbow from your back and an arrow from a quiver at your side. Fix the arrow into the string of the bow, take a long, strong pull, and try to shoot the arrow over the sun. Hear the arrow buzz through the air as it leaves you and feel the slap of the string and the whip of the untautened bow and be aware of the flying arrow, a brief gleam in the sunlight, and then a quivering dark line against the azure sky, before it disappears from sight, to fall you know not where, but in the direction of your aspiration.

Be aware also of two other great figures who build at the bidding of your mind's eye. One is a great-winged archangelic figure who towers over the whole scene before you, robed in blue and gold, the great Archangel Raphael, bearing a pilgrim's staff and a scrip or purse containing the elements of healing.

Also, larger than human stature, see the king and overlord of all the elementals of air, mighty Paralda. As you see him be aware of all the peoples of the element air whirling about in a great spiral of force that is as steady as a strong breeze, and be aware of air flowing through your whole body, cleansing and purifying, blowing all dust and cobwebs of stale thoughts, feelings, and conventions away.

Invocation of the South

Go to the southern point and face outward. There be aware of being bathed in the bright sunlight of noon, the warmth of the life-giving radiation of the daystar soaking through you. See the sun, a great incandescent disk with golden rays shooting forth from it in all directions. It may take up the whole of the sky rather like the Tarot trump of the Sun, a beaming face upon its disk in token of the fact that it is alive, a warm, sentient, and conscious being, that cherishes, nurtures, and loves you and all else upon the planets within its ambit, that circle it in adoration and love. You may see yourself as one of the naked children that dance within a ring in the sun's rays this side of the wall of form, with the high nodding heads of sunflowers beaming over you, reminders of the complete reliance upon the sun for birth, life and breathing by the world of animal life and vegetation. Or you may be aware of yourself as the variant of the Tarot trump that depicts a naked child upon a white horse, carrying a banner.

That banner is the glorification of life, and may have upon it either a simple heraldic device, a red cross on a pure white ground, or alternatively be richly sewn with embroidered flowers, animals, birds, and fish, a great tapestry of all created life under the sun. These various visions may be evoked either one after the other, or as alternatives on different occasions.

The horse may also appear before you as Epona, the great white mare of the hills. You may see her, perhaps in the form of one of the great white chalk hill figures carved by the Celts, or those who came after even to the present time. If so, be aware of the chalk figure, coming alive, and galloping over the green hills in the sunshine. In the bright sunlight that surrounds you be aware of points of diamond light—these are the consciousness of the beings of fire, like fireflies of the day, the salamanders, also called "will-o'-the-wisps." They are capable of giving great spiritual contacts, for they serve the great ones at all levels of being and they are forces of transmutation and transformation behind the fires of life. Now imagine that you have in your hand a long, stripped wand of hazel wood with a hollowed core through which powerful subtle forces play. Something of this may be seen in the raying points of starlight that shine from its endmost tip and can be felt in the almost animal warmth of the end that is grasped within your hand—a warmth that seems to stem from deeply banked furnace fires from within the depths of the Earth, and of the quality of the deep seated fire that is within the Sun. This is the planetary and solar kundalini, the serpent power, a reflection of which you carry within the core of your aura, in the equivalent of your spinal column. Make a sign in the air in the form of a five-pointed star, commencing at the topmost point and swing down right, up left, across, down left, and up to the top again. This is the symbol of man, solar spirit in balanced command of the four elements. Then see yourself standing foursquare facing the south, holding a great spear, its haft on the ground beside your foot and its flaming point, like shining bronze, above your head. Be aware of the great rod as a tool of control, to point and keep things at bay, or to handle virile forces, as a rod is used to stoke a furnace, or to fend off a violent creature. It may also be held two-handed as a weapon of defense, fending off blows but harming none, or being used as a means of exerting pressure or holding a door as with a bolt across a opening. Be aware of your rod as an organ of control.

Then see before you, building in the sky, the red and gold fiery figure of the Archangel Michael, also armed with a long and mighty spear with which he quelled the dragon. Not only the dragon of evil as the vulgar assume but the dragon force that is the virile power of all growing life, the fires of creativity, which create destruction if let run riot but which are the fire-springs of creativity and all manifest life when cooperated with and controlled. Then, associated with the Archangel, be aware of the great king and lord of the elementals of fire, the great fiery heat of the mighty Djinn, lord of all heat and warmth, whether of the animal warmth of the nest, the hearth fire, or the primal fire of the atom. Be aware too of the purifying radiations of heat and fire passing through you from his subjects, many of whom form a part of your being and keep your bodies alive.

Invocation of the West

Proceed to the western point and face outward. Be aware of the soft contemplative hush of eventide, and of being surrounded by the rich gold of autumn colors and of ripe fruits and nuts, and the gathered corn and all good things of harvest home. See yourself at the border of a still lake, upon which there is scarcely a movement, save for the odd fish rising to form an eddy of ripples, or the buzz of insect life about its surface. On the horizon before you the sun, a great dull gold disk, sinks toward the horizon in a soft glory of shades of crimson, and as you watch, it disappears below the ground of the purple mountains in the far west, on the other side of the lake, whence you can see far in the distance a winding path leading up to the heights. As the sun disappears, yet still signals its presence by the afterglow of glories in the cloudbanks of the western sky, you notice in the greening azure of the upper sky a few first faint stars, and shining predominantly amongst them, as herald of them all, the great lamp of Venus, the evening star. At the same time be aware of a last flicker of a point of light from Mercury, the messenger of the gods and attendant of the sun, following its master below the horizon. And then be aware of the mistress of the night sky, the crescent moon, with the evening star between its horns, like a pale lantern in the sky before you.

The darkening clouds of the western horizon almost appear to be like herds of lowing cattle, and you are aware of a great figure of a spotted cow, building over the lake before you. This is Mona, most ancient of sacred symbols.

Within your hands you find you hold a silver cup, and before you on the ground is a cauldron, simmering over a slow fire. Sweet savors are rising from it. You raise your cup toward the great beings of the west and you drink a toast to them that is almost a sacrament. Then you contemplate the rising vapors that ascend above your head in the still air from the cauldron of inspiration, that has images of nine goddesses cunningly worked about its rim. Be aware as you do so of the great archangelic figure of Gabriel, in blue and silver before you, bearing a great horn of annunciation, he who is bringer of tidings and visions. With him, in the lower parts of his aura may be discerned the great elemental lord of water, known as Nixsa. And as you become aware of him you also realize the presence of his creatures, beautiful nymphs and sirens rising from the depths of the lake, some like dolphins, others bearing pearls and sea treasures, and calling on conch horns, and you feel the purifying streams of water flowing through your being.

Invocation of the North

Now go to the northern point of the circle and face the north. Feel that you stand at midnight, in the crystal deeps of winter, looking at the night sky. It is the dark of the moon, or rather just past that point, for a thin sliver of the new moon is visible as a shining silver line that, as yet, casts little light, so that the stars in the sky shine out as brilliant gems of differing sizes and brilliancy, on a backcloth of deep indigo velvet, some flashing or sparkling in various colors or highlights. The scene before you is illuminated entirely by the starlight.

See trees and bushes before you in the landscape without their leaves, save for the evergreens, whose needlelike leaves glitter with frost in the starlight like tinsel on natural Christmas trees, with highlights and reflections from the starshine like glittering fairy lights.

Be aware of the Pole Star in the center of the northern sky before you, situated at the tail end of Ursa Minor, and, circulating about it, the northern constellations of Draco, Ursa Major, Cassiopeia, and the houselike form of the chair of Cepheus. Learn to become familiar with the patterns of the stars; they hold the ancient starry wisdom. Imagine that you hold in your hands a circular disk that is in fact a black mirror of polished stone, which reflects whatever part of the sky whose image you catch in its depths, and which also imparts to you intuitively the meaning of the patterns. Then be aware that you also have a shield that on the outside is of a similar substance and which shines forth your own particular sigil that expresses the innermost star of your being, while the inside of the shield is like a brightly polished silver mirror, that enables you to see yourself in the utter clarity of perceptive wisdom. Then see building before you in the landscape the figure of a great bear, Artor, standing and swaying, clasping a ragged staff—a great protector of his territory and of all of his kind. Be aware that you have the status of one of his bear-cubs, a privilege that in due course of growth in your stature will lead to your taking on similar responsibilities and powers as the bear.

A great archangelic figure also builds before you, that of Uriel or Auriel the giver of wisdom, seen dark against the sky, a shadowy beneficent presence who watches over neophytes. And with him see the elemental form of Ghob, the king of the gnomes, in the colors of Earth, that contain the olive, citrine and russet colors of a ripe apple. He is surrounded by his underground creatures, who can pass easily through solid objects and who are familiar with the mineral deeps of the earth and of the treasures and forces therein. Feel the steady warmth of the stability of earth that holds you in a fructifying steadiness as if you were a germinating seed supported in the dark bosom of the Earth.

BUILDING AN ELEMENTAL SHRINE

You have now formulated the cardinal points of a circled cross, the equal-armed cross of the elements, and if you so had a mind and the space that could be so dedicated, you might build an appropriate shrine at each of the four quarters, perhaps with a small altar containing appropriate symbolism; or also perhaps containing a seat wherein you could sit and commune with the appropriate forces and bring them through your dedicated consciousness. Just as ordinary mortals sunbathe, as they call it, by physically opening themselves to the rays of the sun, so may you also, in balanced turn, immerse yourself in the rays of the four elements. You might also, if you wish, have colored robes appropriate to each quarter—though none of this is essential. The enhanced imagination, vibrating with sympathetic emotion, is the true mode of working to effect. But the ability to "earth" these inner realities is never a bad thing, save when they become the baubles of self-indulgent glamour. Making the symbols and the regalia yourself is of greater worth than simply buying them. Although if they are indeed bought and not made, then a purchase that is something of a sacrifice is of more benefit than one that is easily afforded. There is a tradition about the four principal symbols, that need not be adhered to rigidly but which demonstrates their inner principles.

The sword or dagger of the east should be earned; the wand of the south should be made by yourself; the cup of the west should be received as a gift; the symbolic pentacle of the north should be designed by yourself.

Thus are dedication, spiritual will, love, and wisdom expressed in these cardinal symbols.

As for the colors of the various quarters, think deeply and vividly of the qualities embodied by each direction and allow the images to rise. Have the faith of your own vision in all these matters. This bears greater fruit than all the speculations of intellect. Many are the system builders, but their structures are as lifeless as a scaffold. We seek the actual realms of the evoked imagination—not the maps and travelers' tales of the analytical mind. The mind is slayer of the real: the pin that transfixes the living butterfly to the tabulated board—for its vibrant colors to slowly decay. Follow the living symbols through the meadows of inner vision as a child delighting in the random colors and smells and sounds of nature. You will find it has an inner logic and structure of its own. The principles of discovery are the same on the inner planes as they are on the outer. Simply observe. What you see and hear may amaze you.

Meditation Posture for Westerners

You may stand in the center of your circled cross and realize it as a point of balance—as a condition to which you should aspire. When you have balanced the elements of your nature as represented by the arms of the cross, then may the rose of the spirit bloom. This is one meaning of the rose cross.

Standing is a valid posture for those of the Western Mysteries; so also is sitting upright in a chair. A position of balanced poise is what is sought. It brings comfort without distraction and can be held, if need be, for a long time. The legs should not be crossed, a position that is physically damaging as well as psychically twisted. If the aura requires to be closed, that is if you wish to remain in communion with yourself, then the hands may be lightly clasped, and the ankles crossed. For general work the hands can either rest on the knees if sitting, or hang by the sides if standing. They can also be used for various gestures, of receptivity, invocation, evocation, banishing, rejection, direction, in ways that are best discovered by trial and error. Do and develop what feels right. That is the key to effective work. In the East much has been written about postures and hand and finger positions. This may be well for those who follow the ways of the Orient, but they do not necessarily pertain to the West.

Humankind, more than is realized, is an expression of that part of the Earth upon which we subsist. A rose of the West should not aspire to bloom like a lotus of the East. Though there may be rare instances of those who have such a personal destiny.

Pictures of Egyptian or Assyrian gods and goddesses give a pattern of postures for the West. A footstool of modest size may be a useful addition to raise the feet so that the thighs run parallel to the floor. Feet on the ground is an important part of Western posture. The destiny of the soul incarnate in the West is control of the physical environment. Mark the word *control* and not *abuse*. That of the Eastern soul is more subjective. There, the feet are best raised above the base of the spine, or closely conjoined to it, so forming a closed circuit of the aura not open to objective Earth currents.

THE PILLARS

The concept of the pillars is of great importance. Everything that exists to objective perception is a manifestation of forces in duality. These dual forces, in complement or vortex, are represented by two pillars.

The pillars may be pictured as silver and black, or green and gold, or of other contrasting or complementary colors. Color symbolism is largely subjective, its expression a uniquely personal statement.

The forms are more objective, in their mass and space and relative position, one to another.

At root the pillars are positive and negative, masculine and feminine, active and passive, but remember none of these concepts is synonymous with another. Each definition has its own limitations. The fundamental postulate is that each pillar is the opposite of the other, yet opposite in relatedness; as opposite as the center and the circumference of a circle.

Meditation: Polar Forces Acting on a Point

In terms of esoteric geometry, see a point moving in free space. Left alone, it traces a line moving straight into infinity. See another force impinge on it besides the one that started its first movement. Now instead of tracing an infinite line it moves round upon itself. See it form a circle. Those two forces that acted on this point may be represented by the positive and negative pillars. They are the polarity on one level that creates a form in another dimension.

At whatever level one views a form, it will resolve into two forces at a higher (or lower) plane of existence. These dual forces are depicted by the pillars.

The representation of these pillars also forms a gate. Any two forces in complementary action define another plane of being where they are a unity. Two and one makes three. Thus the triangle is an important symbolic figure as well as the circle and the cross.

The importance of the triangle can be seen in various composite glyphs; whether in simple terms of the Star of David or six-rayed star, or in more complex interrelationships such as the many triads of the Tree of Life.

Constructing the Pillars

It will be no waste of time or effort to make two physical pillars. They need not be of massive size but should be worked upon to invest them with the dignity that the discipline and performance of painstaking and dedicated work confers. In size they need be no broader than the human arm. In height one should be able to walk under them should a cross piece be balanced between their capitals. They need a secure base (as do all things manifest in Earth) and they may be fashioned round or square and appropriately painted. One does not have to be a master carpenter, but all should be able to exercise care and diligence with the hands. To be able to work with simple tools is a fundamental lesson of life. The skill of a handicraft is never too late to be mastered. What is the point of trying to learn to handle the forces and forms of higher planes if one cannot cope with the elementary rules of the physical? There is no escape in trying to flee from the problems of the physical plane before its lessons are learned. To dodge is merely a temporary expedient before an inevitable return to the problem; if not in this life then the next. Therefore cultivate work with the hands. Literally, within your hands lies the health of the soul and the manifestation of the spirit.

In olden temple days the seeker for higher wisdom had first to be a hewer of wood and a drawer of water. There is more to this requirement than simply a willingness for humble service. These acts are basic to life in the world. However exalted one's consciousness, one must have the ability to use and even fashion, bucket and ax. They are each in their way two pillars of a very fundamental wisdom—that which cuts and that which contains—to give water and fire—the necessities of life.

The pillars may be placed about the circle in various ways. Indeed a completely accoutered circle could be seen as a grove of pillars. They may be placed upon each side of an altar in any quarter. Indeed one might visualize, if not physically build, appropriate pillars in such a fashion.

Visualizing the Pillars

Here is a guide to visualizing the pillars in each of the four quarters.

At the east a positive (right-hand) pillar of the gold of the flecks in the rays in the sun, and a negative one (left-hand) of the azure of deep summer sky; at the south a positive pillar of the yellowy orange of flame and a negative of the crimson of a deeply banked furnace; at the west a positive pillar of the silver of reflections on the waters, and a negative one of the deep gray-green-blue of the sea; and at the north a positive pillar of the light green of new earth life and a negative one of the dark tones of ancient rock.

It will cultivate the esoteric sense to contemplate alternative colors for these, and various additional features that may not be practical in physical terms. For instance, see the pillars in movement within themselves. Shooting forth green buds; showing scudding clouds; in restless movement like the wind-whipped sea; brilliantly sparkling with starlight. It is here you may realize the powers of the imagination to be greater than those of the hands. And to see that the physical symbols are but outward signs of a real and vibrant reality that is not of their plane.

In due time, therefore, physical symbols may be dispensed with, but there is no substitute for working with them at first. They are tools of consciousness. With their aid, far greater things may be achieved than leaving the mind untrained and unaided. "Earthing" is also an important principle. The traditional vices of the material plane are disorder and inertia. The physical procurement of symbolic artifacts and finding a place for them in physical life is an exercise in overcoming inertia and creating physical order.

To create a model universe, a temple in the physical of the dynamics of the inner, is to demonstrate one's mastery over minor circumstances of matter. Such a created model may be the vehicle for profound realizations and high mystical experience. It is the dedication of a proportion of physical living space to express universal spiritual principles. It is the building of a life-size talisman; a focus within the material world that will spread, on subtle levels, help and healing by its very existence.

By building this material model, you express the equilibration of the elements that make up the world. The rose of the spirit may bloom therein. By virtue of your tending this mystical garden you will be spreading a sweet spiritual fragrance.

THE ALTAR

We have spoken of an altar at each quarter, between a pair of elemental pillars. This is to effect a focus of intention. In ultimate truth the altar is yourself. As you face the two pillars you may see the altar between them and just beyond. If the pillars were upright sides of a mirror the altar would be a reflection of your soul.

In token of this the altar is sometimes placed before the pillars. It is then termed the altar of sacrifice, for it is only by sacrifice that one passes through the gateway to the inner worlds. This is a fundamental economy of nature. Just as matter can neither be created nor destroyed, but only transformed to another mode of expression, so when consciousness seeks to be raised to another dimension, it needs must exchange energy upon one level for energy on another.

In martyrdom for a cause, this exchange may be dramatic. Such a case is the equivalent of an explosion—the fastest form of physical transformation. Yet all life is in a state of constant transformation in the process of growth and decay. It is likewise with consciousness.

The altar of sacrifice demonstrates that where your treasure is there will your heart be also. Time, effort, money, even friends and reputation may need to be expended in the search for knowledge and experience of the higher worlds, just as sacrifice or allocation of resources would be needed if your desires impelled you to seek knowledge and experience of another part of the physical world.

You may therefore stand in the very center of your circle and be the focused balance of all its parts. This is a useful exercise, but a more solid expression to this intention may be given by placing an altar in the center.

In basic form an altar is simply a table; a focus of consciousness. Convenience should dictate its size and height as it is both practical and symbolic according to preference and circumstance.

It should be of a regular shape—circular, square, or polygonal—and covered with a well-laundered cloth, which most appropriately is white.

The center of the altar is a most especial part. It is the center of your universe. Put something very special there; perhaps a flower, or a sanctuary flame. This represents the perpetual light of the spirit, in balanced manifest expression.

It will help us to pay attention to that central light with some small ceremony. At the heart of ceremony is spiritual intention, enacted with grace and precision.

THE CENTRAL LIGHT

Suppose the center of the altar is to bear a simple candle. Let the stand in which the candle rests be of appropriate simplicity and dignity. Have before you on the altar three matches and a stone. The matches should be of the type that light with friction upon any surface, and of wood rather than impregnated cardboard. One match ought to be sufficient, but two others are set there in case the first one breaks or burns out before the candle is lit. Should more than three be needed then the implication is that conditions within yourself are not appropriate and some other activity should be found.

The appropriateness of creating fire by friction on actual wood should be borne in mind. Although a flame might with efficiency be produced by gas lighter it is not immediately "fitting." In all of this, it is not meticulous rules that we seek to provide, but a developed sense of symbolic appropriateness. We seek efficient function that is a clear expression of a spiritual intention within consciousness. It also has to be within the bounds of practicality. The latter is a containing factor. Ideally, for example, an altar flame might best be kindled by the friction of a fire stick. The rapid twirling of a rod within a depression in a surface with perhaps the use of a bow is one that epitomizes within itself the function of all four quarters (bow of the east, rod of the south, cup of the west, shield or disc of the north). However, except in highly skilled and practiced hands, the length of time it would take to produce fire and the uncertainty of the operation would render it inappropriate, except perhaps in very special circumstances. A wooden match being struck on stone is in our suggestion, a satisfactory compromise.

Flame Meditation

The match should be ignited with due intention and realization of the miracle that is occurring. Were you alone in a wilderness you would the more readily appreciate the wonder of the flame, so easily taken for granted in the midst of modern civilization.

As you strike that match and bring to birth the living flame, be aware that you are participating in the lighting of all the flames and fires that ever existed, from the hearthstones of the most primitive men to the great solar fires that shine upon you as stars from the deeps of the cosmic heavens. And be aware that it is all part of the single living flame that has its originating spark in the heart of God.

In skilled and practiced hands, the lighting of a match and a simple candle can bring with it reverberations and realizations of the very primal creation—of the original Fiat Lux. The power rests entirely within your own imagination and depth of spiritual intention.

As fire is struck from the stone, banish from your mind all negative doubts—about whether in fact the match will break, or whether it will fail to ignite, and so on—the demons of negativity are legion and prolific as flies. Simply *know* that you are going to create fire, that you *are* creating fire, causing light to shine where there was no light before, bringing warmth, bringing change, bringing all the necessaries of created life's expression. This is a moment of supreme affirmation and confidence. In performing this simple act in a spiritually oriented manner you are bringing profound powers of healing to your own soul. You are expressing the divine principle within your environment and sphere of influence. Your whole aura will light up, and the brighter and more vibrant your aura becomes, the greater and wider your powers for good, far beyond your immediate physical confines; they will transcend space, and even time.

If so much can be gained by such a simple act, performed with spiritual intention, think what power for good you have when you bring your spiritual will to bear, in love and intelligent activity, upon the other symbolic realities you build within your circle. The kindling and tending of the flame is a great feminine principle and function. Thus the vestal virgins of ancient Rome were keepers of the hearth fire of the city.

Candle Lighting Ritual

Now take the flame to a waiting candle. The lighted match should take on the significance and power of a mighty flaming archangel, or even the Spirit of God, proceeding through space, to bring light and life to a new creation, waiting in deep latency. See the unlit candle, its wick and its combustible wax as a dark planet, or an unlit solar system, or an as yet uncreated soul, awaiting the touch of the Creator to bring it flaming to life, expressive with light and life and love.

In such a simple action so very much can be expressed. In the course of time and practice of this controlled and spiritual intention, think how your whole life could be transformed, however limited its outward expression might seem.

You are a creative spirit. Only choose to *be* one. Act out your noble destiny—be its current expression in the confines of hospital, prison, or broken home; in overcrowding or loneliness. The greater the darkness, the greater can your light shine. Only start with the small things. Perform them in faith, and the greater will follow, as surely as noon follows the dawn, as the verdant spring the barren indrawing of winter.

The ethic of the physical plane is order. The smooth running of the "machinery of the universe." Students of the Tree of Life will know what this means. But pause not over symbolic theory. Go on to discover the *reality* of all that this means—in the spiritual magic of your circle.

Prometheus, who brought fire to mankind, was a Titan whose name means "foresight." So be prepared for the consequences of your actions. You will need somewhere to place the burned out match. Let a discreet and adequate receptacle be provided. Simply to cast it aside is an expression of *dis*-order. A working for the lords of misrule, the evidence of whose presence is all about you in the world. It is perhaps only the lack of intention that prevents their engulfing the world in a sea of rubbish, of forgotten litter discarded by childish and immature spirits.

Be responsible, which does not mean be dull, authoritarian, priggish, or pedantic. Think out the consequences of your actions and discharge them gracefully. Then you will be truly in a state of grace. God helps those who help themselves. This is a profound truth, not a cynic's wit.

A cupboard or shelf beneath the altar surface can be a convenient repository for unwanted symbolic objects or tools of the art such as incense blocks, tapers, or matches—that is, for all that is needed for the general work yet is not to be an immediate focus of attention.

The lighting of a candle or a lamp upon the altar should be a prelude to all activity within your circle. It affirms the central presence of the spirit. It will serve to lift the mind to a higher level and prepare for the work to come. Conversely, the extinguishing of the flame should be the last act in any work that you do.

Extinguishing the Flame

The act of extinguishing the flame should also be performed with intention—as of putting children to bed at night, or bringing down the curtain on a play, or placing the last full stop in a chapter of the book of life, so that all may return to rest and recuperation for expression at another level of being, completely "other" from that of the flame.

In so doing it is best to use the fingers to snuff out the flame, or to enclose it in some other way. The breath should not be used to blow it out, for the breath is creative, the agency of the Word that calls forth, and so is not symbolically appropriate for the termination of expression.

This final act of extinguishing the flame should bring you back to the level of normal life experience. This is just as valid as what you have been doing, but does not have the concentrated intensity of life within the circle.

THE CYCLE OF TIME

In the magic circle, what seems so little can mean so much! When you are really accomplished in magic, all your life will be expressed with such concentration. But this is not likely to be yet. In its fullness it signifies the grade of the Magister Templi—one who is master/mistress of the temple of expressed consciousness. Deep words. Think upon them. But these early exercises express the fundamental principles, and set you, the neophyte, upon the way. This is a way that leads to theoretical, practical, and philosophical appreciation of the principles of manifest life; and then to adepthood in serving its needs, before proceeding to higher and wider levels of mastery. Note we say higher and wider. Nothing is left behind. As it has been written, even the hairs of your head are numbered. And all is a significant part of the great dance. Your "past," your "future," your eternal now.

Past and future, in so far as they can be understood by incarnate consciousness, may be traced about the circle. Time, in truth, is a series of spirals but can be represented in two dimensions by a circular path. As will be apparent from the designation of the directional stations— east (dawn), south (noon), west (dusk), north (midnight)—this may be trod in a clockwise direction.

A deeper, personal application may be made by regarding these stations in terms of the pattern of the weaving of life's expression, in and out of bodily incarnation. For this purpose one may conceive a veil spread across the circle to make of it two semicircles. In this case the westernmost half is that of manifest physical life; the easternmost half of discarnate life—of so-called death. (Though denizens of that world might, more justly, use that term to describe constriction into the limiting forms of matter.)

If one has a central altar in place, about which to revolve, then two gateways may be conceived, to the south and north of it. The gate of the south is that which leads from inner world to outer world—the gate of birth, or gate of the womb. The gate at the North is that which leads from outer world to inner world—the gate of death or gate of the tomb (figure 1).

It may be helpful to fashion two sets of pillars, one for each gate, particularly if a physical veil is incorporated. A light rod may be laid transversely across the top of each set of pillars, above head height. This can be firmly affixed with small eyelets or hooks, and have a thin muslin veil hanging from it, in two separate pieces, so that there is a divide in the center through which one may pass. Alternatively a hanging bead curtain may be utilized, of appropriate color. Precise detail is left to individual taste and ingenuity, but dignified simplicity is the criterion. A simple blue-gray veil is as effective as an ornate curtain embroidered with complex symbols of birth or death. The latter can readily and effectively be provided by the imagination, using for

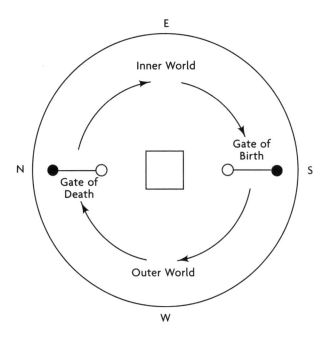

Figure 1

its basis the simple general purpose symbolic furniture of the physical level.

Circling Exercise

Now, as an exercise, we may proceed slowly to circumambulate the circle, in a clockwise direction. Starting from the east, spend some time at that quarter meditating upon your own central core of being, and conceive the idea and desire for physical expression.

When this is assimilated, very slowly proceed towards the gateway of birth at the south. Feel yourself descending the planes of intuitive, mental, and emotional modes of expression until you feel the enclosing instinctual, etheric, and physical warmth of the womb about you, just prior to your passing through the veil between the pillars, which is the actual moment of birth. You may pause here to meditate upon the opportunities and destiny afforded by the chance of a physical life.

Now, in slow procession from south on to the western quarter, feel the forces of growing maturity. The gradual acquisition first of the control of the interpretation of the data from the senses—the meaning of weight, distance, color, perspective, temperature—all that the adult so easily takes for granted. Evoke the wonder of childhood, the great zest for experience. Then a coming out of the dream world of the fantasy of games, towards adolescence. The dawning of the expression of the mating urge; the experience of human polarity away from the parents onto one of your own generation of incoming spirits.

At the western quarter you should pause. Feel yourself as a mature human being, at the peak of outer life expression. This is the polar opposite to the starting point of establishment in the life of the unmanifested spirit. This is a most important position which, if you are young (say under thirty-five), and have not yet achieved, you should earnestly aspire to do so. It is the natural expression of the intention of the current incarnation. If one is not seeking greater material life expression at this time then the reason may be a reluctance to manifest—a seeking of a way of escape from destiny and karma by short-circuiting back to the inner worlds, through the apparent escape route of esoteric study and practice. This intention, despite its high destiny, is in fact no other than a reversion to the fantasy worlds of adolescence and childhood, or a prolonged emotional dependence on surrogate parents. At the western quarter is the appropriate place to rest and meditate deeply upon these matters: on how you are best expressing your inmost powers in the world about you—to associates, family, and friends. Try to descry what was and is your spirit's aim in incarnation and how well you have achieved, are achieving, or propose to achieve this life expression.

Past the nadir of the west, and proceeding to the north one becomes increasingly reflective about the purpose of incarnation. There comes a gradual appreciation of the strength of the inner forces of the soul as the more overtly physical forces wane, with life expression fully established on Earth. This is not a period dominated by forces of ossification and decay even if many human beings allow it to become so. It should be the balanced expression of a natural process whereby the incarnate soul, as it approaches the portal of death, concentrates more on the inner forces. In physical terms this process commences more strongly after the menopause. With advanced physical years the soul looks back, often with enhanced detailed memory, over the lessons learned in the process of incarnation. This assessment is a necessary and preliminary part of the dissolution process. An aspect of this is embodied in the tales of the events of past life reeling quickly before a person faced with sudden death. The natural process is at a more leisurely pace, and the more fully it is achieved in the incarnate body before death, the less will the soul need to tarry on the other side of death—in the condition sometimes called the Judgment Hall of Osiris. It will be able the more easily to proceed through the progression into the higher heaven worlds, or to take up dedicated service, for a period, from the other side of the veil. It is to aid this process that is one of the objects of the well-known esoteric exercise of visualizing the preceding day's events, in reverse flow, each evening before falling asleep.

At the gateway between the pillars at the north be aware that your passing through is the moment of physical death. This should not be accompanied by feelings of grim foreboding or by melodramatic imaginings. It should be affirmed as a natural and peaceful passing from one plane of expression to another. Nevertheless, it is not a light step and here is an appropriate place to reflect upon the mysteries of death; and a recitation or contemplation of requiem prayers for the dead, visualizing yourself in that position, is no bad thing.

The contemplation of one's own death is an important part of many systems of religious observance the world over, and also of systems of esoteric training. The reason is perfectly obvious. It is preparation for a natural and inevitable process; of a movement in the soul. It is an important element in the process of mystery initiation, which we shall proceed to examine in later pages. It is important in preventing pathologies of the newly dead, of their trying to resist the process, and becoming to a greater or lesser extent Earthbound. At worst, such can be virtual vampires of the living, clinging to a wraithlike semi-existence, utilizing not blood, as in the Dracula legend, but the emotions and animal magnetism of former friends and relatives—until such time as they are forgotten on this Earth and have no choice but to move on. The soul who cannot proceed at this stage is in a similar but converse condition to the one in life who strives to remain in the fantasy world of childhood or youth.

Past the northern point of the gate of death, proceed slowly back toward the east, becoming conscious of ever greater expansion, lightness, and light. There should be a sense of a "coming home," bearing all the realizations and experience of a life in incarnation, back to the shining world of the great company of free spirits about the throne of God, or however you best conceive the ultimate heights of the inner worlds in your present limited physical consciousness.

This may bring the exercise to completion; or you may proceed around the circle again a number of times. Remember in this exercise, as in life, of which it is a condensed model, they do best who make haste slowly.

A MODEL OF THE UNIVERSE

We have now fashioned a twofold artifact, in physical expression and in consciousness. This is the means of considerable development and extension of awareness into the inner realms of form. Remember, "form" in its true sense, is not the external appearance of things, but the subtle inner matrix (or series of matrices) that determines external shape or manifestation.

What we have fashioned is a working model of the principles of form, the archetype upon which all archetypes are based.

We have expressed the inmost dual polarity that is inherent in the manifestation of a point, moving in space in spiral fashion, eventually to consolidate expression in a circle.

That duality is now expressed on a lower plane in the static and the dynamic elements of our construction. These are a circle and a cross. The cross represents a static matrix of energies, the circle a dynamic expression of energies within that matrix. Both circle and cross are expressions of the initiating, creative spirit that is represented by the point at the common center of both cross and circle.

That central point is also expressed as an altar, and therefore another dimension of the cross might be envisaged. This would not necessarily be in a third spatial dimension but in a dimension in consciousness, running between the initiating creative spiritual spark and the actual physical altar. In symbolic expression of this, a "perpetual lamp" is often hung high over an altar. One may observe this in certain churches. And the altar is often also a formal foursquare object. In the Masonic tradition which derives from the ancient Mysteries, it is usually in the form of a double cube. That is, a solid figure with a square top, and twice as high as it is broad and long. This form contains, in geometrical symbolism, the figure ten in the number of its square faces (two to each rectangular side and one each above and below).

On the Tree of Life of the Qabalah it is expressed as the all containing universal spark—a perpetual uncreated flame of divine self-expression at Kether, the Crown of all—and the final multi-dimensional form expression in Malkuth, the Kingdom, or Bride.

The altar usually stands between black and silver pillars. They also are to be found associated with the Tree of Life. They represent the loom of creation—the positive and the negative poles whereby interme-diate expression between the highest and lowest is formed.

We have in this dual polarity, of lamp and altar and dual pillars, another form of the cross. This is the cross of manifestation upon which the spirit performs its circular serpentine, spatial, or labyrinthine dance.

In Masonic symbolism this duality is expressed by the square and compass. The square marks out the cross; the compass the circle. This finds another expression in the heavens and the earth. The heav-ens are associated with circular movement, for that is what the stars describe to all who watch them from Earth. The Earth is associated with the straight line—the measuring out of land—and the straight line that is given by a plumb bob or pendulum, or a falling object, that by the force of gravity makes a direct path toward the center of the Earth.

It is now our task to elucidate how the circle of life and the cross of initiation may be used to open consciousness to other realms of expres-sion of spiritual beings.

We might use the analogy of an electrical generator. This is a device for generating electrical potential (power) and movement (current). In a similar way the interaction of circle and cross is a device for generat-ing psychical power and flow of force (see figure 2 on page 34). The electrical generator works on the principle of two coils of wire, one that is fixed (called a stator), and one that rotates within it (called a rotor). Similarly our fourfold cross is the stator, or fixed part, of our psychical generator; our circle is its rotor, or moving part.

An electrical generator works on the principle that a coil of wire

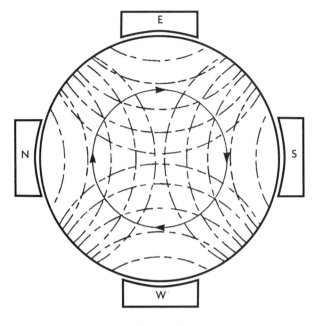

Figure 2

moving within a magnetic field will have an electrical current induced within it. The magnetic field is provided by the stator. Similarly the four points of our cross are rendered psychically magnetic. This is achieved by the body of symbolic meaning that we confer upon them.

Thus, within this psychic magnetic field, the movement of an open consciousness will have a psychic current induced within it. This you should have proved to yourself by the exercises so far described. That is, first by the vivid building in the imagination of a complex of symbolism at each of the four quarters, and second in the physical process with receptive consciousness of treading around the circle.

This movement should have induced various realizations within you; or evoked various images that might be the expressions of a higher reality—tentatively glimpsed; or flashes of memory or foreknowledge of other incarnations. If you have not achieved any of this, then more practice is needed.

As we have seen, the imaginal dynamics of our magic circle are readily attuned to the natural cycles of the Earth. The four stations can represent points in the daily cycle of the Earth's rotation—dawn, noon, dusk, midnight; or the annual cycle of the Earth's path around the Sun—spring, summer, autumn, winter.

Another natural cycle is that of the Moon round the Earth, which is a twenty-eight-day one. The poet W. B. Yeats, through the automatic writing of his wife Georgie, built up a considerable amount of esoteric lore based upon this cycle, most of which he recorded in *A Vision,* a volume most literary critics have preferred to ignore. It forms the basis for a very complex philosophy of the operating of cycles in human history and some momentous images in his poetry.

His natural reaction to the material was a very masculine/intellectual one—seeing it as a quasi-scientific system of philosophy. But much to his surprise, the communicators being channeled by Mrs. Yeats put greater value on its use as providing "metaphors for his poetry." This is a salutary reminder that we should give the feminine side its due. There is no doubt a place for the masculine, intellectual, systematizing approach to inner world realities, but we ignore at very great cost the far deeper way. The less-organized and systematized creativity of poetic imagery and the world of the imagination—which despite being free flowing—reveals its own structures within which we can work. These are structures of organic growth rather than mental scaffolding.

We shall therefore continue to build the poetic (or magical) imagery that naturally forms about the dynamics of the sacred circle. And as we are primarily concerned with the evocation of the Goddess, let us see how the feminine forms relate to its various aspects. We can use any of the traditional cycles for this purpose.

In terms of goddess figures, we can see in the east the virgin goddess, rose-fingered dawn, Aurora. She is also to be seen in another guise as Persephone, the spring maiden, whose steps across the barren countryside of winter cause flowers to bloom in her wake. Her course through the land is being accompanied by springing buds, and bird song, and the building of nests and dens by the wild creatures of the countryside.

In the south we might see the summer queen, the midsummer bride surrounded by all the activities of life and growth and burgeoning—a rustic idyll such as those depicted by painters of the neoclassical tradition; the young Earth mother, who raises her children and continues to produce more; consort of the shining Sun, the healer and giver of life.

We may turn to the west to find the harvest home, and the mature matron, the gatherer in of fruits, an aspect of the Earth Mother who has raised her family of plants and animals and children and who now looks on to see all that is good—but with just a hint of the sadness that comes with the passing of life, for all that it is a continuous natural cycle of passing, that will be regenerated on a new arc in new growth.

And in the northern quarter we might see a dark queen, the queen of night, or the winter queen. Not a sinister figure but one who watches over the secret gathering in of forces in preparation for new life, as the seeds, fallen beneath the ground, seem to die, but only as a preparation for shooting forth new life, when the next spring maiden comes.

Thus we can see the cycle of the natural processes of life upon the Earth in goddess images. And upon this structure it would be possible to place a sequence of seasonal ceremonies and festivities. It is upon such a structure that the pagan celebrants, of today or in former times, form their ritual year—the processes of a natural religion that is rooted within, and geared to, the cycles of the good Earth.

Such a sequence can include the "cross-quarter" points at southeast, southwest, northwest, and northeast that correspond to the dates intervening between the quarter days. A typical cycle of celebrations related to the Goddess might therefore be:

Ostara	March 21	*festival of rising sap*
Beltane	May 1	*festival of flowering*
Midsummer	June 21	*festival of vibrant life*
Lugnasad	August 1	*festival of fruiting*
Harvest Home	September 21	*festival of gathering in*
Samhain	November 1	*festival of returning to soil*

| Yule | December 21 | *festival of beginning of reawakening* |
| Oimelc | February 1 | *festival of green shoots* |

These are the epiphanies of the Goddess in the ritual year, and the natural festivals for any nature-based religious observance. In figure 3 they are shown on the wheel of the year.

There are, however, other ways in which we can celebrate and mediate the feminine principle. The festivals of the natural cycle, holy as they are, are essentially of the elemental world. As human beings, creatures differentiated by a spark of divine fire that raises us above the simple animal condition, there are certain human paradigms, or *super* natural archetypes, that we should not neglect.

In some elements of the feminine tradition this realization has survived as, for example, the Nine Muses of ancient Greece, those cultural deities of the liberal arts who surround the sun god Apollo. Or in the Celtic tradition the nine maidens who tend Ceridwen's cauldron of inspiration.

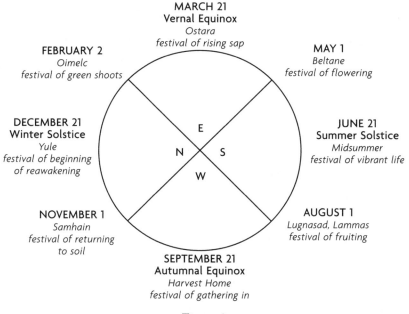

MARCH 21
Vernal Equinox
Ostara
festival of rising sap

FEBRUARY 2
Oimelc
festival of green shoots

MAY 1
Beltane
festival of flowering

DECEMBER 21
Winter Solstice
Yule
festival of beginning of reawakening

JUNE 21
Summer Solstice
Midsummer
festival of vibrant life

NOVEMBER 1
Samhain
festival of returning to soil

AUGUST 1
Lugnasad, Lammas
festival of fruiting

SEPTEMBER 21
Autumnal Equinox
Harvest Home
festival of gathering in

Figure 3

There is another version of this pattern of feminine powers in a more modern and detailed form that we can use. This is the system of symbolic images to be found in the trumps of the Tarot. Close examination of the twenty-two trumps will reveal that they may be split into two equal divisions of male and female images.

The ones embodying feminine principles are:

II. The High Priestess
III. The Empress
VI. The Lovers
VII. The Chariot
VIII. Justice
X. The Wheel of Fortune
XI. Strength
XVI. Temperance
XVII. The Star
XVIII. The Moon
XXI. The World

At first sight the feminine essence of all of these cards may not be readily apparent. This is because the images have suffered some change through the course of time, not always for the better. For a detailed survey of this process, see my book, *Tarot and Magic,* Destiny Books, 1991. Three images listed above are not quite what they seem.

The Lovers, in the earliest designs, prominently showed Venus, the goddess of love, giving her blessing to a procession of lovers, with her son Cupid hovering overhead. Craftsmen producing crude woodblocks for printing the cards evidently felt that more than one set of lovers made for too complex an image for their technology. Hence we have been left with just one pair of lovers, and the modern assumption that the picture represents a young man in a state of indecision between two ladies, sometimes labeled vice and virtue. Essentially, however, this is a goddess-related card and she is the main figure upon it.

The Wheel of Fortune has suffered similar simplification, to the extent of leaving the goddess out altogether! Originally the most important figure on the card was the goddess Fortuna, who turns the wheel of fortune or destiny.

And in the simplification of the Chariot, turning it face-on to get the image more easily onto a narrow card, the goddess has suffered a change of sex. The original designs show the goddess, winged Victory, on a triumphal car pulled by winged horses.

So we have eleven symbolic feminine figures, of which eight may be placed about the circumference of the sacred circle. The other three form a central axis or spindle, for in its fullness our circle is a three-dimensional figure, like a spinning top.

The numerical order of the Tarot trumps is largely a matter of custom and what we wish to make of it, for the earliest versions had no numbers at all. Numeration only became necessary when they began to be used as part of a card game. In placing our goddess figures about the circle, however, we will take the most commonly accepted order of trumps, those found on the traditional Marseilles Tarot. The type of pattern we are now creating is not based on time but upon function. We are making a kind of Round Table of feminine powers. Each one is as important as any of the others, and we may approach them in any order according to our need or desire. We show the feminine Trumps around the circle in figure 4 (on page 40), and the axis to which they relate. This represents an inner temple of feminine powers to enable us to make contact with the goddess, whose various aspects of expression are represented by the surrounding figures.

As an introduction to the circle, we will perform a very basic guided meditation, in which we approach each archetype in turn. After that, it is up to individual practice and inclination to approach the figures either one at a time, or in any preferred order. The circle of goddess images is a key to almost limitless teaching and inspiration, for each figure is the start of a pathway into a realm of psychic and spiritual experience which, if followed, will take the student beyond the need of any books or gurus.

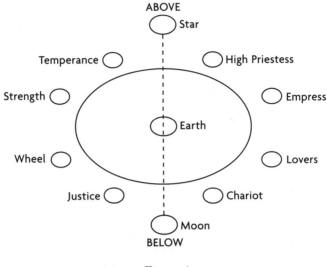

Figure 4

VISUALIZING THE GODDESS

We will begin by visualizing ourselves at the center of the circle, where we feel a deep indigo atmosphere building about us, as if we are in the center of a deep blue egg, which is kept in place and in being by four watchers, whom we can just discern spaced around us. Each has the head either of a lion, an eagle, an angel, or a bull. We find we are sharing this protected space with a dancing figure. One who is at the same time our guide and a representation of ourselves as we are in potential. It is a representation of the naked spirit coming into the worlds of form to seek expression and experience.

If we now look upward, we will see, high overhead, a similar figure, but in the form to be seen on the Tarot trump of the Star. A naked maiden is kneeling by the waters of the lower worlds, holding cups from which she pours the waters of life. Beyond her is a paradisal scene, and a tree (possibly two), dominating the scene, with jeweled and golden fruit, and beautiful birds and butterflies. And beyond is the backdrop of a brilliant canopy of shining stars that seem to stretch into infinity—but an infinity of love and of light, not of cold, impersonal, interstellar space.

We now look beneath our feet, and there we see a long tunnel that runs into the ground, brightly lit from some interior source. At its end a stream crosses its path, beyond which stand two towers, guarded by a dog and a wolf. Between them the full moon hangs low in the sky; a sky; a sky that scintillates with silver points of light, a kind of astral atmosphere of shining dew suspended in the air. In the moon we see the *face* of a benign goddess, who may also reveal herself as a matronly figure on a throne. It is she who presides over the pathway that leads further on and further in, to distant purple mountains, and the secrets of the hollow hills of the Inner Earth.

These two ways, the above and the below, are ways to the Overworld and the Underworld, respectively. They are other levels of *form* expression from those of the everyday world and its psychic dynamics, and with which we shall have more to do as we advance in our studies. (This will form much of the work of the pathways to be described in part 2.) For the present however, we need to establish ourselves in balanced expression in our own world, and to help us to this attainment, we will approach each of the goddess forms in turn, who stand about our circle.

First we approach the High Priestess, who seems to take no notice of our presence, so deep is her inner calm. Yet we have the impression that she is indeed fully aware, not only of our presence, but of our reasons for being here, and all the contents of our soul and the secrets of our inner motivation. Her awareness, beyond the calm and still exterior, is intensely alive and aware upon the inner levels. As we stand before her, we are drawn in to this ambiance of peaceful quietness that is the wisdom of intuition and higher knowledge. It also brings the stimulation of our own intuitive and higher faculties. We simply need to stand and gaze, focusing our attention upon her lavender-blue and gray cloak, her silver triple crown, on the dark and light pillars behind her, with their veil adorned with pomegranates. Upon her breast is an equal-armed cross of silver, sigil of harmony and balance, and on her lap a book or scroll, held slightly open by her fingers, from which opening water is gently flowing, down the folds of her gown, thence into a calm pool at her feet, waters of wisdom in which a crescent moon may be seen reflected. These calm waters are another facet of the Goddess into which we may gaze. And the appearance of symbols within it may be the keys to wisdom or visionary guidance; or the influx of ideas into our mind as we gaze upon the still surface may be another way in which this great feminine wisdom contact communicates with us.

Our next visit is to the figure of the Empress. Here we are bathed in a different kind of ambiance as we enter her powerful aura. It brings a feeling of great fruitfulness, of burgeoning life, of intense expressed creativity. For this figure embodies the principles of all Earth and vegetation goddesses, all those who empower fruitfulness. We feel the vitality within our own bodies rising, an increasing glow to our health aura, a vitality which we can in turn pass on to others if we wish. She smiles upon us, a beneficent figure in a green robe with golden emblems of ears of wheat upon it, a circlet of flowers in her hair. All about and around her are growing plants, from luxuriant grass and flowers to tall trees. And again there is the flow of water, a bubbling stream flowing along behind her at the base of the trees and then out and around us into the world.

We pass now to the figure of the goddess of love. She stands as a commanding presence, as on the Tarot card, a radiant crown upon her head. Although as beautiful as any naked Venus, she is clad in a priestly robe, for she is a director and stimulator rather than an object of erotic desire. About her, in the world of nature, can be seen the courtship rituals of birds and animals, and along the well-beaten path before her a veritable procession of lovers. Over all there hovers, with beating wings that cause such a breeze that standing against it can be difficult, her son the cherubic Cupid, with bow and arrow, the hunter of the goddess of love. His winged darts into the hearts of the lovers causes them to see each other in terms of paradisal perfection, for true love is a state of vision that pertains to the heavenly rather than the mundane world.

We move now to a young and vibrant goddess who sits upon a

triumphal carriage, upon which she stands, holding the many-colored reins, tinkling with bells, that control her steeds—a number of winged horses, as she herself is winged. As we watch her progress we are imbued with the strength of her aura, for success breeds success and brings its own understanding of what we need to do in life to perform our necessary destiny. It is an auric power that brings confidence and faith, not only in the future, but in others and ourselves.

We turn now to a figure who resembles the traditional image of justice, with drawn sword and pair of scales. She may appear blindfolded but this is in some ways deceptive for, like the High Priestess, she is well aware of the inner reality of all that comes before her. She is blind only to the blandishments of error and deception that try to thwart the course of true justice. She represents law in its deepest sense, from the physical laws that keep the world in being to the highest ideals of cosmic balance. She is also a great protector. Within her aura we can evaluate practical problems and disputes calmly, clearly, and wisely. By so doing we can bring ourselves not only the power of balanced judgment represented by the scales, but the will of the sword to take the necessary effective action for the restoration or preservation of the true and the good.

We now approach the goddess Fortuna. She sits, a bright and smiling figure, turning a wheel upon which many cycles revolve—all the machinery of the universe that keeps the worlds in being. If the figure of Justice represents the clear seeing of the state of the soul that embraces a vision of karma and destiny, then the goddess Fortuna sees to its working out in due process of positive and negative circumstance. She is the mistress of all cycles and waveforms and rhythms. By coming within her ambit we are able to look upon the fortunes of life as part of a greater pattern. She is the patron of life experience and for this reason has the bearing of a matronly figure; in some respects almost like a stallholder in the fairground of life, calling all to life expression and experience upon her great wheel.

We now go to stand before the figure of a young girl who holds, with ease, a fierce lion. There is a feeling of quiet control in this maiden, who by her purity and integrity is controller of the beast. She is, in a sense, one who has passed the ultimate test represented by the figure of Justice, and who is thus not prey to the ups and downs of Fortuna, but gently controls all, the accomplished spirit in action. By coming before her we may gain something of her sense of control. She is thus a great exemplar, but at the same time one whose influence and power can help us.

Finally we approach the winged figure of a goddess who stands before a rainbow, between water and land, pouring water from one vessel into another. She smiles upon us, and continues her dexterous pouring without spilling a drop. She may, if we wish, pour her waters over us, catching it all beneath us, in an action of healing, cleansing and baptism to new life. Within her aura we feel confidence through hope and dedicated service in action, and as her title of Temperance signifies, it is to her we may come when we feel in need of balance and self-control.

So ends the building of our magic circle as a vehicle for the evocation of the Goddess as a help in our way through the world. And it is as far as many may wish to travel.

Yet there remain further heights and depths to the power and presence of the Goddess. The further extensions possible are related to the central axis represented by the three Tarot figures of the World, the Moon, and the Star, which signify three levels of inner objective being. At the human level we have at the center the figure of the World, dancing within her charmed circle, held in being and watched over by the four archetypal figures. When we identify with this figure, we identify with the feminine side of our being (whatever our sex), and from this basis we may approach the eight modes of expression represented by the surrounding images.

When we looked up we saw revealed the figure of the Star Maiden; and when we looked down we saw the path through the Moon gate, to the Inner Earth, presided over by the figure of Luna. As we have said, these represent gateways into the Overworld and the Underworld, respectively. They are not synonymous with the superconscious or the sub-conscious, or even the collective unconscious, as formulated by modern schools of psychology.

The Overworld is a real inner place, peopled with angelic and other forms of creative hierarchy, whose being and actions may have a profound effect upon the physical world we know. The Underworld is similarly a real objective place or state, but should not be confused with crude religious teachings about hellfire and damnation. It is not the exclusive abode of evil, which can manifest in any of the created worlds, given the existence of free will. Rather is it the abode of elementals and of fairy beings, intelligences behind the patterns of the natural world, and in human terms the accumulated wisdom of the ancestors—our ties to the land by birth or habitation. As we have before stated, all three worlds are levels of divine expression, and thus equally holy. It is true that in an imperfect state of expression (whether through a cosmic fall, or inadequate evolutionary progress, or both) any of the three can be less than ideal, can manifest abuses.

Middle Earth, the familiar human-dominated world, can be deadening in its banality, convention, self-seeking, commercialism, corruption, snobbism, and the familiar "all too human" modes of false expression, to say nothing of wars and organized crime.

The Underworld can be the cause (on Middle Earth) of irruptions of racial, tribal, and territorial prejudice, ultraconservatism and other atavistic tendencies linked to land or blood ties. Nonetheless, in potential it is the beautiful world of paradisal nature with a place for everything and everything in its place. A creation of elemental pattern-makers, "the creations of the created."

The Overworld can be the cause (on Middle Earth) of impractical idealism, of things being brought to birth too soon or without proper roots, or what feeds the illusions of all kinds of cranks and faddists, and the "holier than thou" assumptions of whose who seek escape from, rather than immersion in and cooperation with, the processes of earthly life.

Yet in essence it holds the pure pattern of all that should and shall be in the ultimate working out of the divine plan, held within the exalted consciousness of angels and archangels and all the company of heaven.

In the part of our book that follows, we shall explore ways to come to awareness of these inner worlds. But this cannot be done simply by reading about it, as an intellectual exercise, for their realities extend beyond the bounds of intellect.

Neither can we enter these realms as uncommitted tourists. This is not an excursion for esoteric day-trippers. The stars we seek to journey toward are real beings, not spots of light on the dome of a planetarium. The ancient figures are real powers, not plastic models in a theme park.

So in our attempt to enter into these inner worlds we shall be committed to doing something. As in quantum physics, the presence of the observer has an effect upon that which is observed, and the observed will have a like impact upon the observer.

We shall conduct our inner journey partly through time, seeing how the Goddess, the source of the feminine powers, has interacted with human consciousness within the western world over some two thousand years or more.

So our journey will be one of the evocation of images of myth and legend in the form of a series of imaginal workings, each representing a stage in the expression of the divine feminine principle. We will need to support this with a preliminary overview of each section, so that the mind is well stocked with a necessary store of evocative information. This will provide resonances for the conscious mind to work upon that will make the practical work the more effective. So we do not recommend skipping the theoretical parts and just doing the workings, for this is likely to result only in a superficial acquaintance with the dynamics involved.

Conversely, we hope that the more theoretically inclined will not just read the text and not bother with the practical working. This again would very much represent a missed opportunity, for unused knowledge has as little worth as superficial experience.

The Goddess calls. How are you going to answer?

PART TWO

Evocation of the Goddess
and the
Planetary Being

Evoking the Goddess

We come now to a major change of gear in our working. The work of part 1 has been largely subjective or psychological, be it in an increasingly transpersonal way. We seek now a more objective approach to the inner worlds, where the powers of the Goddess are discernible realities rather than personal aspirations or ideals.

We have been concerned up to now largely with the process of *invocation*. That which follows pertains more to *evocation*. Although it is important to make the distinction between these two modes of working, in practice there is no real hard-and-fast line that divides them. Invocation, if regularly and faithfully practiced, will lead in time to evocative powers and experience. That is, to an awareness of objective innerworld realities, be they of the Overworld or the Underworld or the higher ethers of Middle Earth. The powers of inner perception that we have been developing in the exercises of Part One will now be turned toward their active interaction with inner-plane powers and forces, and in particular with those relating to the divine feminine principle.

Part Two is divided into branches, and each one represents a stage in coming to a realization of the existence of an entity we may call the Planetary Being. In our sense of the term, this is the consciousness of the planet Earth, which is an evolving elemental entity, specially guided or watched over by archangelic and other beings of the inner creative hierarchies.

It is closely linked to, and dependent upon, the evolving forms of consciousness that inhabit its sphere—which includes of course ourselves as members of the human race. This adds an extra responsibility to our spiritual evolution, in that collectively, humanity is not only answerable for its conduct toward itself but for how our actions affect the general tone of the other forms of evolving life that share the planet with us. This gives an added gravitas to concerns such as animal as well as human rights, and even to the treatment of natural resources, be they rivers or rain forests, oceans or minerals.

The Planetary Being may be imaginally represented by a female human or goddess figure, and we may link into it by actively and intentionally imagining it thus.

The interfacing of human consciousness with that of the Planetary Being has come increasingly to the fore of late. It is in a sense the key realization of late twentieth-century humanity toward the close of an epoch. It shows as a concern for Gaia, the consciousness of the planet, put forward as a serious hypothesis in one way or another by individual scientists of some distinction, and at a more popular and political level in the growing concern for ecology, the environment, and the stewardship of the Earth's resources. It is also present in the increased awareness of the importance of feminine rights.

All of this is not merely a modern concern, however. The Goddess and indeed the Planetary Being have been around long before our own times, and in a variety of ways. It has been ever the same fundamental divine principle, essentially that of *form,* but reacting with and registering upon human consciousness in different ways according to current human needs and capability. In each of the parts that follow we shall highlight a different aspect of this revelation of the Goddess and its relevance to a particular stage of development of the Planetary Being. These link fairly straightforwardly with historical periods in the development of human consciousness in the West. So we shall deal in turn with the following "snapshots" from the past, that do however retain an importance and demand for realization and action in the present.

Branch One: the ancient Greek myth of Andromeda, the chained maiden, and her rescue, by a hero, Perseus, informed and empowered by the primeval triple goddess powers.

Branch Two: the rescued maiden as Psyche, betrothed to the loving sky god, in a sequence from the Mysteries of Isis in Roman times.

Branch Three: the Virgin at the Well, enabled by this betrothal to give expression and form-empowerment to cosmic divine principles, still in a threefold feminine pattern, as revealed in early apocryphal gospels rejected by the church.

Branch Four: the Star Maiden, custodian of powerful divine energies now enabled to circulate through the network of light about the Earth, as depicted in Rosicrucian *ludibria* (seemingly non-sensical stories that pack a profound message).

Branch Five: as Mistress of the Magic Mountain, or Faery Queen, a figure from various folk and mystical traditions, helping to empower a more conscious and profound link with cosmic forces and hierarchies.

Branch Six: the process of cosmic interchange, the interaction between Underworld and Overworld, particularly at sacred sites, for the regeneration of Middle Earth and all who live and move and have their being in it.

Other systems of symbolism, legend, and myth could have been chosen, but these, in a sense, chose us! And furthermore, they have proved their effectiveness in modern magical work and realization. Whoever chooses to follow the path that has been here outlined, by practically working with the material, should soon be vouchsafed further realizations and vistas of personal growth and insight.

There is a blessing on all who serve.

Ancient Heroes and the Goddess Powers

The myth of Andromeda is of fundamental importance to our culture, demonstrated by the fact that its protagonists have been projected into the night sky as the names of constellations that surround the northern pole, the axis of the world's turning. These constellations show the basic pattern of king, queen, hero, maiden and monster; that is, Cepheus, Cassiopeia, Perseus, Andromeda, and Cetus.

In a broad sense the basic story is the simple one of the hero saving the beautiful damsel in distress, as in Saint George and the dragon and later tales of romance. However, in its essence, and as revealed in much of its detail, there is a great deal more to it than a romantic tale of chivalry or derring-do.

THE MYTH OF PERSEUS

The most ancient feminine powers and our relationship to them are enshrined in the story:

In ancient times, almost beyond the dawn of memory, there was said to be a beautiful garden far, far, in the west. There a magical orchard could be found with a special tree from which golden apples grew. This was the Garden of Hesperides. The special tree was guarded at its root by a serpent. And the way to it, which was across a dark and deep underground sea, was guarded by three sets of sister goddesses. From very ancient times the goddess has been associated with the number three, and here we have this principle concentrated in power, by the three sets of sisters three: the Naiads, the Graiae, and the Gorgons. It is to each of these in turn that Perseus goes for assistance in his hero's quest. But first something should be said about Perseus' lineage.

Danäe

Perseus is the son of Danäe, who was coupled by Zeus in the form of a shower of gold while confined in an underground chamber. She had been entombed by her father, who feared that she might bear a son inimical to him.

In this we see an ancient form of divine kingship whereby the reigning king was sacrificed for the coming of the next. These are the hallmarks of a matriarchal society, at one with the Earth, the old king merging with the Earth in burial, for the good of the land and his people.

In the story of Danäe's father, Akrisios, we find the heinous example of one who attempted to evade his divine responsibilities by entombing the holy maiden to prevent her bearing the next divine king. However, such ancient custom, founded upon profound inner realities, is not so lightly set aside. Danäe in fact conceives a divine child without the need of impregnation by a man. Perseus is one of the virgin born.

When the child is born, mother and child are confined in a chest, or ark, and set adrift on the sea. A direct act of killing either of them by human hand would be too blasphemous to contemplate, but giving them over to the hands of the gods in this way is an attempted compromise whereby, it is hoped, the guilty will not have actual regicide and deicide upon their hands and the victims will be taken back to their place of origin in the kingdom of the gods. In notable cases that have been enshrined in myth, such as this story of Perseus and Danäe, things do not work out so easily as this. The divine destiny has to be worked out to the full on the physical plane and the cosmic balance, tampered with by men's fear or ambition, set aright.

Danäe, with her shining divine child in the dark ark on the tempestuous sea, prays to the gods for succor, and they are discovered and rescued by a fisherman. No ordinary fisherman this, for Diktys, the "net man," is of noble lineage. On one side he descends from Poseidon himself, the great god of the sea. In another tradition from Danaos, one of the mighty twin sons of Belos (the prototype of the Phoenician Baal); and in another tradition from Io—the feminine counterpart of Prometheus, an ancient form of the goddess who predates even the Egyptian Isis. In short, Diktys might justly be called a Fisher King.

This ancient link with the later Grail legends is enforced by the similar tradition that, like the Grail King, Diktys has an evil brother, Polydyktes, (whose name means "receiver of many") and who is king of the Underworld. By ancient right, whoever was caught in the net of Diktys became also the prey of Polydyktes. In other words, they embody an ancient teaching of the concept of free spirits being caught in the web or net of space-time, and the cyclic wheel of death and rebirth. Danäe herself becomes a captive of the king of the Underworld, but Perseus, the divine child, remains a ward of Pallas Athene, the goddess of wisdom.

When Perseus grows to maturity, the king of the Underworld throws a banquet. In accordance with ancient custom the status of those invited is assured by the fact that each has to give a horse to the host. Perseus is unable to meet this test of status but announces that he will enable himself to qualify by presenting Polydyktes with the head of the Medusa. In ancient times she was considered to have the body of a horse, and indeed was originally a mare, who mated with Poseidon himself in the form of a stallion. Perseus undertakes this quest as a means of bringing release for his mother.

In psychological terms, we may see a crisis point at a stage in the evolution of human consciousness. It is the point where dependence upon the mother has to give way to assertion of independence. This occurs in the process of growing to maturity in all human individuals, and has its equivalent in the puberty of the human race. This is the dynamic behind many of the hero legends. The hero is one who is compelled to assert himself, to prove his individual worth by the performance of certain tests, or a quest.

This is particularly relevant in the case of Perseus, for it will be seen that achievement of this state of psychic independence will also be a release *for* the mother. On the other hand, failure to win free of the maternal influence, or mother's aura, will produce that petrification of the will that is so graphically described in the imagery of the Medusa's look that can turn her victims into stone. She is the terrible possessive mother, in this aspect, the spider woman who sucks the souls of her victims and renders them dry desiccated shells. These victims are her own children.

The Naiads

In later versions of the legend, Perseus is helped in his quest by the god Hermes, who lends him winged shoes so that he can leave the island upon which he is confined. This island is an image of the physical world as defined by the outer senses; and the winged shoes confer the ability to walk the skyways of inner reality. This assistance from the god of travelers, magic, books, and learning is valid enough symbolically but is a simplification of the original tradition in which Perseus received this assistance from the Naiads, whom he visits under the instruction of Pallas Athene, his protector and the goddess of higher wisdom.

The Naiads gave him three gifts necessary to his task: winged shoes, the cap of invisibility, and a wallet to contain the Gorgon's head.

The Naiads dwell in a cave in a mountain, an image that we shall encounter more than once. They are of the class of being known more generally as Nereides or water nymphs, of whom there are many, all daughters of Poseidon the god of the sea. Whereas the Nereides were creatures of the great waters, the Naiads were associated with inland water sources, particularly fountains.

In Arthurian legend the occurrence of a beautiful lady at a fountain is almost commonplace in the introduction to a story of inner adventures and enchantment. In the subjective economy of things, such a symbolic scene represents a power point in the aura. These are known in the East as chakras. They are upwelling life-giving force centers, sources of kundalini or the life force.

This is a specialized attribution of their nymphlike nature. In general terms nymphs were associated with the sexual creative function. Let us quote Carl Kerenyi in *The Gods of the Greeks:* "The word *nymphe* meant a female being through whom a man became the *nymphios,* the happy bridegroom who had fulfilled the purpose of his manhood. The term could be applied to a great goddess as well as to a mortal maiden."

And further: "Three appears to have been their basic number, the number of the Graces and of the other well-known Trinities, all of which imaged the dispersed form of a great Threefold Goddess . . . Hermes, their constant companion—often in the presence of Pan—represented the male fourth beside the female Trinity."

It is relevant at this point to mention the further fact that the nymphs were particularly associated with trees and sacred groves—an important attribution that we shall meet with more than once: Also that they are associated with counterparts representing male force in the form of the satyrs, or *silenoi.* Many of these were present, it is recorded, on the occasion when Danäe and the infant Perseus were rescued from their ark in the sea by the Fisher King.

Again, from Kerenyi:

such beings . . . were called, in an ancient Peloponnesian dialect, Satyroi, "the full ones": a term descriptive of their "abundant," and therefore sexually excited condition. This was the more general name for them. "He-goats" who played the same role . . . were also called Satyrs. The word *silenos* was also connected with such dancers, who in this role appended horses' tails to their persons. Silenoi, creatures with pointed ears, hooves and horses' tails, but in other respects in human-phallic shape, with snub-nosed faces and unruly manners, had the same privilege, of presenting themselves in the guise of a troop of male deities, as was possessed by the Satyrs.

We see a certain connection with the fact that the Medusa was once a mare, and with the equine theme in the banquet given by Polydyktes, which initiated the Perseus quest. The symbolism of the horse is connected with the sexual energies, in the sense that their full expression is the mark of the mature human being. This signifies a spiritual maturity—the full expression of the spirit in polar relationship through all levels of form life.

From the Naiads, Perseus gains the powers necessary to approach the inner power sources. This is to be expected in that they are guardians of power sources—or fountains—in their own right. The winged shoes and the cap of invisibility are the powers of travel in the imagination body untrammeled by physical form; and the wallet for the Medusa's head is the ability to act objectively, or with power, upon those levels, rather than as a mere observer.

The Graiae

Next Perseus visits another threefold sisterhood, the Graiae, located in the Underworld rather than in the halfway condition of a cave in the Overworld. Daughters of the Old Man of the Sea, like the Naiads, they lived in the far side of a dark and underground ocean, towards the Hesperides of the far west, and not far from the site of the Gorgons. Neither Sun nor Moon shine in this dark sea which leads to the realm of night, where the heavenly bodies disappear into and reemanate from, a land under the horizon. In a psychological sense it is all that is unconscious, all that is in *potentia,* not manifest; held in a cosmic womb; a land of pre-birth and after-death.

The Graiae live on a landfall that is called the Land of Rockroses, a land of pathless forest and rock. In these ancient lands it is probable that even Pallas Athene did not know her way, and it was needful for Perseus to discover the way to the Gorgons from the old gods.

In common with most of the other very ancient female figures, they are generally described as ugly and grotesque forms. This is not necessarily the case, though the fact that they were called the "gray ones" and shared a single eye and a single tooth does conjure an image of grotesque senility. However, grayness does not necessarily mean physical age. Ancient these goddesses certainly are, but, as with other of the "old and lordly ones" it is possible to be ever young. Their grayness might also be conceived in terms of shimmering morning mist, under moonlight or starlight, and their single eye and single tooth conceived as organs of perception of a unique and rare character. The all-seeing eye associated with the omniscience of Godhead; and the tooth being the threefold adamantine emblem of the immortal spirit (in the Qabalah the letter Shin means both "spirit" and "tooth," the latter being the hardest organic part of the physical body).

By his having attained the freedom of the inner sea and skyways as a result of his approach to the cave of the nymphs, the hero Perseus is enabled to approach this other aspect of the threefold Goddess. This is to attain the spiritual power of omniscient wisdom, the possession of which enables him to penetrate yet deeper into the heart of the mysteries of manifest existence, to the home of the Gorgons. It is a deep mystery that he attains this wisdom at the change of the tides, when, in the imagery of the story, the eye is being passed from one sister to another.

The Gorgons

Perseus then proceeds to the very Hesperides themselves, armed with a shield-mirror and a reaping-hook-shaped sword. These were both divine gifts, the shield from Pallas Athene, the sword from Hermes. It is these weapons of higher wisdom that enable him to look upon the Medusa undazzled and to cut off her head in a strange reaping action, just as the heads of the corn are reaped by the sickle. This ancient moon-shaped implement is similar to that used in the earliest Titanic days when Kronos used one to castrate his father Ouranos. That is, it is a cosmic weapon, whose action in one mode created time, and separated the world of space and time from the eternal heavens. It is now used as a weapon of freedom and redemption in connection with the powers of the mother—in their crudest and deepest sense.

Something should be said about the origin and nature of the Gorgons, and in particular of Medusa, who was said to be the only mortal one of the three. The two immortal ones were Sthenno (strength) and Euryale (the wide sea), and it is to be noted that they were also ageless. Their collective name (gorgo) is used as a name for little girls so at root they cannot be identified with the ugly and terrible. Medusa has been described as the beautiful-cheeked one, and one story relating to her apparent ugliness is that Pallas Athene wrought this affliction upon her as a punishment for making love in the Temple of Wisdom.

Other descriptions of her depict, if not an image of conventional prettiness, a strange and awesome beauty, with golden wings, hands that shine like burnished brass, with boars tusks, and with head and body girdled with serpents.

These latter attributes depict the powers of the Gorgons. The boar is a creature of the wild woods traditionally sacred to the goddess. Ancient Celtic heroes went on a boar hunt to the Underworld. The sacrifice of pigs was a feature of the ancient rites of Demeter, the Earth Mother, at Eleusis, and the only surviving line of Aeschylus' tragedy, *The Phorkides,* which tells of these ancient Titanic Mysteries is, "Boar like he passed into the cave."

Serpents are universal symbols for the creative powers of the feminine. In esoteric psychology and physiology they represent the kundalini—the serpent power. This is not only a phenomenon of the human organism but has its planetary correspondence in the inner forces of the Earth. In one aspect it is the reality behind the force fields of ancient sites and trackways, and in a more elemental way in the mighty forces of wind, sea, volcano, and earthquake. It also represents the generative powers of life, "The force that through the green fuse drives the flower," in the words of Dylan Thomas. It is essentially a feminine force, and thus is not easily comprehended or come to terms with by the masculine-dominated intellect. Hence in the paternally oriented Jewish tradition the serpent appears in the Garden of Eden as a bringer of evil, or at least of temptation.

Whether or not there was a Fall, the serpent power was not the cause of it. There may have been temptation to misuse it, born of the misuse of the freedom of the spiritual will, but the power of physical generation, and its subtle equivalent on inner levels, is not an evil in itself. One might as well say that "money is the root of all evil." Certainly money also may be a temptation to the morally weak but it is not evil in itself. Like all manifestations of raw power it simply gives the opportunity for the expression of human motive.

All the old sea powers of the Titanic mythology relate to this power of the feminine, for in ancient times it was predominant in the development of infant man. It is still as much a power today, although during the epoch of humankind's adolescence—which covers the historical period—there has been a reversion from the feminine. This may have been a necessary phase but the feminine principle is not something that will simply go away. It pertains as much to God as does the masculine principle. Only in the balanced union of the two can progress to maturity be made. This does not mean a canceling out of sexual characteristics but a coming to terms with the forces of physically polarized sexuality in balanced expression.

The fact that the developing human consciousness found it necessary to break free from infantile reliance on the Great Mother in order to express its individual Apollonian freedom is what is behind the stories of the wars of the gods—when, for instance in the Greek mythology, Zeus (a male chauvinist, if ever there was one) and the other Olympian deities, replaced the ancient Titans.

Most of these ancient Titans were born of the sea, and their hideous form is but a distortion of their original beauty. The evil and ugliness is in the eye of the beholder. The time has come when these old forces should be recognized for what they are, and redeemed from their neglected, despised, and feared position. In this direction lies health and wholeness for the human psyche and its planetary expression. The apparent ugliness should be transformed to its real beauty, for the fearful appearance has been an act of mercy. These great ancient feminine forces appeared as monsters only because mankind could not stand their overwhelming beauty!

This is resumed in the tradition of the messenger of the Holy Grail, who appears alternately as a fair damsel or a loathly hag. Hero knights like Gawain married such feminine figures, who were under some kind of enchantment wherein they had to be ugly for at least part of the time.

Their restoration to permanent beauty depended on the attitude of the questing knight who courted them. To the pure all things are pure—to the ugly all things are ugly. Blake's "vegetable glass" reflects to us our true condition, and the mirror is essentially a device of the feminine, reflective principle. It is a tool of ruthlessly honest self-revelation, not of vanity.

It is a valuable exercise therefore to reevaluate all the ancient powers of primeval mythology, particularly those associated with the sea and night. For these are the forces of the primal creation, the Ain Soph or limitless sea over which the Holy Spirit breathed the first eddies of manifest form, transforming it into Ain Soph Aur—the limitless light.

Of these are included sisterhoods, (usually threefold) such as the Fates, the Harpies, the Furies, the Sirens, as well as the Naiads, the Graiae, and the Gorgons. Many of them have semiserpent forms; sometimes figured with tails like mermaids or otherwise like dragons.

The Pelasgian creation myth is of particular interest. The Pelasgians were an early Greek people who claimed that they originally sprang from dragons' or serpents' teeth—and of no ordinary serpent or dragon either, but of the primal Ophion. Robert Graves suggests that they may have been the neolithic "Painted Ware" people of ca. 3500 BC.

According to mythology, the first ever divine being was a goddess, named Eurynome, a kind of primal Aphrodite who arose naked out of the sea of nothingness. In her solitude she danced towards the south thus causing a north wind to blow from the motion of her body. She seized the north wind between her hands and it took on the form of a great serpent, Ophion, who grew enamored by her dancing and coupled with her. From the union, Eurynome, taking on the form of a dove, laid an egg around which Ophion coiled himself seven times. This hatched out to give birth to all that exists within the universe. Subsequently, according to Robert Graves' reconstruction (in *Greek Myths*), Eurynome bruised the head of Ophion with her heel; and evicted him from their abode on Mount Olympus to dwell in the caves below the Earth, because he presumed to claim that it was he who had been creator of all. From his scattered teeth sprang the first man, and Eurynome created dual Titanic powers, male and female, to rule over the seven planetary forces.

Thus, according to this legend, Eurynome and Ophion were the equivalent to the Old Ones of the Sea who ruled over the Titans before Kronos and Rhea seized power from Ouranos and Gaia. In later myth, Eurynome still appears, though relegated to a consort of Zeus to whom she bore the three Charites, from which our word *charisma* derives, from a root meaning "to rejoice." They are more familiarly known as three Graces, and are, in a sense, the opposite to the Erinyes, or Furies, the threefold agents of retribution.

According to Kerenyi, quoting Pausanias Periegeta, "a goddess named Eurynome had a temple in Arcadia, in a spot difficult of access. This temple was open only once a year. The cult-image of her showed a woman with a fish's tail and in golden chains. The inhabitants of the region supposed her to be Artemis, but better educated people remembered that, according to Homer and Hesiod, Eurynome was a daughter of Oceanos, and that she and Thetis received Hephaistos in their lap, in the depths of the waters, when he was flung into the sea."

This imagery is important, providing ancient links between the heavenly and the underworld powers. Hephaistos, the great smith of the gods, often depicted as a lame dwarf, was the misbegotten child of Hera, the queen of the Olympian gods, who threw him from heaven into the sea, to be saved and nurtured by the ancient goddesses Thetis and Eurynome, for whom he fashioned jewelry in a grotto by the great underground sea. He also had as his companion the Kabeiroi, another line of ancient Underworld gods and servants of the Great Mother— who were seagods and smiths. And later he became associated with the volcanic powers of Etna and Vesuvius. His importance in ancient myth is preserved in confused and conflicting stories about births engendered by Zeus and Hera. It is said that Hera bore Hephaistos unaided as an act of spite and emulation when Zeus bore Pallas Athene from his head. Another story says that Hephaistos assisted in the birth of Pallas Athene by cleaving Zeus' head with an ax. Then there is the tradition that Hera bore a dragon, Typhaon, in revenge for Pallas Athene, whom she gave to the dragoness Delphine, who in ancient times operated the oracle at Delphi before it was taken over by Apollo. She was also depicted as half woman half serpent. A variation of the story records the mother of Typhaon to have been Gala, the most ancient goddess of the Earth, at the behest of Hera.

Giving birth to a dragon seems more characteristic of the attributes of Gala than of Hera, although the latter might well have provided the motivation. Gaia, according to the cosmology of Hesiod, gave birth to the Titans, as well as the mountains and seas, along with many other forms of Earth life, in union with the great sky father Ouranos. Hera was thus invoking a great ancient dragon form of the primal generative powers of earth. This is described evocatively by Kerenyi:

> Thereupon Hera went apart also from the other gods. She prayed and smote the earth with her palm: "Hear me, Gaia and Ouranos,

thou who art on high, and you Titans who dwell beneath the earth in Tartaros, you who are the ancestors of gods and men: hear me, all of you, and give me a son who shall not be weaker than Zeus himself! As Zeus was mightier than Kronos, so let my son be mightier than he!" She struck the earth with powerful hand. Gaia, the source of life, quivered; and Hera rejoiced, for she guessed that she had her will. (*The Gods of the Greeks,* p. 152)

The power of the ancient Underworld gods may be seen in that even the queen of the Olympians has to invoke them for aid. Also, the connection with the great oracular center of Delphi is significant. This was a center of the ancient feminine powers, for it was Delphine who reigned supreme there, and the later serpent/dragon Typhaon, or Python, who was put in her charge. His lair was in a cave by a spring—a location that is the hallmark of any source of psychic power. Another version has him coiled about a tree—an equally indicative symbolic location. Furthermore, in this case it was a laurel tree, giving an Apollonian connection.

The name Delphine, from which Delphi derives, is connected, according to Kerenyi, with an old word meaning "womb." The oracular priestesses of Delphi were termed Pythonesses, after Delphine's consort Python.

The cause of the later connection of Apollo with Delphi is somewhat confused in the myths. We are dealing with fragments of very ancient oral tradition that are like pieces of patchwork that have to be assembled into a coherent fabric. Some versions depict this as a violent acquisition, others imply that the violence was an error later to be atoned for, while there are other pictures depicting Apollo and Python in accord, mutually guarding the omphalos—the sacred stone considered to be the center of the universe.

Much would seem to depend on the changing character of Apollo—or rather how mankind related to his archetype—for all such relationships are in a process of change with the gradual evolution of consciousness.

Solar heroes in particular tend to transform in this way. The character of Gawain in the Arthuriad is a particularly clear example. In the aspect of the "enlightenment" of intellect, the Apollonian powers can be equated with much that is at variance with the old dark feminine powers of the earth. The conflict, however, is one that should be a polar creative tension rather than a rending source of disaster. The Apollonian powers are the natural urge for growth to individualization. Thus we see a temporary, or temporal, conflict of role but one that is evil only in the overreaction or unbalance of man. In the individual this can be painful, as with all problems of adolescence, but they are for the most part outgrown without permanent damage. When a whole race is undergoing the adolescent phase then obviously the risks and dangers are more far reaching. This is the root of the current concern for a proper regard for the feminine. It is the way to responsible racial, social maturity.

Indeed, the proper balance is clearly shown in the fact that Apollo is the twin brother of the moon goddess Artemis. They were both children of Leto, the ever mild and gracious granddaughter of Ouranos and Gaia, whose father had been the Titan Koios, whose name, Kerenyi records, means the sphere of the heavens, and who was also called Polos, referring to the celestial polar axis. Leto's mother was Phoibe, a goddess of the moon, whose name meant purifying one. It is from her that Apollo was later sometimes to be called Phoebus Apollo. It is said that Leto wandered through many countries seeking a place to give birth to her children—in common with other goddesses who wandered for various reasons: Demeter, Isis, Io, and others. Appropriately the time of birth of the twins was to be dusk, the time of balance between night and day. This time is called "wolf light," and there are also traditions that she was protected by wolves during this time, or even that she temporarily turned into a wolf herself.

Other traditions should be mentioned that show evidence of the connection between ancient sea, feminine, stellar and underworld powers. Leto had a sister Asteria, which means "star goddess," and who was the mother of another moon goddess, Hecate, closely related to

Artemis. After Zeus had fathered Apollo and Artemis on Leto he had pursued her sister Asteria, who escaped him by turning into a stone and falling into the depths of the sea. She emerged as an island on which Leto could give birth to her twins. This is usually identified with Delos which also had the tradition of having once been a floating island, an ocean wanderer hidden from the eyes of men. At the birth of Apollo and Artemis it became firmly anchored to the sea bed with four great pillars, and is described evocatively, as quoted by Kerenyi, as a "widely visible star of the dark earth."

There is a certain alchemical element about the descriptions of rejoicing when Leto eventually gave birth on Delos. All the gods rejoiced, the former rocky and barren outcrop became fruitful, singing swans circled the island becoming mute after the seventh time, nymphs sang a sacred birthing song, the foundations of the island turned to gold, as did the waters of its river and circular lake, and also the leaves of the olive trees.

All of this brings us back to the traditions surrounding Perseus, whose mother Danäe was also associated with heavenly gold. We left him approaching the Gorgon Medusa with mirror-shield and crescent-sword—higher moon powers, in a sense, given by Pallas Athene. By coming to terms with the higher principles of the feminine wisdom, the old devouring mother who sucks her immature children back into the womb, in a living death, can be overcome by the individualized hero. In a very physical symbolic sense, the sack in which the head of the Medusa is contained could be described as the sac of the testes, the scrotum, the filling of which with the creative seed is the prerequisite of manhood.

The Medusa head is later incorporated in the armor of Pallas Athene. This may also be understood to indicate that without the Medusa powers, the higher wisdom is a mere attenuated idealism lacking human substance, and inadequately related to the realities of life experience. It is a weedy growth of a seed with insufficient root, and not at all uncommon in idealistic esoteric circles.

Andromeda

It is on his way back from the Gorgon's lair that Perseus appropriately meets the woman who is to become his wife. This is Andromeda, chained to a rock, the impending victim of a marauding sea monster. With the powers that he now has from confronting and overcoming the Medusa, he is able to release her. These powers are those of a spiritual and psychological coming to maturity. When the Medusa was slain by Perseus, it is said that two creatures were born. Some say this was from drops of her blood falling into the sea—others that she was pregnant by Poseidon the sea god and carried them already in her womb. Either version is adequate to the inner meaning. The blood is the vehicle of expression of the spirit; the sea is the universal creative matrix. Their intermingling is similar to a conception by the god of the sea. In either case the two creatures are the powers represented by the Medusa raised to a higher expression. They are Pegasus, the winged horse, and Chrysaor, a hero with a golden sword.

Pegasus is usually considered to be the emblem of poetic inspiration. He is, however, more than this. The winged horse is an archetype of the type of priest who not merely acts as a channel for divine force but can carry others to great spiritual heights and far inner realms. He is therefore an archetype of the magician-priest—which is of course similar to that of a poet or dramaturge in the highest sense; a bard, or storyteller, a conductor of "path workings."

Perseus, by confronting the threefold triple goddesses, has released mighty creative powers on many levels of being, besides being able to rescue and mate with the heroine Andromeda.

Andromeda is chained by reason of the folly of her mother, Cassiopeia, who, in an act of overweening pride, claimed that her beauty was greater than that of the sea nymphs. As a consequence, the kingdom was flooded by an uprush of the sea and was also ravaged by a fearsome sea monster, Cetus.

There is in this a parallel with the story of Noah's flood, or the Atlantean deluge. Once again overweening pride brings retribution, as it must, for it is an unbalancing of the natural order.

The vanity of the mother must also imply the denigration of the daughter as well as all other expressions of the feminine such as the sea nymphs, hence her being chained to a rock to be ravished or slain by the monster from the depths. It is also a mirror image of the condition of immaturity represented by Perseus before he has conquered the great terrible mother as Medusa. Now that he has achieved his quest not only are the higher powers of the Medusa released, as her progeny, but he can release the feminine principle as mate rather than mother, and so, as in the quest of the Holy Grail, release the land from enchantment or inundation by uncontrollable forces. Andromeda helps Perseus to overcome the sea monster by passing stones to him. This is not without significance. There is a down-to-earth quality in the feminine contact in the role of mate.

Perseus overcomes the monster finally by the powers of the Medusa head. The serpent powers are now his. Following from this he overcomes the male rivals for the hand of his bride, and goes on to rescue his mother Danäe and Diktys the Fisher King. The Gorgon head is dedicated to Pallas Athene who has worn it on her shield and breast armor ever since. The other gifts that had enabled him to journey to the interior, over the underworld sea, are returned to the nymphs, and Perseus returns with his mother and wife to Argos.

The Garden of the Hesperides

The whole of the Perseus mythology is relevant to the Goddess powers, and our consideration of them will not be complete until we have examined their central holy of holies, the Garden of the Hesperides. This was in the far west of the great underground sea of Okeanos. It was sometimes said to lie at the far end of a red sea. This is another allusion to the far west, and the apparent path to it is made by the setting sun inflaming the waters with its reflection.

In later Olympian mythologies it was said that Zeus, the king of the gods, had a palace there. This emphasizes their importance, but their origin is more accurately indicated in the belief that they were the possession of Hera, the queen of the gods, and had been given to her as a wedding gift by Gaia, the most ancient Earth goddess and the source of all life on earth. The marriage bed of Hera was even said to be located here, and the creative aspect was emphasized by the fruitfulness of the earth and by the many fountains that jetted forth. It was the site also of an orchard and in particular of a special tree that bore golden apples. This tree was guarded by a serpent, called Ladon, which is also the name of a river in Arcadia. This is not inappropriate, for Arcadia was by tradition an idyllic pastoral land, and a river is one of the most ancient symbols for the fount of life. One of the ancient Greek creation myths saw all life as having come from a primal river, Eridanus, which also has a constellation dedicated to it that stretches along the horizon between the celestial hemispheres from the feet of Orion toward Cetus, the sea monster, from whence it plunges down to the far southern star, Achernar.

Ladon was variously considered to be either the son or the brother of a primeval serpent goddess called Echidna, who was both male and female in disposition, but in appearance was a young woman of great beauty from the waist up, and of serpentine form from the waist down. As Kerenyi remarks in *The Gods of the Greeks:*

> In the stories, as told in our oldest mythology, of any god or goddess of the great family of Phorkys, Proteus and Neseus [i.e., of the ancient sea gods]—or of the corresponding old gods of the earth, such as Typhon or the Athenian Kekrops or the Kychreus of Salamis—it is always difficult to make out whether the deity concerned was believed to resemble, in the parts below the hips, a serpent, a dolphin or a fish.

The dolphin, it should be added, is a sea creature with a womb. Echidna was, according to Hesiod, immortal and ageless; and she gave birth to many of the creatures associated with the tests of initiation and the boundary between the worlds of life and death. These included Cerberus, the three-headed hound who guarded the entrance to Hades;

and Orthos, a two-headed hound with a serpent's tail—or alternatively with seven serpent heads. Orthos became the hound of Geryoneus, the strongest man in the world, who was the three-headed son of Chrysaor, the hero of the golden sword who had sprung from the womb of Medusa along with Pegasus. Orthos helped guard the red cattle of Geryon, which were the envy of the world, and kept by Geryon in his kingdom of the West. They were identified by some as the red clouds of the evening sky.

Orthos and Echidna between them also begot the Sphinx, which appears in the saga of the hero Oedipus—another who had to contend with the forces of the mother.

Another of Echidna's children was the Chimaira, a composite lion, goat, and serpent overcome by the hero Bellerophon. And it would be right, according to some authorities, to include Ladon in the progeny of this primordial nymph. However his special position, guarding the golden apples of the Hesperides, suggests that it might be more fitting to regard him as the brother of Echidna—both being progeny of Gaia and Typhaon—earth form and serpent power. Like Echidna, Ladon had his dwelling in underground caves beneath the golden apple trees of the west.

He was assisted in his task by the Hesperides. The Hesperides, usually four in number, were beautiful young women as their names imply. Kerenyi gives a selection from various sources, which include: Hesperia—the one of the evening; Aigle—the luminous one; Erytheia—the crimson one; Arethousa, who is a goddess of springs; Lipara—soft radiance; Chrysothemis—golden law and order; Asterope—star brilliant; and even Medusa. They are associated with a number of other female beings, the serpent nymphs, who frequent the Garden of the Hesperides. The double flute is an instrument associated with them, the tones of which, at dusk, called the initiated to their rites. They were particularly associated with the magic of harmonic sound by virtue of their bright song, and Ladon himself had the gift of many voices. So beautiful was their singing that they have been associated with the Sirens.

The Sirens

The Sirens had a similar birth to Pegasus and Chrysaor in that they sprang from the blood of one of the great creatures of ancient time when overcome by a hero—in this case when Heracles overcame the great originating river god in the form of a bull-headed serpent. This primeval creativity became transformed into those capable of ravishingly beautiful song, so beautiful that sailors feared them, for to hear their song was to be entranced by them forever. As a result of these seamens' tales they have been depicted in monstrous guise but in fact were originally fair creatures whose name associates them with the humming of bees.

In other legends they are held to be companions of Persephone, the queen of the Underworld (and in this role, daughter of Clithon, the depths of the earth). Their enticing travelers into the realms of the Underworld is in this respect an alleviation of the pangs of death and indeed hides ancient rites for the safe and proper conduct of the soul at the dissolution of the body—an art that seems retained only in the ritual of *The Tibetan Book of the Dead,* but which once had a more universal practice as other books of the dead testify. A book of the dead is also, of course, closely parallel to a manual of initiation, which is an introduction to the inner realms without the soul completely severing from the body.

The Sirens were also sometimes depicted as birds who carried human souls, or at very least their prayers, to heaven. It is the attempt at pictorial representation of their various attributes that renders most of these ancient deities into monstrous form, bird-headed women with sphinxlike claws for instance; and their association with the realm of the dead, or the Underworld, likewise exacerbated the fears of the ignorant and the superstitious into regarding them as nightmare figures.

Similar fate, in the literature, attended the swanlike maidens known as the Graiae, whom we have already mentioned, and also the Harpies, who were sisters of Iris, the rainbow. They were associated with the wind, and their names variously mean swift-footed or swift of flight. They could carry souls off to the inner realms, hence their rather frightening title of "snatchers"; however, they are also associated with swift-footed horses and so have much in common with the heavenly inspirer, Pegasus. The rushing wind is also a universal title for the Spirit, or the Holy Spirit, the wind that bloweth where it listeth.

The Furies

Probably the most fearsome of all these children of the ancient sea mythology are the three Furies, the Erinyes, or Eumenides, who, like Medusa, had snakes in place of hair. However, they are but agents of karma, or divine justice, and transformed when justice had been done. When they first pursued Orestes for having killed his mother they were black but when, in one version of the story, he chewed his finger off in remorse they turned to white. In the region associated with the Orestian tragedy they were given sacrifices and divine honor in conjunction with the Charites or Graces, of whom they are the counterpart, for another name for them is the Benevolent, which shows they were not mere personifications of anger and revenge.

They were variously held to be daughters of the sea, the earth, or the Underworld. Ouranos and Gaia, Phorkys and Eurynome, Hades and Persephone, among others, are cited as their parents, and all are appropriate in one aspect or another. Their function, and relevance to a matriarchal age, is expounded clearly by Kerenyi: ". . . above all they represented the Scolding Mother. Whether a mother was insulted, or perhaps even murdered, the Erinyes appeared. Like swift bitches they pursued all who had flouted blood-kinship and the deference due to it. They defended the rights of the father, and also of the elder brother; but especially they supported the claims of the mother, even when these were unjust." At the close of Aeschylus' Oresteian trilogy they are redeemed and placated by Pallas Athene, mediating between them and Apollo.

We may conclude our examination of these ancient goddess forms by reference to the Morai, or Fates. They have a particular relevance to the dynamics of the magic circle of birth and death. Their number varied from two to four; although they are more generally recognized as a trinity. When only two are considered, as at Delphi, they are regarded respectively as guardians of the gates of birth and of death.

In their triune form Klotho is the spinner of the thread of life; Lachesis measures the length that the thread is to be; and Atropos cuts it with her shears, bringing about physical death. They lived in a cave in the inner worlds, from whence white water gushes—in one sense the waters of life, in another sense (and closely associated with it in its inner dynamics) moonlight.

They can also be regarded as aspects of a simple primeval goddess, sitting at the center of the circle, spinning the web of life in the worlds of form.

Another star hero associated with the apples of the Hesperides is the mighty Heracles (or Hercules). As with Perseus, so did Heracles need to consult the nymphs for advice on how to cross the inner sea, and he obtained the means of going there by wrestling with Proteus, the shape-shifting Old Man of the Sea to whom they had directed him.

Another version says that he used the cup of Helios once again but there are various ways of attaining the Garden of the Hesperides. An alternative, less direct route is described in the legends that tell how Heracles obtained the help of the great Titans Prometheus and Atlas.

Prometheus was still chained to a rock for his act of bringing divine fire from heaven to aid the human race. Prometheus refers Heracles to Atlas, the Titan who carries not only the Earth upon his back but also the axle upon which the heavens revolve. The two are of course intimately connected in that the circuit of the heavens is an appearance resulting from the axial rotation of the Earth.

It is Prometheus' advice that Heracles should not attempt to seize the fruits of paradise by violence but by request of the aid of the powers that hold the machinery of the universe in balanced motion. Atlas agrees to conform, but while he goes to fetch the golden apples it is needful for Heracles to take his place, holding the balance of the manifest universe. In this part of the task Heracles is also aided by the higher wisdom of Pallas Athene.

Other versions say that it was necessary for him to aid Atlas by killing the serpent Ladon, that guarded the tree, with his bow and arrow. Once the golden apples are achieved the old tale (whereby Atlas attempts to trick Heracles to retain the burden of the earth and sky, and is tricked himself into taking it back) is simply the matter of choice that lies before the spiritually attained human being. The golden apples, as the fruit of the gods, cannot be retained on Earth, and after they have been shown as evidence of the successful completion of Heracles' task, they are returned by Pallas Athene to the Hesperides.

This involvement of superhuman Titanic forces shows the measure and depth of these mysteries. They are somewhat beyond human psychology. Heracles may be an archetypal human figure performing evolutionary tasks but Prometheus is the source of spiritual powers, which he brought down from heaven as a gift to humankind. Atlas is the holder in place of the machinery of the universe while Pallas Athene is divine wisdom that sprang direct from the head of Zeus, fully armed. In other words she represents the eternal mind, wisdom *not* dependent upon worldly experience.

In the imaginal working that follows we shall be using some, but not all, of the images we have discussed.

We ourselves will take on the role of Perseus, assisted by the various goddess forces. Our object is the contact with the Planetary Being, in the form of Andromeda, to see her transformed from chained victim to freestanding cosmic being, with the sea monster transformed along with her.

One of the opening images, culled from another area of Greek myth, may need a note of explanation. This is the goddess in a sea chariot who starts off the action for us by throwing a scarf that enables us to rise onto other planes of experience. She comes from the myth of Odysseus, a nymph who helped the hero on his voyage home from Troy when he had been shipwrecked, for he, like Andromeda and her family, had incurred the wrath of the sea powers. The scarf enabled Odysseus to swim safely to shore despite the ferocity of the waves. Similarly, it enables us to rise on the planes to attain the pure wisdom contact of Pallas Athene—the ultimate mistress of these mysteries.

JOURNEY 1: THE RELEASE OF ANDROMEDA

We are standing upon a flat seashore. Be aware of the waves riding in toward you, to eddy gently about our feet as we gaze out to sea. Something moving across the waters begins to attract our attention. As it comes closer we see that it is like a chariot, pulled by sea horses, and standing within the chariot is the figure of a goddess or sea nymph. She has one hand held aloft, in which she holds a long diaphanous scarf, that billows in the wind. Approaching in a wide curve the chariot approaches and gallops some way off from us, parallel to the shore. As it passes the goddess throws the scarf toward us; it snakes through the air and we catch it. There is a scarf for each one of us, the scarf dividing as it comes through the air for each one of us to catch. As we do so, the wind billows round it, and it encircles us and wraps itself around us. And as it does so, we feel the effect of the waves and the wind within it, and find ourselves becoming airborne, rising upward above the sea and the sands.

After we have risen to a fair height we begin to look around at the scenery below. Toward the land we see a green hill, with a spiral path that goes up and around it. Upon its summit is a brilliant white temple in the Greek style, with seven pillars and a triangular roof. We go toward it, and come to rest on the greensward before it. We pass up the steps and into the doorway that leads to the dimly lit interior. At the far end we see a great figure of the goddess of this temple, which is Pallas Athene. She stands with her familiar attributes of helmet, shield, and spear and with a serpent coiled behind the shield, and an emblem of the Gorgon's head upon her breastplate. As we look, the goddess transforms from being a stone statue into a live figure. The serpent behind the shield coils and hisses. Her armor is of the brightest shining gold, with the head of the Medusa picked out in colored enamels. Brightest of all, however, are her eyes, a translucent gray like the morning or evening sky. They seem to embody the very spirit of clarity, calmness, and wisdom.

We go reverently forward and from a stoup before her feet we splash water upon our foreheads and eyes as she extends an arm in blessing above us. Then looking up, we see that her extended arm is pointing, and our eyes, given a new dimension of vision from the water within the stoup, see through the walls of the temple and far along the rocky coast to a cave high up in the cliffs.

And as we register that sight so we find ourselves flying toward it in our scarves of flight. Approaching the cliff face, we see that from it there comes a stream of water that cascades in diamond drops down to the strand below. Landing upon a small plateau before the cave we gaze in and see sitting there three sisters, they are the Naiads, and in appearance similar to mermaids, with golden hair and fish tails. They smile in welcome, knowing from where we have come and at whose bidding, and hold out to each one of us three gifts.

First a pair of winged shoes, that give us the ability to travel to far-off places. We fit them on carefully, conscious of the birdlike wings at their heels. Then a cap, that as we try on gives us invisibility to all that would harm us. And finally a wallet, a leather pouch, upon which is embroidered in bright colors, the same head of the Medusa that we saw on Pallas Athene's breastplate. As we take the third gift, the source of the stream in the cave jets up like a fountain, spraying ourselves and the three Naiads, who laugh with joy, sporting in the spray. But we realize, as by an intuitive link with Pallas Athene, the goddess of wisdom that we have a further journey to go.

We rise and circle in farewell above the cave of the Naiads and then speed out west across the sea. For some while we go over the marching waves below us, heading toward their source. And then we see, far below, a small island. It is of dark rock, and seemingly bare, but growing up from the sea and all about it, is not the seaweed that one might expect but clusters of rambling red roses. We make our way down toward it, and land upon its shore, among the roses.

Turning our eyes towards the center of the island we see what appears to be a dark wood, impenetrable to the eye. The sun also seems to have gone down, and we are in a twilight world. But as the light fades, so do we see something gleaming at the edge of the dark woods. It appears almost like a will-o'-the-wisp, but then glows more clearly, and we see that there are three gleaming figures of maidens, the Graiae. They are dressed in robes that are patterned with roses, although in their shining the roses might almost be clusters of stars.

The Graiae are aware of our mission and of the source of our authority, and beckon us to approach. And as we do so they turn and lead us into the wood. We follow a dark and winding track, following with some difficulty the three spritelike figures that dance on before us showing the way.

Finally we come to a clearing, and find the three sisters seated at its center upon a large rock, and passing from one to another a great crystal ball that seems to glow with its own evanescent light. It stands upon a silver boat shaped like a crescent moon. And seeing our fascination with it, they hold it out to our gaze.

As we look upon it, so do milky clouds pass across its surface, and then we see a picture beginning to form within. The picture that begins to form we realize to be part of the mysterious lands to the far, far west. And the picture that is arising is that part of where the sisterhood of the Gorgons is to be found. As we gaze, the picture becomes closer and clearer and we realize that the crystal ball is a form of the mirror-shield of Pallas Athene and its silver boat an equivalent of the sickle sword for gaining the Gorgon's head. As we gaze so we see, in the safety of indirect regard, the form of three horrendous sisters, with tusks and claws, and heads like boars, and hair like coiling snakes.

They are somehow aware of our watching them, for they turn their faces in our direction and snarl. But then some realization seems to come to them and they rise, and transforming into actual boars, they rush into the forest behind. We are able to follow their course through our crystal vision, and as they pass farther into the wood where the trees are farther apart and the glades lighter, so they change from boars into three white mares. And finally, bursting into a great wide glade in the center of the forest they transform again into three beautiful naked maidens, pursuing golden apples that roll across the greensward before them. With ineffable grace they each snatch up one of the golden apples, which they hold up triumphantly. They are three graces of such beauty that it can be hurtful to look upon them, and in protection our eyes are shielded by a golden radiance that surrounds them as if from the sun.

Our attention is drawn however to the apples, one of which is thrust toward us so that it takes up the whole of the crystal sphere of vision. As it does so something impels us to hold forth the wallet that has been given us by the Naiads, and as we do so, the crystal sphere itself seems to drop within it. We find ourselves holding a wallet in which is contained a hard round object, and which is warm to the touch as if glowing within, yet the crystal remains before us in its silver vessel. We have, it seems attained the head of the Gorgon, although in a manner we hardly expected.

Aware of our achievement we thank the maidens of the Graiae, and rising upward aided by our winged sandals and carefully holding the bag of the Gorgon's head before us, we make our way back toward the land from whence we started, toward the temple of Pallas Athene.

As we approach the shore, however, we see an unexpected sight. Upon a headland, chained to the rocks, is a fair maiden. She is dressed in a green robe with flowers upon it, and has a coronet of flowers about her head, but she is cruelly chained to the hard cliff face, and below her the seas are whirled to a frenzied spray from which we see the coils and then the head of a furious and ferocious sea monster, which snaps at her with its jaws.

Then it begins to crawl out from the sea, and move slowly and menacingly toward her, with slavering jaws. We realize that before us is the very reason for our journey and for the gifts that enabled us to undertake it.

Averting our eyes, we reach within the wallet we carry, seize what lies within, and hurl it at the monster. It is as if we have thrown a shining sun that courses through the air and strikes the monster. The effect is dramatic. With a flash of incandescent light the monster transforms into a shining diamond serpent with its tail in its mouth. The chains that bind the maiden fall from her, like tendrils of dead weeds. And amid a great and joyful noise, which seems compounded of fairy and angelic trumpets and the cries of birds and beasts of the field, she slowly starts to rise into the air. The encircled serpent rises with her, and together they form an image reminiscent of the Tarot card of the World, or Universe, of a maiden dancing within an oval victory wreath.

We see upon the clifftop, as she rises, all manner of wild creatures gazing up at her, and this is truly a case of the prophecy of how the lamb shall lie down with the lion. Creatures of other evolutions, nature devas and fairy folk, are also among them, the naiads of the woods, and the elemental intelligences behind plants and flowers. Thus the Earth rejoices and we stand looking upward as the two figures proceed higher and higher and as they do so take their places in the world of stars, which become visible in the daylight sky, as the constellation Andromeda, and Draco that coils about the northern star.

Aware that we have contributed something toward the reconstitution of a newly constructed Earth we look across to the temple of Pallas Athene, and are aware of the gaze of the goddess upon us, and with this final wisdom contact, we find ourselves slowly returning in consciousness to the physical world of our place of meditation.

BRANCH TWO

The Mysteries of Isis Revealed

For our next imaginal working we shall take images of the Mysteries of the Goddess from a different period, as revealed in *The Transformations of Lucius Apuleius of Madura,* popularly called *The Golden Ass.* Lucius Apuleius, born ca. AD 120, was an initiate in the Mysteries of Isis, and his book is more revealing of the Mysteries of Isis than most people suspect.

The original is written in a high-flown form of Latin prose, the nearest modern equivalent of which might be "stage Irish." Apuleius' other works, a *Discourse on Magic* and an exposition on the daimon of Socrates, were written in clear straightforward Latin. *The Golden Ass* is a parody of a professional storyteller's style of the times. Robert Graves suggests that the catchphrase of these gentlemen: "Give me a copper coin and I'll tell you a golden story," is in part responsible for the more popular title of *The Golden Ass.* This may be so but we would also suggest that there is an alchemical tinge to this gold—that it indicates a pure and priceless Mystery concealed beneath the surface of the tale.

Just as the wisdom of the Tarot was preserved because it was put in the form of a common card game, so with *The Golden Ass.* It is at base simply an elaboration of an ancient Greek dirty joke and has come down the ages as a comic erotic novel. Human nature being as it is we find that the complete texts of Apuleius' other books have not survived, or are rare volumes in the libraries of academe, whereas *The Golden Ass* has not only survived, but is freely available in cheap paperback form to this day.

There are many hints that this is no ordinary comic story. In his preface, Lucius Apuleius "apologizes" for the rustic Egyptian overtones of his animal-god story. Yet those readers of his own times would know this to be a broad hint about hidden meanings. Egypt was at that time a legendary treasure house of ancient mysteries and magical powers.

He also traces a family lineage for himself, claiming ancestors who lived on Mount Hymettus, near Athens, (famous for its honey, a substance particularly symbolic of the mystery religions), and at Taenarus in Laconia (which is the traditional site of the entrance to Hades). *The Golden Ass* is therefore a form of literature known in later Rosicrucian days as a "ludibrium," a fantastic tale embodying great truths.

The disadvantage of this type of literature is that it can easily be misunderstood, and Apuleius' book is particularly prone to this. More prudish editions of the past have tended to leave out parts, with discreet lines of dots where the plot becomes too vulgar. On the other hand, and perhaps more indicative of our own times, there are versions which leave in the vulgarity and cut out the religious parts. This narrowness of vision is also to be found in the academic world. Some scholars feel that the hand that wrote some of the more earthy adventures of the ass could not possibly have written the beautiful spiritual visions of other parts. Thus do the blind try to deny sight to those who can see. Apuleius is no pornographer who has had his work tampered with by a spiritual hand, for whatever peculiar motive. He is a profoundly wise initiate who is able to regard life as it is, from the spiritual heights to the most depraved depths, and to forge a message of hope and instruction from it all.

In his story, if one reads between the lines, is a very full exposition of the realities of initiation into the Mysteries. To those who have trod a few steps along the way, the experiences described by Apuleius have a familiar ring. This is the Ariadne's thread we may use through the labyrinth of the ass's adventures; for recognition of living experience may prove a surer guide than the erudition of the classical scholar.

The basis of Apuleius' tale is an ancient Greek ribald joke about a man who was changed into an ass by witchcraft, and found that in this guise he was loved by a woman of unusual sexual appetite. Later he manages to change back into human form and eagerly presents himself to his lover, only to find that she spurns him, preferring him in his asinine form because of his superior sexual endowment as an ass.

It is upon this unpromising foundation that Apuleius built a profound story of initiation into the Mysteries of Isis. When Lucius, the hero of the story, is turned into an ass he falls into a semianimal condition from a higher state of being. This is analogous to the Neoplatonic idea of the human spirit falling into material existence, the world of the flesh. The subsequent adventures of the ass are thus parallel to the initiations of the Mysteries, that lead from the material world to the condition of the unfallen spirit.

THE STORY OF LUCIUS

At the start of his adventures Lucius is a very high-minded young man, filled with the noblest of intentions. It is significant that he is going to visit the country of his mother, for Isis is the mother of us all, of all nature.

In her interpretation of the story *(The Golden Ass of Apuleius—A Psychological Interpretation),* Marie-Louise von Franz, a Jungian psychologist, regards this and much that is to follow in terms of a man with a positive mother complex delineating a case study of a negative mother complex. This kind of interpretation may be helpful to psychotherapists but is a somewhat limited view of the great dual Mysteries of the Black Isis and the White Isis. Parallels may well be drawn between analytical psychology and magic, one with its approach to the unconscious, the other to the anima mundi or the astral light, but such terms are not necessarily completely interchangeable. We must beware of substituting one set of ill-understood and inadequate terms for another set of ill-understood and inadequate terms and thinking that we are gaining great wisdom thereby.

The Three Warnings

In the early stages of the story Lucius receives three warnings. In effect these charge him to ensure that his motives are correct. This is in accordance with the prime injunction of all Mystery training. The first warning is a story from a cheese and honey merchant whom he meets on the way. Both products that this merchant, Aristomenes, sells have close associations with the Mysteries, and particularly those of the great mother, in the Dionysian, Eleusinian, and Orphic rites.

Aristomenes' story is what we would nowadays call a black comedy. It tells of his efforts to rescue an intellectual old miser, named Socrates, from the toils of a witch, Meroë, who has seduced him and holds him in bondage. The use of the name Socrates is no coincidence, for however great the wisdom of the original Socrates may have been, he came to be the caricature, in the popular mind, for the logic-chopping intellectualized pedant, one who has cut himself off from his emotional and instinctual roots and is prey to a sudden uprush from them.

In spite of Aristomenes' efforts, Meroë and her accomplice catch up with Socrates and, through a wound in his throat, steal his heart. (The Daath/Yesod and Tiphareth significance of this will be plain to any Qabalist.) The warning to the idealistic young Lucius is not to become too preoccupied with the "higher" things, for the lower have an unexpected and unfortunate way of taking their revenge for being so discounted, betrayed and neglected.

Lucius proceeds to the nearby town and takes lodgings at a household that has a close resemblance to Aristomenes' story. It belongs to an old bore and miser, named Milos, who is married to a seductive witch called Pamphile.

Also in the household is an attractive young slave girl called Fotis, on whose actions much of the adventures that befall Lucius depend. She is, in effect, the Opener of the Ways for him. Her name is in fact derived from the Greek word for light, just as the name Lucius is derived from the Roman word for light. This is a clear indication that we are concerned with a story of illumination.

Lucius, on his arrival at the town, is full of all the naive and superstitious speculations that beset the new student of the Mysteries. In this overheated mood he wanders into the provision market to buy some fish. Here he meets an old student friend and the subsequent exchange with him is typical of relationships between tyros in the early stages of seeking esoteric wisdom. His friend gazes at the fish he has bought, condemns it as worthless, berates the fishmonger from whom it was purchased, and in righteous moral indignation throws the fish on the ground and stamps it into paste. Thereupon he goes off congratulating himself on helping a friend and upon his own moral rectitude. As a result poor Lucius is left supperless. Thus do many newcomers to the Mysteries wantonly criticize the beliefs and institutions of their contemporaries, without being able to replace the faith that they destroy with anything better.

In the same market Lucius has a more productive encounter with Byrrhaenea, a foster sister and cousin of his mother's who had nursed him when he was young. She is thus a surrogate for the goddess, and in this role gives him his second warning. This she does by inviting him to her house where there is displayed an impressive group of statues. They show the virgin hunter-goddess Diana about to bathe, with the face of Actaeon peering through the bushes at her, already half transformed into a stag; he was torn to pieces by his own hounds as punishment for seeking to gaze upon the unveiled goddess. This is a warning to Lucius to look to his purity of motive. However, as so often happens, the warning serves only to inflame his curiosity, and he hurries off with irresistible urge to study the dark magic of his hostess Pamphile.

What in fact immediately transpires is the mutual seduction of Lucius and Fotis. This commences in the kitchen; and, throughout this story, food and the place where it is prepared occur again and again.

They signify spiritual nourishment, the food of the Mysteries. There is also more implied in the union of Lucius and Fotis than the assuaging of sexual appetite, for there is a sustained analogy throughout of the conjunction of Venus and Mars.

Roses also feature largely in this scene. Fotis comes to Lucius's bed bearing wine and roses. The wine she sups like a dove (a bird sacred to Venus), and the roses (also sacred to Venus) she strews on and around the bed. She has a rose between her breasts and puts a chaplet of roses about Lucius' head.

Following this event Lucius receives his third and final warning. This is at a party held by Byrrhaenea and is a story told by Thelyphron, a fellow guest. He has been badly mutilated about the face through becoming involved with witchcraft and sorcery in a skeptical fashion, and indeed he would have fared much worse but for the intervention of an Egyptian priest. This emphasizes the connection of the story with the Mysteries of Isis and Osiris, wherein the body of Osiris is mutilated by Set and restored by Isis.

Following hard upon this final warning Lucius finds himself the subject of a ritual initiation—although he does not realize this at the time. He returns late to his house where he sees three villains trying to storm the gate. He thereupon attacks and kills them. The doorway and the three villains are the start of an initiatory sequence.

The next day he finds himself accused of murder and is dragged to court with a great crowd in attendance. So great is the crowd that the case has to be transferred to a theater—another suggestion that we have a ritual drama. Here he undergoes trial, and is berated by a mourning mother and a wife and child of the murdered men. As a final preliminary to being sentenced, tortured, and put to death he is ordered, as a salutary humiliation, to withdraw the cloths that cover the bodies of his victims. Much against his will, he is pressed to do so, only to find that instead of human corpses they are inflated wineskins. The whole assembly breaks into laughter and it is revealed that he has taken part in a festival of Risus, the god of laughter.

Whether or not a public joke, this has been a profound initiation for him. As Dostoevsky pointed out, who was once similarly condemned to death and reprieved at the last minute, after such an experience one is never quite the same again. Lucius has entered, through this initiatory drama, the porchway entrance of the gates of death—and as an innocent victim. This has profound parallels in pagan and Christian theology. The wineskins suggest the Dionysiac Mysteries, references to which occur throughout the story.

An initiation ceremony often presages or confirms actual events, or stages of realization, in daily life. Following upon this one Lucius has the choice of taking up or refusing the adverse side of magical operation. Pamphile is in the midst of great conjurations and Lucius and Fotis plan to spy on her. Following upon this resolution of deceit and overweening curiosity it is not insignificant that their sexual relationship takes a twisted turn, first "in Bacchic fury" and then "as though she were a boy." Expressions of outer and inner life go hand in hand.

Soon after, they see Pamphile rub ointment upon herself and turn into an owl, whereupon she flies off into the night. Lucius is determined to emulate this act, which, as a flying soul, might be likened to etheric or astral projections. He prevails upon Fotis to steal some of the ointment. In keeping with the atmosphere of intrigue and betrayal, however, they choose the wrong box, and instead of turning into an owl (a creature sacred to Persephone and Pallas Athene and associated with wisdom) he turns into the Set-like beast most abhorred by Isis—an ass.

Not only this, before any counterpotion can be taken (which is the apparently simple expedient of eating roses) their own act of theft takes on an objective reality. Thieves break into the house, steal all the valuables therein, and kidnap the ass to carry off the loot.

At the bandits' hideout we find the elements for another Mystery drama. There is a young bride called Charitë, who has been seized and carried off on her wedding day by the bandits. Typical of the god/goddess relationship of ancient Egypt (for example, Isis and

Osiris) she and her bridegroom, Tlepolemus, are also cousins and have slept together since infancy.

Cupid and Psyche

To console the desolate and weeping bride an old crone who lives with the robbers tells the story of Cupid and Psyche. This is perhaps the most spiritually inspired tale of pagan antiquity to portray the condition of the human soul.

Psyche is one of three royal daughters, and so beautiful that many take her to be the incarnation of a goddess. This is also her misfortune for, whilst her plainer sisters are successfully married, Psyche is so adored that she has no normal human contact. All who see her seek to place her on a pedestal. This excites the wrath of the goddess Venus whose shrines are being neglected. As a lesson Venus instructs her son Cupid to cause Psyche to fall in love with some degraded outcast. By a neat ironical twist the "degraded outcast" turns out to be Cupid himself.

In the meantime Psyche's father seeks advice at the oracle of Apollo and receives the prophecy that she shall be wed on a mountaintop, and not to a human but to a feared and mischievous winged terror. In fact the mountaintop may be conceived as the heights of human mystical aspiration, and the "winged terror" is Cupid himself, the embodiment of divine love. Taking the prophecy in its literal sense, with much grief Psyche is taken to a mountaintop and left there to her fate.

A gentle west wind however wafts her to a beautiful land where, in an enchanted castle, she is tended by invisible servants ministering to her every wish. And when night falls she is taken in marriage by an invisible husband. This is Cupid himself, who tells her that she must never seek to gaze upon him.

So life goes idyllically on in this paradisal condition but Psyche conceives an ever stronger desire to see her sisters and to show them her circumstances of life. She is counseled against this by Cupid but in the end he lets her have her way. Her sisters come to visit but are consumed by jealousy and rabidly curious as to who her secret husband might be.

When they return home they hide the gifts of jewels they have been given and say nothing about the visit to their mourning parents, who still grieve the apparent cruel fate of Psyche.

When Psyche wishes to see her sisters again Cupid once more warns her about the dangers that might ensue, particularly as she is now with child by him. She can see no danger however and persists in her desire that her sisters come again. When they do so they tell her that they are much concerned for her, that they have discovered she is married to a hideous evil monster. They advise her to hide a lamp and a knife near her bed and when her husband next comes to her in the night to raise the lamp and cut his head off with the knife.

Deceived by their wiles Psyche does as they suggest, but when she raises the lamp to strike with the knife she is struck helpless by the beauty of the naked god. Even the blade of the knife turns at the vision, and a spot of hot oil from the lamp awakens Cupid. For her betrayal and disobedience Cupid rebukes her and vows the evil sisters shall have their just deserts. As for Psyche, her punishment shall simply be—the cruelest that a god of love can inflict—his absence.

Desolate in her fallen condition Psyche meets Pan, the most earthy representative of the power of love. He advises her not to despair but simply to have the faith and loyalty to go on loving the god of love, as this is the only way that he can be invoked to reappear. She returns to her own country.

One of her sisters, on learning that Psyche's husband was in fact a god, mad with envious desire, runs up to the mountaintop and casts herself off. But no gentle sustaining west wind comes and she crashes to her death on the rocks, which cut her to pieces, and the birds and beasts of the mountain consume her remains.

Psyche finds herself an outcast. She is turned away from the temples of Ceres and Juno, who tell her that her only hope is to reconcile herself with Venus. Venus however is enraged at Cupid's disobedience of her original edict and at his mating with a mortal. When Psyche approaches, Venus has her scourged by two servants, Anxiety and Grief, and in mockery gives her a series of impossible tests as the only means to reinstate herself.

These are:

1. to sort a huge pile of seeds in a single night;
2. to collect a skein of golden fleece from a flock of ferocious rams;
3. to fill a cup with water from the high spring that feeds the Styx, the river dividing this world from the Underworld;
4. to descend into Hades and return with a box containing some of the beauty of Proserpine.

Psyche, however, succeeds in performing these tasks, with the help of others. The ants, emblematic of industry and civilization, sort the seeds for her. The simple wisdom of the riverside reeds advises her to collect the fleece from briars while the rams are asleep. The eagle, who was helped by Cupid to raise the cupbearer Ganymede to heaven at Zeus's command, returns the favor by procuring the cupful of water for Psyche. To perform the final test Psyche ascends a tower with the intention of throwing herself from the top to her death. The tower, however, tells her that although this is a way to reach the Underworld it is a way that precludes her returning. The wise tower (obviously a structure of initiation) gives her detailed advice on how to enter the Underworld, find her way through its passages and tests to Proserpine, and how safely to return. Psyche follows this advice and returns with the box of Proserpine's beauty. Even here she almost fails, when her human curiosity gets the better of her. She tries to peep at the beauty inside the box but on opening it is overcome with sleep. Cupid, however, comes to her aid, and all ends happily. Zeus regularizes their marriage and makes Psyche immortal.

So ends the story told by the hag (another form of the goddess) to the captive Charitë. Like Psyche, Charitë seeks the help of lower creatures and begs help from the ass. He, although he is lame (a parallel with the lameness of Oedipus and the supreme lame god, Asclepios) gallops off with her on his back—beauty and the beast. In this scene is embodied the relationship between higher self and lower self as taught in esoteric psychology. As so often happens, rider and ridden have a difference of opinion as to which way to go. Charitë wants to ride straight home; Lucius the ass knows that this is the way the robbers have gone. They are still disputing at the parting of the ways when the robbers return and recapture them.

Further rescue comes in a most unexpected way. The robbers elect a new chief who seems to be a very superior kind of robber. In fact it is Charitë's bridegroom in disguise. He overcomes the robbers, delivers them to justice, and marries his bride. Thus we have the drama of a savior god coming among men to restore things to rights.

For his attempt to save Charitë, the ass is rewarded in a fashion thought most likely to please an ass. He is sent to a stud farm. However, all does not go well for him there. His further adventures parallel the Mystery drama that has been enacted by Charitë (the stolen and ransomed virgin bride) and Tlepolemus (the savior-bridegroom descending to a lower condition to effect her rescue and redemption).

The couple do not live happily ever after. Tlepolemus is betrayed by a former rival for her hand. He is invited on a hunting expedition, and although he has vowed never to hunt horned or tusked beasts (sacred to Isis), things are so arranged that he is cornered and gored by a ferocious boar. The rival, Thrasyllus, finishes him off and then, feigning innocence, proceeds to woo the widowed Charitë.

She, however, is informed of the facts by the ghost of her murdered husband. She pretends to welcome the murderer's advances, and even to agree to a secret love affair before their marriage. However, on the night that she promised to come to his bed she drugs him and blinds him with a bronze pin from her hair. She then flies to her husband's grave and kills herself with his sword, plunging it under the right breast—where Jesus also received the lance thrust from Longinus.

There are interesting parallels in all of this story with Christian and pagan mysteries, and also with some of Shakespeare's plots. Of particular significance is that on her husband's grave Charitë erects an image of the god Dionysus, endowed with her husband's features. Tlepolemus, a savior like Dionysus, is torn by a wild beast as Dionysus was by the Bacchanals. This death of the savior is occasioned by a rival whose name means "rashness," or the impiety that comes from presumption and envy. This gives the opportunity for a noble, martyr's death, in a love that transcends the grave, for Charitë, whose name signifies hope and love. This episode shows the close parallels that lie between certain pagan Mystery cults and the Christian interpretation of the significance of Jesus, who is an historical embodiment of pagan spiritual insights as much as a fulfillment of the Old Testament Jewish prophetic tradition.

The Trials of the Ass

In parallel to these events, the ass's stay at the stud farm is not a happy one. First he is shunned and persecuted by the horses, who look down upon him as inferior to themselves. And in defiance of express orders for his honorable treatment, the steward's evil wife sets him to work slaving at a mill. He is also cruelly overworked and tortured by a sadistic boy. The theme of evil wife and mill turning appear more than once in the narrative. The evil wife is the adverse side of womanhood, and a distorted aspect of Isis, invoked by Lucius' underhand means and motives in his approach to her Mysteries.

The mill is an interesting symbol in that it represents harnessed power. It can be beneficent in its technological results or a form of slavery. The symbol of the swastika derives from it, being the plan view of a mill spindle driven by four beasts via transverse poles.

Just as the evil wife, the nagging shrew, is the adverse side of the goddess, so the sadistic boy is the adverse side of the divine miraculous child. Poor Lucius certainly reaps as he has sown in his impious approach to the Mysteries.

This is the nadir of his treatment. Having been well punished by the circumstances evoked by his own attitude (the true operation of karma) his sufferings are brought to an end by a she-bear killing the sadistic boy. The she-bear is another emblem of the goddess Isis, and signifies her intervention. This is in the nick of time for, as a result of the boy's falsely accusing him of trying to molest little girls, plans were afoot to castrate the ass. Even so, he suffers a cruel beating from the boy's avenging mother, who blames him for her son's death.

We may consider this episode as a period of purgation. It is an established step in any initiation process, and precedes the next stage of initiation, which is a desert or wilderness journey.

This journey is brought about, in the story, by the steward and his wife deciding to abscond with all the goods and chattels on hearing of the death of Tlepolemus and Charitë. Thus Lucius finds himself once again in the hands of thieves, but with the slight improvement that these are amateur rather than professional thieves.

The initiatory character of the wilderness journey (in this instance, through a forest) is shown by its having three crisis points within it. The first is their fear that they will be attacked by wolves. In fact they are attacked by the mastiff dogs of the village where they seek refuge. The villagers also throw stones at them in the belief that they are bandits. There are two interesting aspects to this. First the principle that what one fears does not generally happen in the way that one expects. Secondly, that although they are not the bandits the villagers fear, they are certainly thieves, and thus not undeserving of the treatment they receive. So divine justice (or karma) acts through ordinary levels of causation in a seemingly arbitrary but, at root, just fashion.

The second crisis is where they are duped by an old man who allegedly seeks help to rescue a child. In fact he is custodian of a dreadful snake monster who lures unwary travelers to their death. Again this reflects themselves as betrayers of trust.

The third crisis is their confrontation with the fate of a false bailiff (as they themselves are), who because he betrayed his wife and child (a particular sin against Isis) is sentenced to be tied to a fig tree smeared with honey where he is eaten alive by ants. The ants we have met before in the story of Cupid and Psyche; and figs and honey are both sacred to the Mysteries of the Goddess.

In the normal sequence of events, after the Mystery journey through the wilderness, the candidate for initiation would come upon a temple. We are enacting, however, in the story of Lucius, a distorted shadow of the true Mysteries. This is partly to warn of the consequences of their desecration; partly as a convenient "blind" for Apuleius not to reveal too much to the "profane." Consequently we have a distorted portrayal of an initiate's reception into a band of devoted brothers. Lucius, the ass, finds himself purchased by a wandering group of holy men. These are described as eunuch-priests (as indeed many priests of the Goddess were) but in fact they are homosexuals of a most predatory kind, who make their living by performing ecstatic dances of self-flagellation and collecting money from the impressed onlookers. They require the ass to carry a statue of the Eastern goddess Cybele, whose adherents they purport to be.

Lucius describes his falling into their hands as the work of "merciless Fortune" which is what we might nowadays call karma. A changed attitude can bring about a changed circumstance so, at root, any "lack of mercy" is a lack of repentance.

A couple of interesting points are made in the text about pseudoreligious experience and pseudooccult knowledge. The first is in his description of pretended ecstasy of one of the priests—"heaving deep sighs from the very bottom of his lungs, as if filled with the spirit of the Goddess, he pretended to go stark mad." He goes on to comment: "A strange notion, this, that divine immanency, instead of doing men good, enfeebles or disorders their senses." The other amusing point, which might well be applied by occult charlatans of today, is their all-purpose oracle. To any who come seeking prophetic guidance they chant:

The patient oxen plough the soil;
And harvests rich repay their toil.

This can be applied to any conceivable problem as a welcome generally optimistically toned answer from the gods.

The ass remains with the eunuch priests for some time, carrying the
image of the goddess and the ever-full offertory bags. "I was at once a walking temple and a walking larder" he says, again emphasizing the recurrent
symbolism throughout the whole novel of the sacramental symbolism of
eating and feasting. This again is universal symbolism found from the
ever-flowing cauldron of Ceridwen to the table of the Last Supper.

While he is with them he faces the first of three tests of moral
integrity. At some risk to himself he raises the alarm when the eunuch
priests attempt to rape a young farm worker. Thus although an ass, he
shows more than an ass's concern for the well-being of others.

Later he exposes the deception that a cook intends to play in serving up ass's meat instead of venison, although there is a certain degree
of self-interest here in that it is he who is likely to provide the ass meat
if the cook's scheme goes through. There is an overtone here of the
savior-god theme, the hero being eaten. There are more immediate
spiritual developments required of Lucius, however, as he is eventually to become an initiate of the Mysteries for which his experiences in
animal form are a prelude. The test here is one of superasinine intelligence in that he saves himself by smashing up the dining room and
then sheltering in the master's bedroom, where he spends the night.
There is another interesting piece of symbolism here in the role of
the dog. Anubis, the Egyptian Opener of the Ways, is a dog-headed
god, and the ways are opened in this episode first by a dog stealing the
haunch of venison (which is the circumstance that leads the cook to
kill and serve up the ass), and then he is left unmolested in the bedroom because another dog is found to be rabid and so all fear to go
near the ass in case he too has rabies, his actions in smashing up the
dining room being thought the symptoms of the disease.

Following this episode the eunuch priests are arrested for having
stolen a golden cup from the temple of Juno. This is an apt symbolic
statement of their spiritual condition, for their assumed effeminacy is

a travesty of the true principle. The ass is sold again, once more coming under the dominion of an evil and adulterous wife at a mill, and the ass's third moral act is to expose her deception of her husband by revealing her lover.

An interesting historical sidelight here is that the woman appears to be a Christian, and in the author's words: "She . . . professed perfect scorn for the immortals and rejected all true religion in favor of a fantastic and blasphemous cult of an 'Only God.' In his honor she practiced various absurd ceremonies which gave her the excuse of getting drunk quite early in the day and playing the whore at all hours; most people, including her husband, were quite deceived by her."

Plainly Apuleius has no great love of Christians and this early example of relations between the new religion and the old is an interesting one. If this travesty of early Christian belief and practice was the common attitude of intelligent pagans then there is small wonder that when Christians came to power they took such unsympathetic views of paganism. Following the successful completion of these tests of moral initiative, Lucius meets with some better luck when he passes into the hands of a market gardener and earns his keep helping him to take his food to market—another instance of spiritual food symbolism.

This does not last however. It is a phase quickly followed by what is called in the mystical terminology of Saint John of the Cross, "the dark night of the soul," or in terms of alchemy, the *dissolutio*. Everything falls to pieces.

There are, first of all, a series of frightening portents. The ancient world took portents seriously. In the histories of Livy, for instance, along with the historical details of the year's events, the major portents or omens are also listed. The modern mind tends to sneer at this preoccupation, but as Jung has found and reported in his work on synchronicity, when one approaches the inner worlds particularly, whether in analytical psychology, Mystery initiation, or the psychic upsurge caused by great national events, signs preceding (portents) and signs following are to be expected. Admittedly, interpreting them may be difficult, but the inner worlds have a way of making their presence felt in no uncertain manner. They are, after all, levels of causation, even though the effects of that causation work out in a perfectly ordinary "accustomed" way.

The strange portents are swiftly followed by bad news of corruption and death, and following upon this the most unlikely things happen, the most significant of which is the old market gardener turning upon a centurion who tries to commandeer the ass and beating him up and leaving him unconscious. They then become fugitives, for assaulting a Roman army officer is a serious offense, and they go into hiding. Their hiding place is betrayed however by the ass's shadow showing up against a wall. Thus are we all betrayed by our "shadow" side. It is that which constitutes the dweller on the threshold of initiation and causes all the life problems that we have, as our own adverse side is projected onto the world about us.

These unfortunate occurrences are, however, the prelude to initiation and are at least a sign that progress is being made. From now on Lucius is on a plainly discernible upward path that leads first to his leaving behind his asinine form, and then his higher initiation into the rites of Isis and Osiris.

We need to bear in mind however, if we are to avoid the pitfall of vainglory and ego inflation, that although it behooves us to try our best, it is not by our own merits alone that we achieve initiation. We need help from others, and we need divine grace. This is signified by the story that is interpolated here of an innocent victim only being saved from evil machinations by the intervention of a deus ex machina in the form of a holy medical man.

Having got his attitude right through the numerous tests, realizations, and retributions that have gone before, Lucius is set for initiation, the stages of which follow in the narrative, beginning from the point where he is put into kitchen service (again the symbolism of spiritual food) with the lord chief justice. This symbolizes law, order, and the civilizing process represented by initiation and the aims and aspirations of the Mysteries.

From the time that Lucius in his asinine form is taken into service by the lord chief justice, his development shows rapid progress. Working as a pack animal attached to the kitchen, he begins to leave his hay and to feed on human food left over from the banquets.

He is discovered in this, but his masters, far from punishing him, encourage him to do more human tricks. They teach him to sit at table, to wrestle, to dance, to nod or shake his head in answer to questions, and even to wink at the wine waiter when he needs a drink. He soon becomes quite famous as a result.

We have in this episode an analog of spiritual initiation. Just as the ass is being trained to become more human, prior to resuming his original and proper human form, from which state he has fallen; so in the initiation process is the human personality trained into more spiritual attitudes and patterns prior to regaining its original and proper spiritual condition from which it has fallen.

In *The Golden Ass* this process reaches its peak in the visit of a noblewoman who takes the ass and trains it to be her lover. Keeping in mind the consistent symbolic parallels, we see how Apuleius has transformed the original dirty joke into an initiatory parable, for this represents the human soul being taken into close consummation with the goddess—the higher realms of inner, nature—or Isis unveiled.

However, just as the highest mysteries are capable of the greatest profanation, so in the story do we get a degrading of the situation. The relationship between the noblewoman and the ass is treated by Apuleius with considerable literary skill and good taste. It is a genuine love that is depicted, which reminds one of the delicacy of the feelings of Titania the fairy queen for Bottom, the ass-headed, in Shakespeare's *Midsummer Night's Dream*. In the story, word gets out, and it is decided that it would be amusing and profitable to make a public spectacle of this new feat of the ass.

This kind of divertissement occurred frequently in Roman times. Scenes from mythology were used as the material for public spectacle. In this instance the show is to be the Judgment of Paris, which provides an excuse for a display of feminine nudity. And as a sequel to this, a condemned criminal woman is to be coupled with the ass, before she is torn to pieces by wild beasts.

However, the ass has by now achieved a measure of sensibility and morality superior to his human owners, and rather than take part in such public profanation of the Mysteries, he runs away—renouncing a life of asinine ease, fame, and fortune.

Evocation of the Goddess

Lucius runs to the seashore and there makes a sincere and passionate supplication to the goddess Isis to save him and restore him to his rightful form. This, his invocation and the subsequent appearance to him of the goddess, is possibly the most moving and evocative passage in ancient literature. To the occult student it is the very stuff of "pathworking" and similar meditational image building. Some may, at some time, be fortunate enough to experience such a vision themselves.

About the first watch of the night, when as I had slept my first sleep, awaked with sudden fear, and saw the moon shining bright as when she is at the full, and seeming as though she leaped out of the sea. Then thought with myself that this was the most secret time, when that goddess had most puissance and force, considering that all human things be governed by her providence; and that not only all beasts private and tame, wild and savage, be made strong by the governance of her light and godhead, but also things inanimate and without life: and I considered that all bodies in the heavens, the earth, and the seas be by her increasing motions increased, and by her diminishing motions diminished; then as weary of all my cruel fortune and calamity, I found good hope and sovereign remedy, though it were very late, to be delivered of all my misery, by invocation and prayer to the excellent beauty of this powerful goddess. Wherefore shaking off my drowsy sleep I arose with a joyful face, and moved by a great affection to purify myself, I plunged my head seven times into the water of the sea; which number of seven is convenable and agreeable to holy and divine things, as the worthy and sage philosopher Pythagoras hath declared. Then very lively and joyfully, though with a weeping countenance, I made this oration to the puissant goddess:

"O blessed queen of heaven, whether Thou be the Dame Ceres which art the original and motherly nurse of all fruitful things in the earth, who, after the finding of thy daughter Proserpine, through the great joy which Thou didst presently conceive, didst utterly take away and abolish the food of them of old time, the acorns, and madest the barren and unfruitful ground of Eleusis to be ploughed and sewn, and now givest men a more better and milder food; or whether Thou be the celestial Venus, who, in the beginning of the world, didst couple together male and female with an engendered love, and didst so make an eternal propagation of human kind, being now worshipped within the temples of the Isle Paphos; or whether Thou be the sister of the god Phoebus, who hast saved so many people by lightening and lessening with thy medicines the pangs of travail and art now adored at the sacred places of Ephesus; or whether Thou be called terrible Proserpine, by reason of the deadly howlings which Thou yieldest, that hath power with triple face to stop and put away the invasion of hags and ghosts which appear unto men, and to keep them down in the closures of the Earth, which dost wander in sundry groves and art worshipped in divers manners; Thou, which dost luminate all the cities of the earth by Thy feminine light; Thou, which nourishest all the seeds of the world by Thy damp heat, giving Thy changing light according to the wanderings, near or far, of the sun: by whatsoever name or fashion or shape it is lawful to call upon Thee, I pray Thee to end my great travail and misery and raise up my fallen hopes, and deliver me from the wretched fortune which so long time pursued me. Grant peace and rest, if it please Thee, to my adversities, for I have endured enough labor and peril. Remove from me the hateful shape of mine ass, and render me to my kindred and to mine own self Lucius: and if I have offended in any point Thy divine majesty, let me rather die if I may not live."

When I had ended this oration, discovering my plaints to the goddess, I fortuned to fall again asleep upon that same bed; and by and by (for mine eyes were but newly closed) appeared to me from the midst of the sea a divine and venerable face, worshipped even of the gods themselves. Then, by little and little, I seemed to see the whole figure of her body, bright and mounting out of the sea and standing before me: wherefore I purpose to describe her divine semblance, if the poverty of my human speech will suffer me, or her divine power give me a power of eloquence rich enough to express it. First she had a great abundance of hair, flowing and curling, dispersed and scattered about her divine neck; on the crown of her head she bare many garlands interlaced with flowers, and in the middle of her forehead was a plain circlet in fashion of a mirror, or rather resembling the moon by the light that it gave forth; and this was borne up on either side by serpents that seemed to rise from the furrows of the earth, and above it were blades of corn set out. Her vestment was of finest linen yielding divers colors, somewhere white and shining, somewhere yellow like the crocus flower somewhere rosy red, somewhere flaming; and (which troubled my sight and spirit sore) her cloak was utterly dark and obscure covered with shining black, and being wrapped round her from under her left arm to her right shoulder in manner of a shield, part of it fell down, pleated in most subtle fashion, to the skirts of her garment so that the welts appeared comely. Here and there upon the edge thereof and throughout its surface the stars glimpsed, and in the middle of them was placed the moon in mid-month, which shone like a flame of fire; and round about the whole length of the border of that goodly robe was a crown of garland wreathing unbroken, made with all flowers and all fruits. Things quite diverse did she bear: for in her right hand she had timbrel of brass, a flat piece of

metal curved in manner of a girdle, wherein passed not many rods
through the periphery of it; and when with her arm she moved these
triple chords, they gave forth a shrill and clear sound. In her hand
she bare a cup of gold like unto a boat, upon the handle whereof,
in the upper part which is best seen, an asp lifted up his head with
a wide-swelling throat. Her odoriferous feet were covered with
shoes interlaced and wrought with victorious palm. Thus the divine
shape, breathing out the pleasant spice of fertile Arabia, disdained
not with her holy voice to utter these words unto me:

"Behold Lucius, I am come; thy weeping and prayer hath moved
me to succor thee. I am she that is the natural mother of all things,
mistress and governess of all the elements, the initial progeny of
worlds, chief of the powers divine, queen of all that are in hell,
the principal of them that dwell in heaven, manifested alone and
under one form of all the gods and goddesses. At my will the planets of the sky, the wholesome winds of the seas, and the lamen-
table silences of hell be disposed; my name, my divinity is adored
throughout all the world, in divers manners, in variable customs,
and by many names. For the Phrygians that are the first of all men
call me the Mother of the gods at Pessinus; the Athenians, which
are sprung from their own soil, Cecropian Minerva; the Cyprians,
which are girt about by the sea, Paphian Venus; the Cretans which
bear arrows, Dictynnian Diana; the Sicilians, which speak three
tongues, infernal Proserpine; the Eleusians their ancient goddess
Ceres; some Juno, other Bellona, other Hecate, other Rhamnusia,
and principally both sort of Ethiopians which dwell in the Orient
and are enlightened by the morning rays of the sun, and the
Egyptians, which are excellent in all kind of ancient doctrine, and
by their proper ceremonies accustom to worship me, do call me by
my true name, Queen Isis."

Isis instructs Lucius to attend a public ceremony of hers the following
day, when the high priest will be carrying a wreath of roses for him as a

result of being instructed to do so in a vision that she will give him.

This occurs, and Lucius resumes his human form, becomes a three-fold initiate in the Mysteries of Isis and Osiris, of which he says he can tell us nothing save that:

> I approached the very gates of death and set one foot on Proserpine's threshold, yet was permitted to return, rapt through all the elements. At midnight I saw the sun shining as if it were noon; I entered the presence of the gods of the underworld and the gods of the upper world, stood near and worshipped them.

The solemn rites end at dawn and he emerges from the sanctuary wearing twelve different stoles—no doubt corresponding to the wholeness of the zodiacal signs, elsewhere symbolized by the initiatory twelve labors of Hercules, the archetypal man.

Although he vows he can tell us nothing of the Mysteries, Apuleius has told us a great deal. Not that all will be readily apparent to surface consciousness without a fair bit of meditation, intuition, and parallel inner experience on our part. But at least he has indicated the type of images with which we should work, and that is the most that any elucidation of the Mysteries can do.

We are not talking about a readily explainable "mystery" as in the sense of a detective story or mathematical puzzle. But about a Mystery in the sense of deep and hidden truths that are beyond the reach of the intellect. It is not a question of intelligence, it is a matter of level. It is barely possible to explain the unexplainable, but it is possible to experience it, and then it needs no explanation.

In our next journey, we shall be using some of Apuleius' powerful imagery, but we shall not be retracing all the steps of the ass. Indeed, that would be beyond our purpose for the ass's adventures are in one sense a description of what *not* to do, or the consequences of having taken the wrong attitude to the Mysteries in the first place, (that is, intellectual curiosity and the desire for strange powers).

It would, however, be a useful exercise for anyone to repeat the invocation of the ass at the seashore, for this is a genuine and heartfelt approach to the Goddess. It is not immediately to our main purpose though, for it is simply a repetition, in slightly different symbolic terms, of the invocation of the ninefold goddess we have conducted in our magical circle in Part One.

We are now concerned with a more objective level of working, and the next stage of our appreciation of the needs and dynamics of the Planetary Being. We shall thus concentrate upon the core imagery at the very center of *The Golden Ass,* the story of Psyche, who for our purposes will take the place of Andromeda as the feminine power. (It is interesting to note in passing the similarity in the origin of each of these figures, both as a consequence of overweening pride on the part of others, or of being equal or superior to the gods.)

And so in the next sequence we see the Planetary Being, no longer as a chained maiden needing rescue, like Andromeda, but as a being restored to a higher level (a process we saw at the end of our first journey). She is now in the process of being betrothed to the divine masculine power, which we shall see depicted as a composite figure somewhat allusively depicted with attributes of Orpheus and Dionysus, but in reality and fullness being the all-embracing Son of Light, subsuming all the gods, as the Goddess subsumes all goddesses.

JOURNEY 2: THE LOVER OF PSYCHE

We are at the foot of a range of mountains. As we look up we see a stony, winding path that leads between the rocks. About us are a group of people who try to bar our way, and who deride our intention to climb this path. We take no notice of them, however, and they make way before our determination and spiritual will.

Leaving behind all cries or hubbub from the crowd below, we climb energetically up the steep path. As we gradually ascend, the vegetation becomes more stunted with the increased altitude until eventually we are moving among rocks bare of all growth except a few patches of moss and lichen.

Our way leads to a passage between two peaks and as we approach the pass we see that the path leads between two tall, rough-hewn, upright stones. Between these pillars is what appears to be a crude stone altar, and upon the altar are the remains of rusty chains.

We stand before the low gray altar stone and look between the rough pillars and find, to our dismay, that the path does not continue. Beyond is nothing but a sheer drop, the bottom of which cannot even be seen. The wind blows gustily about us, and we begin to think that perhaps the folk below were right, and that this is a dead end to a fool's journey that leads nowhere. But as the wind blows so it seems to sing through the pillars and we listen to it, and it's as if it contains voices that bid us to mount the sacrificial altar.

Somewhat hesitatingly we do so, and as we do we hear the wind voices again. They seem to bid us to leap into the chasm below. Looking out into the empty space before us, there appears nothing but wisps of cloud. But as we gaze, within the cloud there is the hint of a golden light. And taking our courage in our hands, and with our faith in our own intuition and that golden light, we step forth into the void.

For a moment there is a kind of sinking feeling, but then as a misty cloud envelopes us our slight fall is arrested and we find we are standing upon solid earth. Looking down we see springy mountain grass beneath our feet, and before us a clear, fast-running mountain stream.

We look across the stream, and although at first it is just like looking into the sky from the heights, gradually our perceptions clarify and we see forming in the air before us a beautiful maiden. She smiles, and holds out her hands to us in welcome, inviting us to jump the stream.

It is quite wide, but taking a short but determined run we do so, and as we land before her so our eyes are opened to the fair country in which she stands. As far as the eye can see is a plain high in the mountains with meadows, streams, and farmsteads.

She smiles at our surprise and bids us follow her, and she leads the way along a path that soon becomes a lane between flowering hedge-rows. Eventually we see that she is leading us to a fair palace, that stands brilliant in the sun in the midst of beautiful gardens.

She leads us on through the gardens and into the palace, across a great marble hallway and up broad marble stairs and along a passage-way until we come upon a wide door, surrounded by golden decora-tions. She bids us enter and we find a great room, around the walls of which are tables covered in snow-white linen with plates of food and drink. She bids us to take it, as invisible servants bring plates and cups and goblets to us, and we find that the food and drink is the fairest that we have ever tasted.

We now notice that in the center of the room is an unusual sight for a banqueting hall. It is a huge bed, a massive, white, circular divan with golden hangings.

The princess proceeds to lie down upon the bed, and we see that she is now dressed in a pure white wedding gown that spreads out all around her. She composes herself for sleep and as she does so a quiet comes upon the room, and the light begins to fade to a twilight. As it does so we see that in the roof above the bed there is a domed window. It is fashioned in a mosaic of colored glass and shows the figure of a god, clad in a white tunic and holding a lyre, and a serpent-twined staff with wings and a pinecone at its top.

As we gaze up, the window becomes illuminated, perhaps by bright moonlight, and we find that we are all standing in a great circle about the bed, each holding a lighted taper.

The image of the god grows brighter until it seems no longer just a picture in stained glass but an actuality. At the same time the thyrsus, or winged and serpent-twined pinecone wand, bursts forth into a blaze so bright that we cannot see the one who carries it. Our gaze is domi-nated by the great wand that descends down toward the sleeping figure upon the sea. The silver wings beat like those of a gigantic swan, the cone at the top glows and vibrates with red and golden light, pulsations of energy run up and down the interior of the hollow staff like divine fire, and at its bottom tip is a golden arrow point that coils and quivers like a scorpion's stinger.

The princess upon the bed holds forth her arms in an arc shape of acceptance of the god, and as she does so the vibrant tip of the staff penetrates her solar plexus. At this moment there is a blaze of rainbow light and we see, as it subsides, that the thyrsus has been transformed into a figure of a goddess, the winged Isis, radiant behind a rainbow veil.

She holds out her hands in blessing to us as she slowly ascends, in ecstasy, through the dome of the nuptial chamber. As she does so, we find we are standing in the midst of sweet-smelling flowers that shower down upon us, while the bed in our midst has become transformed into a green grassy bank covered with wildflowers.

And as we look around we realize we are no longer standing in a palace room but are in a mountain vale that instead of growing nothing but coarse grass and heather is ablaze with every kind of exotic bloom and the hum of honeybees.

Looking up we realize that we are standing in bright sunlight, and looking toward the sun we see it as a gold orb in which stands a god and before him, held within his arms, is the figure of the winged Isis, the transformed princess of the mountain, who also gazes down upon us. They give us their blessing.

We bathe in this atmosphere of divine love and benediction until, when we feel ready, we turn back toward the pylon gate. Stepping through the stream and then up between the pillars, we find ourselves, as we pass through them, back in our normal mode of consciousness and in the familiar physical place from whence we started our inner journey.

BRANCH THREE

The Trembling of the Veil of Orthodoxy

Just as few may realize that mysteries of the Goddess are being revealed by Apuleius in his comic erotic novel, so is there little realization about the extent to which the powers of the Goddess have permeated and influenced the overtly paternalistic and masculine-oriented expressions of religious orthodoxy in the Christian West.

If Apuleius had misgivings about the cult of Christianity in his own times, he would have been considerably surprised, not to say shocked and horrified, to learn of its eventual cultural dominance. Although perhaps his feelings would have been mollified by the realization that the powers of the feminine principle are far greater than the intellects of theologians. And like green shoots growing through concrete, there has been no stopping the expression in various ways of the feminine principle within the Church.

Christianity, with its roots in Judaism, has had to labor under a curious masculine bias, although in the beginning this was simply a characteristic attitude of the times.

It should not be forgotten that the pagan Mysteries were also pater-

106

nalistic and male-oriented, despite the worship of the Goddess. Initiates were not only male, but from the higher echelons of society. It was an elitism far removed from modern democratic and egalitarian assumptions. Indeed it was a scandal to the pagan world that Christianity opened up its Mysteries to women and to slaves.

It is instructive, however, to look closely at the Christian story to see the function of women within it. Who stood at the foot of the cross? Who was first at the tomb on the morning of the Resurrection?

The dark figure of the mother at the foot of the sacrificial cross is more than a mourning Jewish woman. She is this too, for in the Christian story the universal finds expression in the particular. Yet she is also a representative of the great dark Mother of Form, who gave birth to the Savior, and now stands under the wood of the cross to witness his passage through the gates of death. Jesus had presented his challenge and his credentials on the olive-clad mount of the Garden of Gethsemene. He had crossed the brook Kedron between worlds of existence, and their values. He had met the dragon in the form of the mob, with its dual heads of priestly and secular power. Now he enters the Underworld, between the pillars of two other crosses, for a three-day journey from Good Friday to Easter Sunday.

The Passion of Jesus Christ is indeed a Mystery story, a process of initiation. But more than this: Christians would see it as a unique, once-for-all cosmic event, taking place at a point in time and space, in the body of the Earth, and thus raising the spiritual quality and opportunity of planetary life.

The great Feminine power gradually began to make itself felt and to assert its presence, despite the world view of Judaic Christianity, that at first almost completely excluded the female principle and even saw it as the root of all evil in the figure of Eve. However, in the dramatic personae of the Garden of Eden story, there are all the elements for redemption through the feminine principle. The serpent and the tree in the Garden are familiar figures from the Garden of the Hesperides.

THE RETURN OF THE GODDESS

The gradual increase in the realization of the importance of the divine feminine principle can be traced over the twenty centuries of Christendom. From the unpromising beginnings in the synoptic gospels, where even the nativity stories relating to Mary are thought to be later interpolations, we find, by the second century, the appearance of the apocryphal gospels of the Book of James and the Gospel of Thomas, which attempted to fulfill a natural demand for details of the "Mother of God."

This process has been condemned as a "throwback" to paganism, a view which is as shallow as it is narrow. The process is rather an enrichment, an expansion of inner truth, a realization that the historical life and death of Jesus Christ was a talismanic act of astounding significance and vast proportions. It was the overshadowing of inner forces to a unique degree. The full truth of this can only be realized by a gradual expansion of human consciousness and even then only in symbolic terms. Hence the stories of Mary are not "mere mythologizing" but a gradual filtering through of profound metaphysical truths about the cosmic place and function of the feminine principle. The image of the Blessed Virgin is the new Isis, if one may so phrase it. The raising of her status from simple Jewish virgin to Queen of Heaven has been a gradual process of realization of the cosmic destiny of the human race.

This was all foreshadowed in the Canticles of Solomon, the great lover king and builder of the original Temple. It is also found in the Revelation of John of Patmos, and his vision of the New Jerusalem, decked as a bride.

It may help to summarize the gradual unfolding of this process of the emergence of the feminine principle.

By AD 200, paintings of the Virgin Mary were appearing in the catacombs of Rome, which sheltered the early Christians, and the Book of James had been written. This dealt with the birth of Mary herself, which in its own way was attended by prodigies, in that her mother

Anna is barren until she is visited by an angel in her garden. The tale is a poignant one. The visitation occurs while her husband Joachim is wandering in penance in the desert for forty days. His offerings to the Temple had been rejected by the high priest who interpreted their continuing childlessness as a sign of the Lord's displeasure. In the absence of her husband the distressed Anna dresses herself in her old bridal array and wanders into the garden. She sits under a bay tree and becomes more distressed at the sight of a nestful of baby sparrows within its branches. Then the angel appears and promises her a child. At the same time an angel appears to Joachim who rushes back in joy, to be met by his wife at the golden gate of Jerusalem.

Their child, Mary, is dedicated to the Temple. She walks seven steps at the age of six months, and her mother catches her up, vowing that she shall walk no more upon the ground until she is taken to the temple. Thereafter her bedchamber is made into a sanctuary, nothing common or unclean is taken into it, and the infant is tended and carried by dedicated maidens.

When she is one year old her father holds a great feast and she is blessed by the high priests at a great assembly of the priests, scribes, elders, and people of Israel.

At her third year, in a ceremony involving a procession of virgins with lights, the child Mary is taken and dedicated to the Temple. Here she sits upon the third step of the altar, and then, filled with the grace of God, dances before the assembled people.

The priest who receives her makes a speech of welcome and dedication that is close to the Magnificat in wording and intention: "The Lord hath magnified thy name among all generations; in thee in the latter days shall the Lord make manifest his redemption unto the children of Israel."

Mary is hereafter described as being like a nurtured dove, fed by the hand of an angel. When she reaches the age of twelve a council of priests is held to decide what is to be done with her, as it will not be possible for her to remain in the Temple when she reaches puberty. The high priest, in prayer in the Holy of Holies, is instructed by an angel to call together all the widowers of the people of Israel. Each one is to bring his staff and a sign will follow showing which shall take Mary as his wife.

In due course all the widowers assemble, with their rods, including the carpenter Joseph. The rods are taken in and then returned, at which point a dove appears at the head of Joseph's staff and alights upon his head. He is therefore regarded as the chosen husband.

At first he strongly protests saying, "1 have sons, and I am an old man, but she is a girl: lest I become a laughing stock to the children of Israel." However, the high priest insists, warning Joseph against disobeying the Lord. Joseph therefore takes Mary into his house but does not lie with her as a husband.

The Spinner and Weaver

Shortly afterwards there is a need for a veil to be made for the Temple, which is to be made by seven pure virgins of the tribe of David. Mary is chosen to be one of these and, the tasks falling by lot, is appointed to spin and weave the purple and scarlet parts of the veil—the others being white, gold, and hyacinthine colors.

In short, in this highly symbolic sequence, to her go the colors of kingship and blood in the veil of the Temple, which is a thinly disguised form of the veil of Isis, the veil of phenomenal appearance that cloaks inner reality.

Mary begins to spin the scarlet thread. She is thus a "new age" representative of the age old Fates of pre-Olympian myth. Then she goes, in another reenactment of ancient symbolism, to a source of water to fill her pitcher. Here the angel of the Annunciation appears to her, saying "Hail, thou that art highly favored; the Lord is with thee; blessed art thou among women."

She returns to her house with the pitcher of water (a female Aquarian image if ever there was one) and there starts to spin the purple thread—the one signifying royalty—and the angel appears to her again. "Fear not, Mary, for thou hast found grace before the Lord of all things, and thou shalt conceive of his word."

Mary mentally questions this awesome statement. "Shall I *really* conceive of the living God, and bring forth after the manner of all women?"

The angel then amplifies his statement, answering her unspoken thoughts. "Not so, Mary, for a power of the Lord shall overshadow thee: wherefore also that holy thing which shall be born of thee shall be called the Son of the Highest. And thou shalt call his name Jesus: for he shall save his people from their sins."

To which Mary replies, with the now time-honored words that epitomize the human soul unsullied by sin, sounding forth a knowledge and acceptance of its destiny, in grace, faith, and love. "Behold the handmaid of the Lord is before him: be it unto me according to thy word."

She then weaves the purple and scarlet thread and takes her portion of the veil to the priest—just as the purple and scarlet of the lineaments of the embryo of the god-man are to be woven within her womb. The priest blesses her, saying: "Mary, the Lord God hath magnified thy name, and thou shalt be blessed among all generations of the earth."

Mary rejoices, and in due course visits her kinswoman Elizabeth who is to be mother of the forerunner, John the Baptist. This story is taken up in the Gospel of Luke, but here the weaving symbolism is followed through, in that Mary finds Elizabeth weaving scarlet wool. (This is a symbolic comparison to the fine linen and silk with which she, as mother of the divine one, has worked.)

We have quoted at some length from the Gospel of James because it is representative of the first workings of "tradition" in the growing Christian community, which at that time had little power and was subject to intermittent persecution at the hands of pagan authority.

The Cult of Mary

From here on, as the Church grows, there is a gradual and inexorable tide of recognition of the importance of the Virgin and what she stands for. Before AD 400, we have the first recorded liturgies and invocation to her, and the legendary founding of the great shrines of Saint Maria Trastavere and Saint Maria Maggiore in Rome. By AD 500, the Temple of Isis at Soissons is dedicated to the Blessed Virgin Mary (B.V.M.), as is also the basilica at Salonika. The Feast of the Annunciation is kept at Byzantium (at the vernal equinox) and the Feast of the Commemoration of the Virgin is observed during Christmastide in Europe. In 431 the Council of Ephesus (the great old center of Diana) proclaims her as *theotokos,* God-bearer, and in 451 the Council of Chalcedon proclaims her as *aeiparthenos,* ever virgin. The empress of Byzantium, in the middle of the fifth century, begins a collection of her relics.

By AD 600, the Parthenon at Athens—the temple of Pallas Athene, goddess of wisdom—is dedicated to the Virgin Mary. A church of Saint Mary is founded in Jerusalem, the city of the original Temple of Solomon. And Saint Maria Antiqua is founded in Rome. In Byzantium, always a leader in recognition of the feminine principle, and where mosaics of the Virgin and Child had begun to replace those of Christ Pantocrator, the feasts of the Nativity of the B.V.M., of her Presentation at the Temple, and the Dormitian or Falling Asleep (now known in the West as the Assumption) were kept. The latter, which implies her freedom from the toils of death, falls on August 15, one of the ancient feast days of Isis, when the Dog Star Sirius rose to announce the eagerly awaited inundation of the Nile in ancient Egypt that brought new life. Another ancient Isiac feast was commemorated on February 15, the Festival of Lights, when little boats carrying lights were floated upon the waters. This was replaced in the fourth century by a Christian feast closely associated with Mary, the Presentation of Jesus in the Temple. This was the occasion of the moving testimony of the ancient Simeon: "Lord, lettest thy servant depart in peace according to thy word, for mine eyes have seen thy salvation, which thou hast prepared before the face of all people; a light to lighten the Gentiles and the glory of thy people Israel." When this feast was recognized by Rome the emphasis became centered upon the purification of Mary herself. Through a change in calendarization the Feast of the Purification is now celebrated on February 2.

The image of the Virgin also began to be used as a protection in battle. In 610 the emperor Heraclius flew her banner at the masts of his battleships; in 626 the Virgin and Child were painted on the gates of the besieged Constantinople; and in 717 the same picture was paraded round the city walls to help repel the Arabs.

Pope Sergius I (687–701) instituted great candlelit processions in Rome on the major Marian feast days and John VII (705–7) took upon himself the title of "servant of the Mother of God." The Theophilus legend also began to circulate widely in the mid-eighth century, extolling the powers and virtues of the Virgin as protector against the works of the devil. The tale of Theophilus is of a sixth-century Faust figure, who allegedly made a pact and sold his soul to the devil in return for worldly riches and success, after he had been passed over in ecclesiastical preferment. He was, however, saved by the Virgin.

By AD 900, a further dimension to the feminine principle was enacted in the institution of feasts dedicated to the mother of the mother of God, Saint Anne. Although the cult of Saint Anne did not gain great force until the fifteenth and early sixteenth centuries, its seed appeared in the institution of the Feast of the Conception of Saint Anne at Byzantium some six hundred years previously. At this time too, tradition has it that the Holy Roman Emperor, Charles the Bald, the son of Charlemagne, left in his will the treasured relic of the shift that Mary had worn at the Annunciation. It was to provide a fitting edifice for such a priceless gift that the present cathedral of Notre Dame at Chartres was constructed in 1194, after the original church had been destroyed by fire, and the relic had miraculously survived the conflagration.

It is easy for the modern secular mind to be cynical over such medieval beliefs but here is symbolic magic of the highest order at work. Qabalists will see the connections of the robe, the body's veil, with the principle of Binah, the archetypal feminine principle. And the fact that belief in this talismanic object should result in the building of a religious house of worship (in itself another Binah symbol) that is the jewel of Western Christendom, indicates a powerful reality at work on inner levels of expression.

Black Madonnas

By AD 1000, Saturdays were dedicated to the Blessed Virgin and one of her greatest shrines was founded, the abbey of Montserrat in Catalonia. Here the focus of worship is a black madonna—and there are other shrines of considerable importance that have similar dark images, including Chartres, and Saint Maria Maggiore in Rome. Black madonnas are particularly renowned for their wonder-working properties and have an ancient lineage in the Black Isis, who, in mourning for the lost Osiris in ancient Egyptian legend, was either black robed or herself black. In this guise, she was regarded as a goddess of healing, and the black madonnas have a similar reputation. In this aspect Isis is also patron of lovers because of her devoted seeking for Osiris, and the Black Madonna of Montserrat is particularly venerated by the newly married, for she is held to preside over sexual love, pregnancy, and childbirth.

Other ancient dynamics of the feminine are associated with the Black Madonna of Montserrat. The image was allegedly found in a cave. Tradition has it that it was fashioned by Saint Luke, and given to Saint Peter, who took it to Spain. It had been hidden when the Moors invaded, and was subsequently revealed to a group of shepherds by a choir of angels. So much for tradition. In material terms the statue appears to be twelfth century Byzantine, though of unknown provenance. An interesting aspect of it is that, besides the infant Jesus, the Madonna has in her lap a Dionysian pinecone.

She carries sufficient power to have attracted immense wealth from the rulers of Barcelona, Aragon, and Castile; and she also inspired Saint Ignatius of Loyola, the founder of the Jesuit Order, to abandon his military career in 1522, and become a soldier of Christ.

The Rosary

In the eleventh century there is evidence of the use of a form of rosary, although a precise date for the advent of this form of prayer is not known. It is generally assumed that the crusaders brought it back with them. In 1041, however, Lady Godiva of Coventry left a circlet of gems on which she used to say her prayers; and in the terms of her will she instructed that it be hung round a statue of the Virgin. The rosary subsequently became a form of prayer pre-eminently associated with the virgin.

Visions of the Madonna

The twelfth century was remarkable for the building of great cathedrals. A number of these were dedicated to Saint Mary, or Notre Dame. Famous ones are at Paris, Noyon, Laon, and a little later at Mantes, Coutances, and Amiens. The temple, or holy place of worship is, as Qabalists will know, a symbol of the feminine principle. Of particular interest in this respect is the Holy House of Walsingham. This was built in 1130 following a vision in which the Virgin appeared to a Norman widow, Richeldis de Faverches. She was taken in the spirit to the house wherein Mary had received the Annunciation from the Archangel Gabriel, and raised the child Jesus. The measurements of the house were given to her, together with the instruction to build "England's Nazareth." This became a miraculous shrine until despoiled by Henry VIII four hundred years later.

Another important visionary of this time was Elisabeth of Schonau, a German nun, who, amongst other visions, saw the Virgin rising bodily to heaven. These visions achieved wide circulation and profoundly influenced ideas of the Assumption, which in time replaced earlier conceptions of the more passive Dormition or Falling Asleep.

A vision of the B.V.M. that occurred in 1251 had far-reaching consequences. This was her appearance to an English hermit called Simon Stock, so named because he lived in a tree. Again we have a resonance with very ancient symbolism in that a tree marks the entrance to the portal of initiation. In this instance Our Lady presented Simon with a cloak of the type known as a scapular, a narrow garment that laboring monks used to wear over their habits to prevent them from getting soiled. A confraternity was formed that is still popular among Roman Catholics, although the scapular has shrunk to the form of a medallion. It has been the subject of some contention in the claim that anyone wearing it at their death would be preserved from hell.

BEATRICE AND DANTE

The idea of the intercession of the Virgin to protect the sinner from the consequences of sin in an afterworld hell plays a dominant role in the *Divine Comedy* of Dante. This masterpiece of the high Middle Ages provides a sequential Mystery system that is the Western equivalent of the highest flights of Tibetan Mahayana Buddhism.

Dante is conducted by Virgil (the embodiment of the highest possible intellectual attainment possible to humans) through various forms of hell that are the equivalent of the various hells within the iron mountain in the Buddhist Mount Meru system. The subsequent ascent of Mount Purgatory to the Earthly Paradise is the equivalent of the slopes of Mount Meru that lead to the great palace of the gods at its summit. And the ascent through the heavens beyond is a similar experience to that of the Buddha Fields of the formless worlds that lead to Nirvana.

Dante's poem is a culmination of the revelation of the feminine principle to the medieval mind. This principle had by now expressed itself in many ways. Some of these were to be regarded as heretical or secular, such as the courts of courtly love. Others, such as the burgeoning of the cult of the Blessed Virgin Mary, were considered more theological and orthodox.

In Dante's vision the masculine intellect, even at its highest and most poetic or magical levels, can only go so far in the comprehension of reality, and that is to the external limits of the Earthly Paradise.

Therefore when Dante, having traversed the deepest pits of Hell, and climbed the spiral path of Mount Purgatory, comes to the brook that circumscribes the Garden of Eden, he is able to go no further under Virgil's guidance. Virgil can only return to Limbo, the noble but loveless state of the intellect, that can only see the world on its own terms and within its own limitations. To go further, the force of love is necessary.

This force is embodied by Beatrice, who expresses not only mortal love but carries the blinding, transfiguring power of divine love as well; that which created the worlds and holds them in being. It is she who meets Dante at the limits of the Earthly Paradise and escorts him through the Heavenly Spheres to the limits of the Uncreate Empyreum beyond the Heavens.

It is in fact she, the embodiment of the feminine principle, who is responsible for the whole Divine Comedy anyway, for it is upon her initiative that Dante, wandering lost in the dark wood of the world, is given the opportunity to embark upon his conducted tour of the inner conditions of the soul.

In fact, in accordance with the most ancient goddess symbolism, this feminine initiative is threefold. Dante's condition had first been the concern of the Virgin Mary, the noble Lady of Heaven. She calls it to the attention of Saint Lucia, described as the enemy of all cruelty, and whose very name signifies light. She in turn asks Beatrice, whom he loved in mortal life, to intercede. Beatrice then appears to Virgil, beseeching him to conduct Dante on the first stages of this errand of mercy.

It is not until Virgil has led Dante through the depths of Hell and up the spiral path of the terraces of Mount Purgatory in a form of alchemical or initiation process, that Dante can face the purity and beauty of the heavenly Beatrice. This is a meeting of great power and significance for it is the moment of the purified soul coming face to face with the reality of divine love after sloughing off the limitations of the vales of illusion.

The Earthly Paradise

When Dante finally approaches the verges of the Earthly Paradise he finds it represents the world as it should have been. Sweet gentle breezes blow through beautiful glades in which songbirds sing. A clear stream runs under the shady trees at its perimeter and on the further side he sees a maiden gathering flowers. She is singing like one in love, and wending her way like a nymph through the woodland shades.

Woodland nymphs, we may recall, were also associated with the Garden of Hesperides. Indeed they were also associated with the Mysteries of the ancient world, and any who heard the call of their double pipes in the woods knew well to keep well away, for that was the call for the initiates to assemble.

The singing maiden, like an initiatrix of old, bids Dante to look and listen; and through the wood there comes the most beautiful music, running on the shining air. On the far side of the brook, a resplendent pageant approaches them. This marks the return of love, the personal presence of Beatrice. It also prepares Dante for his return to the conditions of the Earthly Paradise, long lost.

What is to come is the core of the Mysteries of the feminine principle. It is akin to the awakening of the sleeping goddess in naked glory and splendor in *The Chymical Marriage of Christian Rosencreutz*. And also the appearance of the great goddess Isis in all her splendor to the repentant Lucius the ass. Or to the sky-walking dakinis who are the consorts of the highest compassionate buddhas in the Tibetan system. Or to the source of the golden apples of the Hesperides that were the key to the possession of Atalanta, the pure maiden huntress. It is therefore not unfitting that at this point the author of the *Divine Comedy* pauses to invoke the virgin Muses on their heights on Mount Helicon, and in particular the Muse Urania. It is she who inspires knowledge of astronomy and heavenly things. The most divine secrets of love are, in short, held within "the starry wisdom."

The Pageant of the Divine Feminine

The interpretation of the symbolic Divine Pageant that then appears strikes even the poetic genius of Virgil dumb. It is better imagined and contemplated rather than explained. Seven golden candlesticks precede, akin to the seven lamps mentioned in Exodus that are a part of the symbolic accoutrements of the Ark of Covenant. They are also "the seven lamps of fire burning before the throne, which are the seven spirits of God" in Revelation. In ancient Eastern esoteric lore they might be associated with the seven rays or seven modes of divine expression in the solar system. The light from these candlesticks spreads a rainbow canopy over all that follows.

This includes, first of all, twenty-four ancient men, two by two, crowned with fleurs-de-lys—or stylized lily flowers (the equivalent of the oriental lotus) that signify mystical wisdom. They are akin to the twenty-four elders mentioned in Revelation seated about the throne of God but here they are singing a hymn in praise of the expression of the feminine principle: "Blessed art thou amongst the daughters of Adam, and forever blessed be thy beauty."

Then follow four magnificent beasts, each with six wings, that like a peacock's tail are full of eyes. They are crowned with wreaths, and are described as following the twenty-four elders as inevitably as star follows star in the whirling heavens. Dante, despairing of doing justice to a true description of them, refers the reader to the vision of Ezekiel. In the New English Bible this reads:

> I saw a strong wind coming from the north, a vast cloud with flashes of fire and brilliant light about it: and within was a radiance like brass, glowing in the heart of the flames. In the fire was the semblance of four living creatures in human form. Each had four faces and each four wings; their legs were straight, and their hooves were like the hooves of a calf, glittering like a disc of bronze. Under the wings on each of the four sides were human hands, all four creatures had faces and wings, and their wings touched one another.

They did not turn as they moved; each creature went straight forward. Their faces were like this: all four had the face of a man and the face of a lion on the right, on the left the face of an ox and the face of an eagle. Their wings were spread; each living creature had one pair touching its neighbors', while one pair covered its body. They moved straight forward in whatever direction the spirit would go; they never swerved in their course. The appearance of the creatures was as if fire from burning coals or torches were darting to and fro among them; the fire was radiant, and out of the fire came lightning. (Ezek. 1:4–13)

It may be instructive at this point to quote also from the first eleven verses of Revelation 4:

After this I looked, and there before my eyes was a door opened in heaven, and the voice that I had first heard speaking to me like a trumpet said, "Come up here, and I will show you what must happen hereafter." At once I was caught up by the Spirit. There in heaven stood a throne, and on the throne sat one whose appearance was like the gleam of jasper and cornelian; and round the throne was a rainbow, bright as an emerald. In a circle about this throne were twenty-four other thrones, and on them sat twenty-four elders, robed in white and wearing crowns of gold. From the throne went out flashes of lightning and peals of thunder. Burning before the throne were seven flaming torches, the seven spirits of God, and in front of it stretched what seemed like a sea of glass, like a sheet of ice.

In the center, round the throne itself, were four living creatures, covered with eyes, in front and behind. The first creature was like a lion, the second like an ox, the third had a human face, the fourth was like an eagle in flight. The four living creatures, each of them with six wings, had eyes all over, inside and out, and by day and by night without pause they sang:

Holy, holy, holy is God the sovereign Lord of
all, who was, and is, and is to come.

As often as the living creatures give glory and honor and thanks
to the One who sits on the throne, who lives forever and ever, the
twenty-four elders fall down before the One who sits on the throne
and worship him who lives forever and ever; and as they lay their
crowns before the throne they cry:

Thou art worthy, O Lord our God, to receive
glory and honor and power, because thou didst
create all things; by thy will they were created,
and have their being!

We have quoted this at length to show the magnitude of the honor and
glory that is being paid to the one who rides in the chariot in the midst
of the procession. It is directly equivalent to that accorded to the Most
High God.

The chariot or car might be considered indeed a moving equivalent of the throne of God. It is indeed of almost indescribable mag-
nificence. It is drawn by a fabulous beast, described as a red-and-white
griffon with golden wings arching so high that their extremities cannot
be seen.

As for the carriage, even the light of the sun would look dim beside
it. Around one of its two wheels, three maidens are dancing an intri-
cate measure. One of them is red as fire, one green like a precious emerald, and one white as new-fallen snow. About the other wheel are four
maidens clad in royal purple, their leader possessing a third eye.

Although common exegesis regards these figures as an allegory of
the three virtues and the four cardinal virtues, there is a much deeper
esoteric meaning. They represent the feminine expression of the seven
rays which are the inner dynamics of the universe, which in the heavens are associated with the Pleiades.

Following the car and the seven dancing maidens are seven aged men. Dante describes them as being seven counterparts of the seven maidens, which in esoteric stellar symbolism equates them with the seven *rishis* of the Great Bear. Instead of garlands of lilies about their heads like the maidens, their brows are wreathed in red roses, so that from a short distance it appears as if their heads are aflame.

With a great thunderclap the whole procession halts, the carriage opposite Dante, and at this moment Dante chooses to compare it with the constellation of the Wain or the Great Bear. This is an important passage esoterically, and indicates a deep knowledge of spiritual star lore, about which very little has been written.

The "pointers" of the Great Bear are alluded to in *Esoteric Astrology* by Alice Bailey as major stars of direction. The one nearer the Pole Star (Dubhe) is a focus of the expression of the will of the individual; the one further from the Pole Star (Merak) is the focus of a great reservoir of the energy of divine purpose, or the will of God. The earthly planetary center of Shamballah is related to all this, as also those psychic centers in man that concern the spiritual will. Dubhe is the "pointer" for mankind on the path of the *involution* of consciousness, seeking expression in manifestation. Merak comes into play in guiding the achieved human being into discipleship under the planetary hierarchy. And the pattern for the planetary hierarchy is to be found in the great star of Isis, Sirius the Dog Star, in Canis Major.

The griffon-drawn carriage coming to a halt before Dante is an event which seems as pregnant with meaning as if the very heavens themselves had ceased to revolve. The figures about it face toward it. Dante calls them the "people of truth" and they chant, three times, a phrase from the canticles, "Come, bride of Lebanon" (Song of Sol. 4:8). The Canticles or Song of Solomon is one book of the Old Testament from which the recognition of the feminine principle has not been excluded.

Then with a cry like the paean of praise at the Last Judgment angels arise round the chariot singing. One phrase they sing is adapted from the cries of the multitude when Christ entered Jerusalem in triumph (Matt. 21:9), a passage from Psalm 68, "Blessed is he that cometh in the name of the Lord." In this case the phrase is slightly changed to "Blessed art *thou* who comest." This is as if not to proclaim overtly the possibility of a feminine Christ. Indeed how Dante avoided being condemned for heresy remains something of a miracle. The other phrase the angels cry is from a pagan text: "Oh, give lilies with full hands." This is from book six of the Aeneid (6:883) and by Virgil himself, Dante's guide to this point. Lilies are, of course, the feminine flower par excellence in religious symbolism. They are the equivalent of the oriental lotus, and are also associated with the Virgin Mary. The archangel Gabriel is commonly depicted carrying them in paintings of the Annunciation.

Then with flowers showering about her from the angelic hosts there steps from the car one whose coming is likened to the very dawn itself. She is veiled in white, with a cloak of green worn over a dress that is as red as fire. The theological interpretation of these colors seems less appropriate than their relevance to the Isis of nature—that of a living fire within, clad in a mantle of green vegetation, veiled with white clouds. Above all she is crowned, not with gold, but with olives—the fruit of wisdom, associated with the goddess of wisdom, Pallas Athene, the virgin goddess who arose fully armed from the head of Zeus, the king of the Olympian gods.

At this point of revelation Virgil, the great exemplar of the heights of human intellect, poetic inspiration, and magical power, disappears. He can take Dante no further. His instructor from henceforth, who leads him through the heavens, is the great feminine power of divine love. This is no theological or Platonic abstraction, for she announces herself as a flesh and blood woman. "Look at me well: truly I am, truly I am Beatrice," the girl whom Dante had loved in Florence.

We will leave this great pageant of the ascent of the soul of man at this point. It has its equivalent in the Buddha Fields high over the city of the gods in the Mount Meru system of Mahayana Buddhism.

Enough has been examined, we trust, to indicate the great power and transforming energy of the feminine principle, in this work of medieval genius. This same principle was known to the ancients under the various forms of the Goddess, and its power and influence continued into the Christian epoch as the image and lore of the Blessed Virgin Mary.

AFTER DANTE AND BEATRICE

Dante was writing at the beginning of the fourteenth century. At about this time, seats of learning such as Oriel College, Oxford, began to be dedicated to the Virgin. In the fifteenth century there followed the period of great Renaissance paintings of the Madonna, such as Piero della Francesca's *Madonna della Misericord* (1445) and Leonardo da Vinci's *Virgin of the Rocks* (1481–83). And with the coming of the printing press the Office of Our Lady was printed for wide distribution by Gutenberg's successor in 1457.

Another holy house became famous in the beginning of the sixteenth century that rivaled that of Walsingham. This was at Loretto, officially recognized as a place of pilgrimage in 1507. This was the focus of a legend that angels had actually transported the house of the Annunciation through space and time.

With the Reformation, abuses of superstition accumulating around such places excited the reforming bodies to action, Indeed Henry VIII razed Walsingham to the ground at the Dissolution of the Monasteries in 1538, even though he himself had given generous endowments to it in his youth. Its miraculous statue was taken to London and burned.

Different Protestant bodies took differing lines of reaction according to local and national temperament, but it seems more like chauvinist spite that utterly destroyed, in the Lady Chapel at Ely Cathedral in 1539, the two-hundred-year-old carvings of the life and miracles of the Virgin. Had they survived they would have been a most precious spiritual and historical heritage.

There is scope for the analysis of the psychology of group souls to try to identify the cause of such barbarous ferocity that was akin to the vandalism of repressed adolescence. It was in some instances like a reaction to the feminine, or fear of it, welling up from deep levels. This had a strange aftermath in the Puritan areas of East Anglia and New England, with the witch cults and the paranoid persecution of women as witches. This was almost like a visitation upon a society that could not come to terms with the feminine principle. It had to project it outwards and then persecute it.

THE MODERN CULT OF MARY

The Reformation, however, did not completely stamp out the use of images in religious worship. Nor could it for long repress the feminine principle. When abuses are overcome, then genuine expression is free to gain greater recognition. Since the nineteenth century, the legends and iconography of the Blessed Virgin Mary have gradually increased in importance and spiritual significance.

Of particular note are the promulgations of the Dogma of the Immaculate Conception in 1854, and of the Assumption of the Blessed Virgin Mary into heaven in 1950. The psychologist C. G. Jung has drawn attention to the implications of these ideas, and it is not without significance that the general movement toward acceptance of the feminine principle in economic, social, and political, life expression has been gaining impetus. There is still a long way to go, and the movement is not without its unbalanced adherents who bring disrepute through overstatement, but that is common to all human movements for change.

In 1954, the Coronation of the Blessed Virgin as Queen of Heaven was established as one of the mysteries of the Rosary. This is the ultimate recognition of the principle of form, the Earth itself, being as holy as any so called higher state. In its full implication it is the preparation of the New Jerusalem adorned as a bride.

These are highly metaphysical matters that are beyond the reach of intellectual analysis.

The potential literature for an intellectual study of this is vast. We hope we have provided a few simple pointers on the way. It is however, a "centering in," rather than a wandering in the labyrinthine fields of intellectual speculation, that is the direct way of truth. The rose blooms at the center of the cross. And those who are prepared to contemplate the imagery and take it unto their inmost hearts are the more likely to be met by Beatrice from the triumphal car, and led to places where even the intellectual genius of a Virgil cannot go. To this end we can hardly do better than to survey the body of images that are presented in the litany of the Blessed Virgin Mary. Any of these images will infinitely repay meditation, contemplation, and appropriate acts of symbolic or ritual intention. They may be grouped under the three heads of Mother, Maiden or Virgin, and Queen.

Mother of God, of Christ, of divine grace, most pure, most chaste, inviolate, undefiled, most lovable, most wonderful, of good counsel, of the Creator, of the Savior.

Virgin most prudent, most venerable, most renowned, most mighty, most merciful, most faithful; Mirror of righteousness, Seat of wisdom, Cause of our joy, Spiritual vessel, Vessel of honor, Wondrous vessel of devotion, Mystical rose, Tower of David, Tower of ivory, House of gold, Ark of the Covenant, Gate of heaven, Star of the morning, Health of the sick, Refuge of sinners, Consoler of the afflicted, Help of Christians.

Queen of Angels, Patriarchs, Prophets, Apostles, Martyrs, Confessors, Virgins, all Saints; conceived without original sin; taken up into heaven; Of the most holy Rosary; Queen of Peace.

In our imaginal working for this section we find a threefold "sisterhood" arising. These are: the young virgin, the matron watcher, and the scarlet woman. All are Christianized forms of ancient goddess figures.

The virgin and the matron, as the child Madonna and her mother,

Saint Anne, are figures from the apocryphal gospels of James and Thomas, not recognized by the Church as part of the accepted canon, but miraculous accounts popular in early Christian times. These deal with wondrous events surrounding the childhood of the human mother of the new savior god. And this includes her very conception, for her mother, Saint Anne, had been past child-bearing age and conceived only by divine intervention. (This became known in medieval theology as the Immaculate Conception, which is often confused in modern popular belief with the virgin birth.)

Mary Magdalene, the regenerate prostitute, makes tantalizing and fleeting appearances in the Gospels, but comes very much into her own in the Gnostic texts, most of which have been suppressed. Here she was either the initiatrix to high mysteries of the resurrection, or she was credited with being the bride of Christ in more than a figurative way, a tradition that has come down in certain Holy Grail legends.

In the threefold imagery before us we therefore have the divine feminine principle represented as bride, mother, and grandmother of the incarnate god. Unorthodox though this might seem, it is capable of carrying a fair head of spiritual power, as any who care to work with these dynamics may discover.

In terms of objective work with the Planetary Being, it is the next stage on from her rescue (as Andromeda), and her betrothal (as Psyche), whereby it is now possible for the feminine principle to bring through cosmic spiritual dynamics into the physical levels of form expression. In the familiar Christian story this is represented by the Incarnation, observed at least commercially and sentimentally every Christmas, illustrating the power of the imagery even in a secular society.

In the forms that we are going to use, the heavenly or cosmic dimension is represented by the dual images, first of great light emanating from the temple (itself a feminine image), and then a gushing forth of the waters of life from the further feminine imagery of well and tree.

JOURNEY 3: THE VIRGIN AT THE WELL

We are standing in a town square. It is hot and dusty, but before us rise up to its entrance is a young girl, about twelve, playing in the square. She seems to be drawing something in the dust with her bare foot.

We edge forward to try to see what it is. It is a sign, made up of two Greek letters, one shaped like a modern *p*, the other like an *x*. It is the Chi-Rho sign. Having drawn it, conscious of our gaze, she does a little running dance, leaving the prints of her bare feet in the dust of the square. The tracks leave a wavy serpentine trail and then, approaching the center of the square, she turns sharply and bangs her heel firmly upon the ground. At this there arises all about her and around us a cloud of dust in which it is difficult to see anything but vague shapes.

As the dust cloud soon subsides we see that we have been joined by a group of men. They are elderly and carry staffs of office. There are twelve of them and they form a ring about the girl, who remains standing at the center of their circle.

A bearded priest appears at the entrance of the temple and descends halfway down the steps. He seems to be about to conduct a ceremony with the men and the girl. We also notice an elderly woman who has approached from a side street and who now stands looking on, beneath a tree that grows by the side of the square. We realize that she and the priest upon the steps are mother and father of the girl, whom they have apparently begotten in the evening of their years.

We look round again at the circle of elders and now notice the tops of their staffs. Each is carved in the form of an animal or a human effigy, and we realize that they represent signs of the zodiac. There is a ram, a bull, a pair of twins, a crab, a lion, a virgin, a pair of scales, a scorpion, a centaur, a goat, a man carrying a water pot, and a pair of fish.

As we look on, the priest on the temple steps raises his arms in prayer and supplication. A sudden wind whips round the square, raising the dust again and shaking the branches of the tree under which the old woman sits. It forms a kind of spiral dust whorl about the girl and the men, and at its passing, as the dust settles again, we see, to the amazement of all, that the rod of the elder with the staff representing Aquarius, the water bearer, has burst forth into green life and is thick with blossom from top to tip.

He goes forward and embraces the maiden in the center and the other elders disperse. As they do so we become aware of a pair of pillars that appear on either side of the maiden, and just beyond them a spinning wheel.

The remaining elder, the priest, and the old woman beneath the tree are forgotten as we focus our attention upon the girl, who now sits behind the pillars, at the spinning wheel. She sits on a three-legged stool that rests upon what looks like a golden fleece, which lies beneath it, and from the wool of the golden fleece she is spinning a fine thread. As she does so we see that not one, but two threads, are coming from her wheel, one is of scarlet and the other of purple, each being wound upon a different spindle or shuttle.

Having spun sufficient thread she takes up her shuttles and approaches the two pillars. As she does so she is joined by a group of eight other maidens, who stand about her in a circle, at each cardinal point, and at the cross-quarters. They now turn and look toward the temple.

From within its dark interior we see a bright and golden glow that gets gradually brighter, as if a light is being brought from the interior recesses of the temple to the outer door. Then a light appears at the doorway and a male figure appears, shining like the sun. Advancing halfway down the steps, to stand at the spot where the old priest had stood, he holds out his hands to the nine maidens in love, recognition, and blessing.

At this all the maidens cluster round the pillars and begin to weave a veil. Each maiden has two shuttles, one filled with silver and one filled with golden thread, with the exception of the one whom we saw spinning the purple and the scarlet. As they weave they sing a song that has a strange lilt to it combining joy and devotion, and as the veil nears completion we see that it depicts a man, similar to the figure who stands upon the temple steps.

The veil between the pillars completed, the maidens step back from it, and at the same moment, a cloud seems to come across the sun, and the square is plunged into shadow. The shining figure on the temple steps disappears, as do all except the original maiden, who, standing upon her stool, with some difficulty lifts down the veil from between the pillars. As she does so, it falls heavily about her. She gathers it about her, as best she may, and carries it slowly across the shadowed square, and as she goes it seems to be growing heavier and heavier, until, as she approaches the far side of the square she is staggering under its weight and hardly able to lift it.

There, at the far side of the square, is an old tree. It appears to be dead, perhaps struck by lighting in some long time past. It has, however, one dark branch that extends out from its gaunt trunk. With prodigious effort, the girl throws the veil over the extended branch, from which it hangs like a curtain. But we see that in the course of the journey across the square, it has become dirty, darkened, and stained, and even has holes rent in its fabric. She sits down wearily beneath it, upon the low wall of an old well, which from its deteriorating rope and tackle, appears to have been long dried up.

As she sits she sees that some fragments of the veil have fallen to the ground at her feet. She picks them up, and sits looking at them disconsolately. As she does so, she is quietly joined by two other women. One is the old woman we have seen before, who carries a pair of shears, which she offers. The other has long red hair, a heavily painted face, and her body-revealing dress is spangled with tawdry finery. She offers a needle to the maiden.

With the aid of the needle and the shears the maiden begins to embroider a small piece of the fabric from the veil. It is in the form of a red and purple heart, transfixed by gold and silver swords. When she has finished it, she stands and holds it before her breast, and the other two women look on, as do we, at her standing alone under the stricken tree by the dried up well.

As we gaze however, the heart begins to glow, as if it were alive and pulsing with blood. Then we see that it is coursing and glowing with fire, and the swords that transfix it are becoming rays, shooting out from it as from the sun.

At the same time there is a rumbling sound as of an impending earthquake, and we see that the well shaft is lighting up as if a great light were in its depths. The three women back away from the well in wonder, as the light grows brighter, until suddenly there springs from the depths the golden figure we saw standing upon the steps of the temple. He carries a great pitcher on his shoulder, full of water, which he empties with a sweep of his arms. This is met by a great cry of joy and triumph, as from an invisible multitude. The water spreads across the square and at the same time the sun comes out from behind the clouds.

As it does so we are aware of joyous crowds of people flocking into the square, and of the three women at the wellhead, inviting all to come. They dip cups and jars and all manner of vessels into the well, which is now full almost to overflowing. And over their heads the tree bursts into leaf and blossom, like the old man's staff at the beginning of our vision, and birds sing in its branches.

We absorb what we can of this joyous scene, in the hope of mediating some of it to the world about us when we return, as we do now, slowly and in our own time, to normal consciousness and awareness of our own bodies and the physical place from whence we started.

BRANCH FOUR

The Lady Venus in Rosicrucian Alchemy

With the Reformation and the breakup of the monopoly of the Roman church on worship and belief, the way was open for a great deal more freedom of religious expression, although it took some time for this to take effect, for very often the reformers were narrow and bigoted.

We have seen how the divine feminine had made itself felt within the institutional church by means of saints days and hallowed traditions and legends, particularly in relation to the cult of the Virgin. The Protestant sects threw all of this out, and thereby the baby with the bathwater. Hence the Protestant tradition was denuded of the feminine principle.

However, it is just not possible to deny for all time the existence of such powerful psychic and spiritual forces, and so the Goddess began to return by many and devious ways, like green shoots breaking through the concrete shell of masculine intellectual dogmatism. And a notable way in which this occurred was through esoteric societies, particularly those that espoused an approach to form what might best be called "spiritual alchemy."

Such societies, and they were usually called brotherhoods, were still children of their times and so the Goddess came through often in somewhat obscure and disguised form—the "veil of Isis" has many manifestations. In a typical script that we shall examine, she is found in part as the maiden Alkymia who aids the protagonist on his quest, or as the winged, starry messenger inviting him to it, or as the Lady Venus who lies asleep and naked in her secret vault.

We find ourselves flung into a plethora of obscure but somehow strangely moving symbolism. We will do our best to draw a guiding thread throughout its labyrinth but the secret, as ever, lies not in trying to come to some intellectual explanation *of* the imagery, but in direct experience of it by spiritually intentioned visualization. This, it may be realized, is a very feminine form of mental perception, as opposed to the masculine mode of intellectual analysis.

The text we choose is known as *The Chymical Marriage of Christian Rosencreutz*. It was first published, anonymously, in 1619, although it had apparently circulated in manuscript some time before that. Indeed there are coded links in the text with the famous Elizabethan magus, Dr. John Dee (1527–1608).

THE CHYMICAL MARRIAGE OF CHRISTIAN ROSENCREUTZ

The Invitation of Isis Urania

This symbolic story commences on Easter Eve, with all its connotations of transformation and resurrection. The protagonist, who is called Christian Rosencreutz, is approached by a fair glorious lady. She wears sky-colored garments spangled with stars, and has beautiful wings full of eyes, like a peacock's tail. She is obviously a form of the Heavenly Isis—Isis Urania—the heavenly or cosmic aspect of the feminine principle. She carries a bundle of letters in all languages and a golden trumpet. She leaves Christian Rosencreutz a letter, which is an invitation to a wedding, and departs with a resounding blast of her trumpet.

Christian Rosencreutz, or C. R., dreams that night that he is confined in a dark underground dungeon. It is packed with other prisoners who swarm all over each other, regardless of inflicting injury. Their overriding desire is to heave themselves over others. In short it is an image of the outer world. Trumpets and drums sound and the cover of the dungeon is lifted. The prisoners scramble toward the light and an old man speaks to them from above. He tells them that if they would be less selfish and self-centered *his mother* could help them the more.

As it is, a cord can be let down seven times, and whoever can cling to it will be released. There is a mad scramble to seize the descending rope but C. R. is successful without joining in this mêlée, for he earnestly prays to God for help. At this the rope swings toward him. He happens to be standing at the side on a great stone and so can grasp the rope. The stone is significant of his standpoint on the rock of faith and, more esoterically, it is the outermost form of the stone of the philosophers.

As he is drawn up, however, his head strikes on another sharp stone and he is wounded. The significance of this wound is recounted later. It is concerned with the force of love—and even at the shallowest level of interpretation the treasures of the heart are shown to be paramount over the analysis of the head.

The names of all those who are saved are written on a golden tablet and they are freed from their chains and given a piece of gold. Upon this is inscribed a sun at dawn, and the inscription D. L. S. This is variously interpreted as Deus Lux Solis, God is the light of the sun, and/or as Deo Laus Semper, God be praised for ever. There is always a tone of reverence in genuine Rosicrucian documents. Knowledge is not elevated into a self-sufficient false god. Hence these teachings conform to the old principle of the Mysteries that the candidate for initiation must genuinely be able to say: "I desire to know in order to serve."

The old man can be equated with Saturn—the outermost of the traditional planets and so guardian of the bounds of the Solar System. That is, lord of its space and time. His mother is older even than he. She is in fact, by definition, the most ancient feminine principle, who *was* before all worlds. Yet she is not a remote abstraction or unapproachable deity. She laments for all the poor souls left in the dungeon and enters into a personal relationship with all who are saved, each of whom is presented to her.

She consoles C. R. for the wounds he has received from his earthly chains, yet at the same time laughs at him. This is not a callous laughter but that of a loving mother, for from the heavenly viewpoint these wounds are but the scrapes and scratches of cosmic childhood. The lesson is not to dwell in self-pity upon them but to be thankful for blessings and to regard these wounds as badges of experience. "My son," she says, "let not this defect afflict thee," as he stands fancying himself unable to proceed, "but call to mind thy infirmities, and therewith thank God who hath permitted thee even in this world, and in the state of thy imperfection to come into so high a light, and keep these wounds for my sake."

The trumpets then sound, and they have the usual effect of esoteric trumpets in that they call those who hear them from one plane to another. Accordingly C. R. awakes.

First Day: The Journey to the Castle

He determines to attend the wedding and dresses ritually for it. That is, with the emblems of a Rosicrucian—a crossed red ribbon over a white linen coat and with four red roses in his hat. In other words, the center of the cross is over his heart, and the equilibration of the elements blossoms over his head.

He takes bread, salt and water—all emblems of life—and typically, and essentially for the aspirant to the higher mysteries, gives thanks to God. (The principle of thanksgiving is of incredible power at any level of expression.) He also vows that whatever is revealed to him he will use in the service of God and his fellow man. He then goes into the forest, with birds singing all around him, as in a dawn chorus.

All initiation systems have an especial commencement point. This is often associated with a tree or a grove of trees. In this case it is a green plain beyond the forest from which four ways diverge. It is marked by three tall cedar trees which offer "an excellent and desired shade." One is indeed reminded of the Rosicrucian motto which appears at the end of the *Confessio:* Sub Umbra Alarum Tuum Jehova—Under the shadow of thy wings Jehovah. Under the trees is a tablet describing the nature of the four ways. In fact only three are practicable, for the fourth is passable only by the pure—that is, by those with incorruptible bodies.

The right choice is beyond the powers of intellect, and C. R. chooses the right way by apparent accident. This is significantly by the actions of a black raven—an emblem found in alchemy as a symbol for dissolution. It is a bird ever associated both with wisdom and with death. It is found in ancient Irish myth as the Morrigu, the great terrible goddess of the battlefield, who collects the souls of the slain. C. R. sees a white dove and begins to feed it with his bread, whereupon the black raven appears and chases the dove, which flies off towards the south. C. R. runs after them, to find himself automatically upon one of the ways and unable to return for his bread and belongings, by dint of a strong wind that blows from behind him. This is the breath of the Holy Spirit, whose other aspect is the guiding dove.

C. R. keeps to the path with the aid of a compass. This is an important symbolic direction-finding instrument. The lodestone (which is often meteoric in origin, and therefore literally from the heavens) is a natural object that automatically seeks the direction of the polar axis about which all the universe spins.

At sunset he comes to a stately portal. It is the first of three gates, and at each of these he receives a token. First in exchange for his water and his salt, and at the last gate he loses a part of his coat.

The first gate is surmounted by the traditional warning cry of the guardian of ancient mystery rites "Begone, profane ones." It is also surrounded by an orchard. Thus within this very baroque symbol structure we find mystery symbolism of great antiquity, for the orchard is to be found also in the Garden of Eden and in the Garden of the Hesperides, to say nothing of the Celtic Avalon or Isle of Apples.

Added to this, a virgin robed in celestial blue lights lanterns on every third tree. In a sense she can be looked upon as a celestial angel lighting the stars that appear in the heavens. This is an image of very considerable significance for it is the all comprehending feminine power.

At the second gate C. R. is confronted by the figure of a roaring lion. At first it is grim and frightening but when confronted with pure dedication, it no longer threatens.

C. R. has to hasten to the last gate, in increasing darkness, but is aided by a feminine figure, the celestial Virgin of Lights. She runs with him and behind him, affording light for him to run by, until he reaches sanctuary between the two pillars of the final portal.

Here his name is recorded and is sent to the bridegroom of the mysterious marriage. He is also given a new pair of shoes with which to walk the marble floor of the castle. This signifies activity upon a higher plane and is the reason why special shoes are ritually worn by those who tread in holy temples. In Qabalistic terms, the magical weapons of Yesod, the etheric/astral sphere of the Tree of Life, are sandals. They signify the means to walk the inner ways.

The hair of C. R.'s head is then cut into a tonsure. This is an indication of the opening of the crown chakra, the spiritual center of the aura, called in the East the thousand-petaled lotus. He is then left to meditate between two flaming torches struck into holes in the floor, like flaming pillars of an inner gateway.

Then he is taken to a banquet in a great hall where many others are present. A number of them consider they are there by right of their own merit rather than through the grace of God. They laugh at what they consider the over-pious humility of C. R. and see no need of God in their endeavors. They even wink and make fun during the saying of grace, and continue through the feast to boast of their esoteric accomplishments. However this is curbed when a beautiful music commences. These are evidently heavenly harmonies for they impel silence even upon the most ignorant and garrulous, who are physically struck into silence.

This is the prelude to trumpets and drums outside and the amazing spectacle of a procession of thousands of little lighted tapers, like stars. They accompany two pages clad in sparkling white-and-gold robes who hold pillarlike flaming torches before the Virgin of Lights. She is similarly robed and seated in glory upon a moving golden throne. This is another aspect of the great cosmic figure represented by the Virgin of Lights in the orchard and is worthy of much meditation and reverent contemplation.

She announces that all who seek to attend the wedding must be weighed in the balance to see if they be found worthy. Those who feel that they are unworthy, however, will be allowed to sleep on the floor of the hall and will be given release on the morrow to return to their homes. Most of those present assume that they are self-evidently worthy and are conducted to their chambers.

C. R., however, feels that he is unworthy of such great and holy mysteries and, with eight others, elects to remain, bound and in darkness, in the discomfort of the hall, where they are enjoined to silence.

Second Day: The Castle of Wonders

The next day the guests return to the hall, some of them deriding C. R. and the others for lacking the will and courage to submit to the forthcoming test. There follows a further tattoo of trumpets and drums, and the Virgin reenters. She now wears scarlet velvet, relieved by a white scarf, and has a laurel wreath on her head. She is an image of power and justice and her throne is hauled by two hundred men, who are also clad in red and white and bear swords and ropes. On descending from her throne, she congratulates those who have remained in the hall all night as being "sensible to your wretched condition." She shows, however, amused surprise at finding C. R. among them, for, as it turns out, he is far more worthy than the whole concourse of seekers; a fact which is apparently quite obvious to her.

Great gold scales are erected and each one of the company is weighed in turn, to see if their spiritual weight is sufficient. This is a test very similar to that found in the *Egyptian Book of the Dead,* where the soul is weighed in the Judgment Hall of Osiris to determine its inner-world fate. To their dismay, the majority of those present fail— even those who try to make themselves weighty by heavy books. Nor does wealth or rank serve to help any of them.

The few who pass the test are clad in scarlet, and given a laurel wreath, like the Virgin, and permitted to sit on the steps of her throne.

Even those who elected to stay in the hall are in fact weighed, though without risk of retribution should they fail the test. C. R., indeed, to his great surprise, proves to be of greatest spiritual weight, and accordingly is allowed to release one of the captives. He chooses to assist one who had shown great humility despite having high earthly rank, and who had just barely failed the test.

The Virgin then presides over the judgment of those who failed and punishments are meted out according to the gap between their pretensions and their actual performance. Those who had remained in humility in the hall risk no retribution. The swindling esoteric charlatans are most savagely punished. For most of those present, the worse punishment is the realization of their lack of real worth in the scale of spiritual values, and their consequent banishment from the higher degrees of the Mysteries of attendance at the wedding.

In all these events it is the Virgin who is mistress of the ceremonies and she is, in this role, an aspect of divine justice, and pictorially she resembles the Tarot trump Justice. She presides over the ceremony at noon when those not worthy to take further part are dismissed from the company. They return to the outer world, after having drunk a draft of forgetfulness. This is similar to Lethe, the river of forgetfulness, found in the classical conception of the divide between the inner and outer worlds. This means that there is normally no memory of past lives before the present birth or of the inner life in the hours of sleep.

Of considerable importance in this sequence, although easily overlooked in the welter of symbolism, is the fact that this process of dividing the worthy from the unworthy, at the border between inner and outer levels, takes place in a garden around a fountain. The fountain, together with a garden, orchard, or grove of trees, is an almost invariable feature of entrances to the inner planes in esoteric mythology. The fountain has upon it as its guardian a lion holding a sword, a symbolic creature with which we have already become familiar. After the unworthy have been dismissed there is a pregnant silence within the garden. This silence is itself a mighty symbol. It is the stillness of the great feminine archetype, whether in the silence of Binah on the Tree of Life, the great temple of form of all the spheres; or in the great silent unmanifest sea of the Ain Soph beyond Kether, the ultimate feminine principle.

In the silence a unicorn approaches wearing a golden collar. It bows to the lion. The lion thereupon breaks the sword in two, and casts the pieces into the waters of the fountain. The testing having been done, the way to the higher worlds is clear, and the lion no longer bars the way. The roaring lion in the path, the dweller on the threshold or shadow self, is no longer a barrier to progress. A white dove now appears with an olive branch of peace and wisdom. The lion devours it and is quieted, and the unicorn joyfully departs.

All present then descend by a winding stair, and wash their hands and heads in the waters of eternal life of the fountain. The departing Virgin announces that they will meet the king on the morrow.

For the rest of the day the wedding guests are free to explore the castle, each guided by their individual page. One of the principle things to be seen is a library containing a great catalogue of all the contents of the castle, but more important than this, it is said, is a royal sepulchre from which may be learned *more than is extant in all books.* It is covered with many symbolic sculptures including that of a lion, an eagle, a griffon, and a falcon, but above all by a glorious phoenix.

This is an important passage. The page allocated to each guest is in one sense an inner guide, in another a form of the holy guardian angel of each one, or an aspect of the higher self. In practical terms it is often difficult to differentiate between these categories of contact with the outer world personality; they function similarly, and with the same intent. Certainly, however, for the personality to tread the inner pathways, some form of guidance is needed.

There is on the outer levels of the inner Mysteries a great source of knowledge that is sometimes referred to as a great library. It is, in another sense and form, the akashic record, that is impressed with all occurrences in the world as a kind of reflecting ether with a permanent afterimage. This knowledge of all conditions and events is there for those enabled to read it. Of greater importance, however, is not the record of the past but the secrets of the present and future state of the soul. The knowledge and wisdom of this is to be found in a tomb, moreover a tomb upon which is prominently displayed the image of the phoenix—the bird of resurrection and transformation.

It should be said that totem animals formed an extremely important part in the mystery beliefs of our remote ancestors. They remain important in folklore and mythology, whether the animal-headed gods of the Egyptians or in the creatures of fairytales that often give guidance into hidden realms or bring aid or information. Thus more attention might well be paid to the mythical creatures that appear in Rosicrucian and alchemical symbolism. They are guides and bearers of force and influences beyond the normal frontiers of human cognition.

Another symbol of considerable importance that is here mentioned is a terrestrial globe, thirty feet in diameter, which serves a dual function. One is of indicating the position in the world of all initiates by the presence of gold rings set thereon. More importantly, the globe also opens up so that one can enter inside. A planetarium is there, with all the stars of the universe *inside* the Earth.

This is a very ancient worldview that may seem ludicrous to modern habits of thought, yet which has a profound validity of its own. It is interesting to see this represented, almost in passing, in a seventeenth-century document that ostensibly seems to be merely reveling in mechanical contrivances. In fact the whole Rosicrucian castle is represented as a model driven by clockwork. It is indeed a moveable representation of the "machinery of the universe," the inner world of the astro-etheric that keeps the outer world in order and motion.

The real force that drives the "machinery of the universe" is, however, the topic of much riddling conversation at supper that evening, which is how to measure love. That night C. R. dreams of a locked door finally opening. We are indeed at the threshold of the Mysteries of the feminine principle.

Third Day: The Magic Rites

The following day all those accepted to the Mysteries return to the golden fountain. The lion now bears a tablet of instruction in place of the sword. "Drink of me who can: wash in me whoever so wishes: stir me whoever dares." The waters are revealed to be those of Hermes—that is, higher wisdom, an analog of the powers of Pallas Athene who helped the ancient heroes. The final injunction is "Drink brethren, and live." In other words, all who have achieved to this point *are* able to drink of these waters of higher wisdom; to take them within themselves. And the ability so to do makes them part of a great brotherhood, as well as bestowing conscious participation in a higher or eternal life.

This is ratified, after they have drunk from the golden cup of the fountain and washed therein, by their being conducted by the Virgin of Lights into a hall. Here they are decked in gold robes decorated with flowers, given a golden fleece set with jewels, and also a gold medal depicting the sun and moon conjoined. This indicates the union of higher and lower self, and the glory of the unmanifest spirit flowing through the conjunction. A more common depiction of this is by two equilateral triangles conjoined to form a radiant six-rayed star. The motto on the reverse of the medal confirms this:

> The light of the Moon shall be as the light of the Sun, and the light
> of the Sun shall be 7 times lighter.

They then process, with stately harmonies, up a winding staircase of

365 steps (the number of rotations of the Earth in circumambulating the Sun), go through a painted arch at the top (the arch of heaven familiar to certain Freemasons), to find themselves in an upper hall decked like paradise. Here they are greeted by sixty virgins bearing laurel wreaths. Each of the initiates is also given a laurel wreath by the Virgin of Lights. She then presents each one of them to the king of the castle who, with the queen, is revealed behind a curtain. The queen, it should be said, is clad in garments so brilliant that the eye cannot look upon them.

The Virgin of Lights lays down her branch upon the ground and silence falls upon the assembled company. In this holy quietness the figure of Atlas steps forth and welcomes them on the king's behalf. Again we find ourselves in the presence of most ancient symbolism. Atlas is one of the Titans, and particularly associated with the Hesperides, from whom Heracles sought aid in obtaining the golden apples. One of his functions is also to uphold the sphere of the heavens.

Atlas then bids the Virgin to continue the ceremonies, and we note that these mysteries are run by feminine forces. She leads the company to another room where, under a great arch in the west, are three royal thrones. Each throne has a couple seated upon it, with a semicircle of elders behind them, and a great golden crown over all. The central throne bears a young couple, the bride and bridegroom of the Mystery wedding, and a figure of Cupid plays about them and round the golden crown. We should by now be aware that the figure of Cupid is no sentimental convention, but represents an almighty force that drives the worlds in their motions and fires the vital forces of all living creatures upon them.

Before the queen is an altar, dressed with symbols relating to the Mysteries about to be encountered. These are a black velvet book inlaid with gold; a taper in an ivory candlestick; a celestial globe; a striking watch; a fountain of blood; and a skull wherein dwells a white serpent.

Each of these symbols will repay long and deep meditation. They are each in their way aspects of the Mystery dynamics of life and death, of transformation and regeneration. The intention of such symbolism is to reveal, not to explain, and although it may seem obscure it is in fact not so. It is the plainest possible representation of a truth that is beyond the grasp of the intellect. A symbol is a door or gateway. It is to be gone through. By meditating upon, visualizing, taking the symbol to heart, with aspiration and spiritual intention, one is enabled to pass through it.

Returning in procession to the lower hall the virgins play a game with the candidates which is based on the number seven. They all stand in a circle and count round in sevens, to choose bedfellows for the night. In doing so, however, they find they are so disposed by sexes round the circle that all the virgins are counted out first, leaving the men standing alone. This is an indication that these mysteries are connected with the sexual forces but not in the usual physical expression of them.

Cupid then reappears with a golden cup. They all drink from it and dance before forming up in procession again, led by the queen. She carries a small crucifix of pearl, which is imbued with great significance, for it is said that it was "this very day wrought between the young king and his bride." We say no more than to provide the hint that the crucifix is the paramount symbol of vicarious sacrifice and that pearl represents by its appearance a solidification of the life forces. This is sometimes referred to as the "gluten of the white eagle," more familiar to nineteenth-century psychical research in the form of "ectoplasm," or more subtle etheric forms of it.

The Queen is attended by six virgins who bear the symbols from the little altar, referred to now as the "King's jewels." The three kings and three queens follow, with the bride and bridegroom in black, and Cupid bearing the bride's train. They are followed by the rest of the company with Atlas bringing up the rear.

They go to a theater called the House of the Sun and there witness a play in seven acts. This enacts the story of a maiden disinherited and then seduced by a wicked Moorish king. She is rescued by a king's son to be his bride, but falls again perversely and willingly into the evil king's clutches. She is then sadly degraded by him. The young king battles for her again in spite of her defection. Although it appears at first that he is killed, he in fact has the victory and commits his intended bride to the safekeeping of a steward and a chaplain. These two subsequently become insolently wicked in the exercise of their appointed power. They are overthrown by the young king in the last act, who then marries his bride.

All of this is an allegory of Christ and the human soul. Saved once more by the Incarnation of the Christ the soul of humanity is put under the stewardship of the Church, which however betrays its trust in hubris and ambition. It is prophesied that this will be overturned at the final coming of the Christ.

As Dante, three hundred years before in the pageant in the Earthly Paradise, allegorized the institutional Church as betraying its spiritual trust in search of political power, so do the Rosicrucian documents, and plainly demonstrate themselves to be on the side of the Reformation. After the play a banquet is held, for the most part in an awesome silence as if portending some great event. At its end all sign a book, dedicating themselves to the King's service. They then drink a "draught of silence."

A bell tolls. The rest of the royal party put off their festive white garments and are clad in black. The Queen blindfolds them and six coffins are brought in. A tall black man enters with an ax and beheads each one of them. The blood is caught in a gold cup and the heads wrapped in black cloths. Finally the executioner is himself beheaded, by an unknown hand at the door.

The Virgin of Lights bids the company not to lament. She enigmatically states that the lives of those beheaded even yet rest in the hands of the assembled company.

All retire for the night, but at midnight C. R. looks out of his window. He sees over the lake seven ships proceeding with the coffins, each one with a flame over its masthead.

Fourth Day: The Vault of Lady Venus

At dawn the next day, which is the wished-for day of the intended wedding, C. R. is secretly shown some very significant hidden mysteries of the castle by his guiding page.

First they go down an underground stairway where they find a great iron door. Upon it is inscribed in letters of copper, "Here lies buried Venus, that beauty which hath undone many a great man both in fortune, honor, blessing, and prosperity."

Beyond the door is a dark passage that leads to a small door. This, the page reveals, was first opened only the day before, to bring out the coffins. It has since remained open. We are on the threshold of deep Mysteries of love and the creative principle revealed only by sacrifice.

Within the little door is a marvelous vault, lit by the glow of precious jewels. This, C. R. is told, is the king's treasure. We may recall that to reach this place we have come an underground way, and that in Greek mythology the king of the Underworld is associated with great riches.

The main wonder of the place is a central sepulchre, fantastically adorned with precious jewels and of a peculiar and significant shape.

It is triangular, which Qabalists will recognize as the principle of form, and has a great polished copper bowl at its center. Within the burnished copper bowl stands an angel, holding in his arms a strange and mysterious tree, from which the fruit fall into the bowl. As they do so they liquefy and run into three small golden bowls standing by. These form a little altar, supported by an eagle, an ox, and a lion. These are three of the holy living creatures of the vision of Ezekiel. They are normally four in number, the fourth being represented by a man or an angel—who in this instance may be identified with the angelic figure in the central copper bowl.

The page then repeats the message that was found in mysterious copper script on the outer iron door, and shows C. R. a copper trapdoor set into the floor of the vault. They go through it and descend into pitch darkness. The page opens a little chest to reveal a perpetual light (ever a symbol of the inmost spirit and source of our being) with which he lights a torch so they can see.

C. R. is overtaken by great fear at their temerity in advancing so far into these hidden Mysteries, but the page assures him that all is safe as long as the sacrificed royal persons are still at rest.

He then shows C. R. a great bed hung about with rich curtains. Drawing one of these aside, and heaving up the coverlets, he suddenly reveals that which in the ancient Mysteries was held to be unknowable and unseeable by mortal man. That is, the naked form of Lady Venus—or Isis unveiled.

She is in fact sleeping, which may explain the page's remark that this is a unique occasion and opportunity. It is a time in the process of sacrifice and regeneration when all is quiescent; and the dynamics involved may be revealed to the rare soul who is worthy to see them. Over the bed of the sleeping Venus is a tablet inscribed with an esoteric script. The page declines to translate it, saying that C. R. will learn its import through his own experience. In fact it says, "When the fruit shall be quite melted down then I shall awake and be the mother of a King." The page extinguishes the torch after drawing the covers again, and they climb back to the vault of the triangular sepulchre. C. R. is now the better able to examine the place and sees that the tree is melted by heat radiated from the shining precious stones in the walls. These to clearer sight seem to be not only precious stones but mineral tapers burning with a uniquely clear fire. The tree, as it melts in their heat, continually produces new fruit.

The page then tells C. R. what was written above the bed of the Lady Venus, and that this information emanates from Atlas. At this precise moment the little Cupid flies in and discovers them. It is plainly a matter of great enormity that someone has penetrated to these depths, and come so close to discovering the sleeping Venus. Cupid hastily seals the copper trapdoor. C. R. and his page do not dare admit that they have in fact penetrated into the *sanctum sanctorum*. Even so the Cupid says that he must punish C. R., at least in token, for coming so close to his mother's couch. Accordingly he pricks C. R. on the hand with one of his darts, which he has heated in one of the glowing stones that provide the heat for the transformation of the magical tree. This draws a drop of blood from C. R.'s hand.

There is more to come as a result of this incident, for it is pregnant with hidden meaning. Cupid, jesting, bids the others take good care of C. R. as his wound will soon bring him to the end of his days. By this he means not physical death but the death of initiation.

Serious mysteries may be describable only in terms of paradox, or in what passes for jest. Cupid continues to jest and make merry during the following funeral arrangements. Indeed jesting deception is the rule in the ceremonies that follow. The six coffins are solemnly laid in a sepulchre, even though from his observations of the night before C. R. knows them to be empty. Thus all the funeral pomp is a charade.

The coffins are laid in a wooden edifice of seven columns surmounted with a crown and a flag depicting a phoenix. The fact that the building is of wood, rather than the gold and jewels we have come to expect, suggests that it is a mere emblematic show. As the phoenix flag is raised, the Virgin of Lights tells them that if they are constant in their endeavors the dead will rise. To this end she bids them go with her to the Tower of Olympus.

Fifth Day: Journey to the Island

She leads them through a little door to the shore, where seven little ships await them. They sail off in one of them surrounded by the other six, displaying planetary symbols. Saturn leads and Venus brings up the rear. To either side of them are Mercury and Mars, and immediately behind them the ships representing Sun and Moon.

They pass over the inland lake, and then into a narrow channel that leads to the open sea. These descriptions have their analogs in the structure of human consciousness. As they strike the open sea they find themselves surrounded by creatures of the deep—sea nymphs, sirens, sea goddesses.

The seven ships are drawn up in formation. The two representing Sun and Moon remain in the center whilst the other five stand about them. Saturn opposite Venus, Mars opposite Mercury, and that representing Earth, upon which the candidates ride, at the head of this five-sided figure. Apart from the significance of the pentagram as a sigil of the power of the spirit over the elements there is also in the disposition of the ships a correspondence with the slain couples. The Sun and Moon represent bridegroom and bride; Saturn and Venus represent the old king with the fair young queen; and Mars and Mercury the dark middle-aged king with the veiled uncrowned beautiful matron as his consort, representing the *materia* of transformation that is to be paired with the fiery, transformatory alchemical process.

The sea creatures present to the company, in honor of the wedding, a "costly great, set, round and orient pearl, the like to which hath not at any time been seen, either in ours, or yet in the new world." Plainly this is a very special mystery from the depths. It is a recognition of the transformation process and marriage about to be performed, and not unconnected with the pearl crucifix in the possession of the queen, that had been wrought between the royal bride and groom. The assembled sea nymphs and goddesses then sing in delicate sweet voices a hymn to love.

Despite the allurements to stay, the presiding Virgin of Lights gives to the sea creatures, by way of return, a red scarf—an emblem of corporeal life—and the little fleet passes on. C. R. realizes that the wound on his hand he received from Cupid is the same as the blow to the head he received from a sharp stone in his initial dream.

They approach a square island surrounded by a thick wall. Within it is a fine meadow with little gardens containing strange fruits. In the center is a great round tower of seven stories. An ancient warden of the tower comes to greet them in a golden pinnace, attended by guards in white.

They are taken to the base of the Tower of Olympus in which they find a laboratory, and they are set to labor preparing juices and essences. Rude mattresses are slung on the floor for them to sleep on at night.

Before retiring however, C. R. wanders outside and stands on the top of the wall surrounding the island. He sees in the bright moonlight that the planets in the night sky are about to form a most rare conjunction. Then, as the clock strikes midnight, seven flames pass over the sea to the top of the tower. The winds rise suddenly, the sea becomes rough and threatening, and the moon disappears behind clouds. C. R. hurries back in from the tempestuous dark and lies down on his mattress. He is lulled to sleep by the gentle purling of a fountain that is in the laboratory.

Sixth Day: The Alchemical Tower

The following day is taken up with a detailed alchemical process on successive levels of the Tower of Olympus. This is entirely under the direction of the Virgin of Lights, assisted by maidens and musicians. At the commencement of each stage she opens a trapdoor in the ceiling and bids them ascend to her level. They do this according to their ability and temperament, figuratively described as some climbing ladders, others ropes, while a few have wings.

On the first floor they tend a fountainlike apparatus in which are distilled the bodies of the sacrificed ones. The heat for this operation is generated from the executioner's head. A deep yellow essence distilled from this process is collected in a golden globe.

On the second floor the globe is heated in a room of mirrors. They concentrate the rays of the sun upon it from all angles. Eventually it shines as brightly as the sun itself and when it cools they open it with a sharp-pointed diamond. This reveals a snow-white egg.

On the third floor the egg is warmed in a square copper sand bath. A chick hatches from it which they feed with the blood of the beheaded ones, collected on the day of execution, diluted with liquid that they have prepared. The bird grows very quickly. At first it is black and fierce but then molts and becomes tamer, growing snow-white feathers. Finally its feathers become multicolored and beautiful, though the head remains white. It is now very tame and they release it.

On the fourth floor they prepare a bath for the bird in a liquid colored with white powder to resemble milk. The bird drinks some of the milky liquid and appears pleased with it. Lamps are placed under the bath and a lid placed over the top with a space for the bird's head to emerge. The bird's feathers boil off until it is as smooth as a baby, the dissolving feathers turning the liquid blue. The bird is led up and down, smooth and glittering, wearing a gold collar and chain. The blue liquid is meanwhile boiled away to precipitate a blue stone. This is ground down on a stone and used as a tincture to paint the bird's body blue—though still leaving the head white.

On the fifth floor they find an altar identical to the one before the queen in the hall with its six symbolic objects—the book, the taper, the globe, the striking watch, the red fountain, and the skull with a white serpent.

The bird is added as a seventh object. It drinks from the blood-red fountain and pecks the white serpent, which bleeds copiously. The blood is caught in a cup and then poured down the bird's reluctant throat. The serpent is revived by dipping its head in the fountain, and disappears into the skull. The celestial globe on the altar turns successively to those particular stellar configurations or conjunctions and the watch strikes one, then two, then three. The bird lays its head on the gold-tooled black velvet book, willingly allowing its head to be struck off by one of the assembled company who is chosen by lot. No blood flows until the bird's breast is opened. Then it spurts forth like a fountain of rubies. A fire is kindled and the bird's body is burnt to ashes. These are cleansed and laid in a box of cypress wood. C. R. and three other selected ones are taken up secretly to a further stage from which the others are now debarred. These others tend an alchemical furnace and assume that the transmutation of elements on the seventh floor is the highest mystery.

C. R. and his three companions are instructed in a higher mystery by an old man who tends a small round furnace. He instructs them to moisten the bird's ashes with the prepared water until it is like thin dough; to heat this over the fire and then cast it into two molds. They thus produce two little transparent images as fair as the body of the sleeping Venus. These are placed on satin cushions and fed from a gold cup with drops of blood of the bird. The two figures grow and are placed on a long table of white velvet covered to the breast with a white cloth. Eventually they become of full human size. The old man covers their faces with a white silk cloth, torches are placed about the table, and the Virgin of Lights brings in crystalline garments which are laid by them.

Above the figures are seven concentric hemispheres. The topmost one has an opening in it but this is, however, closed.

Six virgins appear with large trumpets wreathed about with green, glittering, flaming material. The old man removes the face cloths and three times places a trumpet to the mouth of each figure. The wreath bursts into flames, the source of fire coming, as lightning, through the opening in the roof of the tower, and bringing life to the figures. Only C. R. sees the true source of the flame.

All lights are extinguished. The figures are enwrapped in the velvet cloths and left to sleep. Meanwhile the brethren on the seventh floor have succeeded in preparing transmuted gold.

Finally Cupid comes to awaken the couple. They think they have slept since the beheading. They are dressed in the crystalline garments and adorned with gold chains. All then descend by a winding stair to a waiting ship upon which the royal couple embark, attended by Cupid and some of the virgins.

The company is then entertained by the old warden of the Tower of Olympus. He conducts them through many secret chambers in the walls surrounding the island. Within them are many wondrous devices "which man's wit in imitation of nature had invented."

The lord himself is also a master of wisdom and instructs them all profoundly on diverse matters. Finally, wearied of learning, they sleep in stately rooms within the walls, lulled to sleep by the gentle sound of the surrounding sea.

Seventh Day: The Return and Investiture

On the seventh and final day they have some difficulty in finding their way out through the labyrinthine corridors within the walls. Finally, however, they do so and are invested with yellow robes and their golden fleeces. The Virgin of Lights tells them that they are now Knights of the Golden Stone.

Each one receives a gold medal upon which are inscribed abbreviations of Latin mottos: *Ars Naturae Ministra* and *Temporis Natura Filia,* which mean "Art is the priestess of Nature" and "Nature is the Daughter of Time." The warden of the tower exhorts them ever to bear these principles in mind in all their works. The need for man's ingenuity to follow in the footsteps of nature is a precept that is a feature of Rosicrucian and alchemical literature, and a hallmark of the new learning advocated by Francis Bacon. Much can also be read into the second phrase. It has regard to the great phases of terrestrial revolution in which the movements of the Earth itself are akin to a simple cog in a great universal clock.

The company embark upon twelve ships for their return journey. Each ship sails under the banner of one of the signs of the zodiac. The one upon which C. R. and his fellow initiates sail is dedicated to Libra, whose ruling planet is Venus, and which signifies balance, between Scorpio and the Virgin.

Upon their ship is to be found, prominently placed, a wondrous clock. The sea upon which they sail is now perfectly calm, and they are enthralled by the discourses of the warden of the tower.

The twelve ships are met by a great welcoming fleet awaiting them in the lake. Atlas makes an oration that is answered by the warden of the tower, who hands over a mysterious casket containing wedding gifts for the royal couple. This is placed in the keeping of Cupid.

As they disembark each is personally greeted by the young king and queen. They form a horseback procession and C. R. finds himself accompanied by no less than the warden of the tower and the young king.

Each one bears a snow white ensign upon which is a red cross. C. R. also wears upon his hat the gold tokens that he originally received at the threefold gates of the castle.

Attention is drawn to the similarity between C. R. and the warden of the tower. Both have long gray beards and hair. This is commonly a symbolic indication of great wisdom. The king also makes the cryptic remark, disguised as a jest, that C. R. is his father. He also remarks, on hearing about the episode of the dove, the raven, and the bread, that C. R. is obviously not only very wise but under the blessing of God.

At this point they approach the gates of the castle where the Porter, clothed in blue, awaits them. He bears a supplication. This porter was once, like C. R., highly esteemed for his wisdom. He is said to have been a famous astrologer. He had, however, committed an act which condemned him to remain as guardian of the gate of the Mysteries. This act, it transpires, is the same that C. R. has committed, of beholding the Lady Venus unveiled. The porter has to remain in this function until he is replaced by whoever next commits this rare and grave act. The supplication asserts that the Lady Venus has again recently been unveiled and the porter now seeks his release.

In the meantime it is announced that, as a reward for their diligence, each one present shall receive as a gift, the thing that he most desires. While they reflect on this the king and queen play a species of chess where all the pieces represent vices and virtues.

After a final banquet it is announced that they must all take the vows appropriate to being a member of the order of the Knights of the Golden Stone. These are, in brief:

1. That their esoteric order shall be firmly ascribed to the service of God and his handmaiden, Nature—not to any intervening daimon or spirit. (This is important, as it is dangerous for an esoteric group or individual to give unquestioning allegiance to a mere discarnate entity.)
2. That they abjure sexual promiscuity, incontinence, or similar

deviance. (This is particularly important in modern permissive times. The powerful nature of the occult forces can easily spill over into the projection of glamors. The ensuing sexual license can be corrosive, inflicting great harm to the young by the resultant emotional instability and even destruction of a home. Thus the innocent become disinherited even in the cradles of their fundamental human rights. Esoteric practice, especially in its so-called tantric forms, demands a strict moral code, not a lack of it.)

3. That they be ready to assist with their talents all who are worthy. (The purpose of esoteric training and initiation is service. It is service to others that is its entire justification. That service, however, is given to those "who are worthy." There are occasions, and many of them, when the service required is not at all what the recipient thinks it should be. That is another angle on the mechanism and motivation of prayer. We should ask for what we need, rather than for what we think we want. The two seldom coincide.)

4. That they do not employ their membership in the order as a means to worldly pride or authority. (The values of the spirit are not those of the world. These strictures not to use the occult arts for gain are very much deeper in implication than a disapproval of commercial clairvoyance. The spiritual principle of love and service is indeed an antithesis to seeking worldly power and glory. There is a spiritual power and glory that shines through those great in love and service, but it is not necessarily coincidental with personal wealth or a position of power or influence.)

5. That they shall not be willing to live longer than God will have them. (This seems a strange condition. It is however an acceptance of death, or the conditions of mortality. Initiation is indeed rightly considered a form of death; it is a going forth into the "shining kingdom" while still in the flesh. This is no mere figure of speech.)

These promises are vowed upon the king's scepter and dedicated in a chapel, where C. R. leaves his hat with the golden tokens, and his golden fleece, and records his name in a book. Above his name he also writes a curious motto: *Summa Scientia Nihil Scire,* "The highest wisdom is to know nothing."

This is not merely an injunction to humility. It is an affirmation that intellectual learning is not enough, or indeed even necessary. The "nothingness" is the spiritual condition above all intuition and intellection. It is beyond what Qabalists call Kether, the Crown, the first emanation of God. It is at the heart of the unmanifest light known ultimately as Ain—nothingness. A similar conception is found at the heights of oriental mysticism as the void, which is beyond the bliss of Nirvana. It is also found in the classic Western treatise on the "via negativa," *The Cloud of Unknowing.*

Each brother is then granted a private audience with the king and his ministers, to tell what it is he desires above all things. At this point C. R. confesses that it is he who has penetrated to the hiddenmost depths of the mysteries of the castle and seen the naked sleeping Venus. That is, he has done that which no living man can ordinarily do, gaze upon Isis unveiled—the conscious creative principle behind the manifestations of the natural world.

This is "naturing nature"—the active principle (*natura naturans*)—that gives life, variety of form, vitality, evolutionary processes, transformation to "natured nature" (*natura naturata*). Even simple perception at this level is guarded from mortal man. For were he to be able to go on, and bring influence to bear at this level, then he would be able to control the manifesting forms of life. With an unredeemed will the deed would result in disease, malformation, monsterism, rather than transformation and transmutation to more beautiful and functional life-forms. Even so, with scientific tinkering on the outer limits of form, something of the dynamisms involved is revealed in the malformations and malfunctions attendant upon subatomic radiations, to say nothing of the genetic engineering implicit in experimentation upon cellular life-forms.

The implications of alchemy are thus seen to be grave indeed. It is not merely a matter of mixing and processing various ingredients in order to obtain a precious metal. The ability to transform and transmute the forms of manifesting life would give an horrendous power. Hence the strictures of purity of motive and dedication to the service of God in alchemical texts. These are no mere empty formalities of assumed piety. One may here catch a glimpse of the type of evil that necessitated a whole civilization being wiped off the face of the Earth in volcanic fire, earthquake, or deluge, in the tradition of Atlantis. Once the springs of life-form are controlled by unregenerate man the types of exploitation, slavery and degradation possible exceed even the vilest abuses of human and animal life performed by man in the current historical epoch.

As a consequence of his attaining this degree of knowledge and power, which is implicit upon his having unveiled the Isis of nature, C. R. is told by Atlas that he may not now return home. He must take the place of the old porter as guardian of the castle gate. Furthermore, no release can be expected until another penetrates the same Mystery, and this will not be until the next chymical marriage, in a new generation, of the current king/bridegroom's future son.

C. R. now realizes why he was so warmly welcomed by the porter initially, who indeed said, "Now welcome in God's Name unto me the man whom of long time I would gladly have seen." This describes a particular function of esoteric grade or office: that one so privileged has to train his successor before he may pass on himself.

This particular office is custodian of the Rosicrucian Mysteries. It is a high one, as is implied by the long wait that is envisaged before another may be found sufficiently worthy. In the higher grades of the planetary hierarchy this may entail a period longer than the normal human life span. C. R. is also evidently of an equal grade to the lord of the tower and even Atlas, with both of whom he shares a glorious lodging.

Here the manuscript abruptly breaks off on the pretext that the last two leaves of it are missing. However this is a device that conceals the fact that the three remain sleeping, like the uncorrupted body of Christian Rosencreutz, or the Lady Venus, or heroes such as King Arthur of Avalon, or Merlin of the hawthorn tower of Nimuë, until such time as they are awakened by one who is found worthy. Then the remaining pages of the manuscript will be written in terms of the life experiences of the one who performs the awakening.

The imaginal journey upon which we are about to embark is not one where we undertake such high personal esoteric ambitions as Christian Rosencreutz, but we may recognize certain elements from the *Chymical Marriage* on our way. There are also some things new, or at any rate, not overtly incorporated in the Rosicrucian ludibrium.

The first of these is our point of commencement. This has its place as a physical location, although the building described no longer exists as a physical entity in terms of bricks and mortar. On the higher physical ethers it may well exert a continued presence. This is the house of Dr. John Dee, the Elizabethan magus, at Mortlake, on the south bank of the Thames to the west of modern London.

Dee was a man of many parts: scientist, philosopher, mathematician, geographer, technologist, magician, and confidant of Queen Elizabeth I in her girlhood. He remained a guide, philosopher, and friend to her for most of their lives. He built the beginnings of a national library at his own expense, and it was to him that the Elizabethan discoverers, adventurers, and sea-dogs, such as Drake, Raleigh, Gilbert, Hawkins, and Grenville, came for the maps and charts for their journeys. Dee owned the first terrestrial globes to be found in England. In the 1580s he spent much time in Europe, researching alchemy and probably acting as a government agent in the years immediately prior to the conflict with Spain and the consequent Armada. Psychical research was another of his interests and his crystal ball and obsidian magic mirror can still be seen at the British Museum. In his travels on the continent, under the patronage of various crowned heads of Europe, he probably helped lay the foundations of much of what was to emerge as the Rosicrucian documents a generation later. His personal sigil, called the Hieroglyphic Monad, a symbolic compendium of esoteric teaching, appears prominently in the margin of *The Chymical Marriage of Christian Rosencreutz.*

His study in Mortlake is a suitable place therefore from whence to commence our journey, which includes various power symbols from the Rosicrucian tradition. The summoning of the Rosicrucian form of Isis Urania is the prelude to a journey upriver, an inner river, (although in this connection it coincides with the River Thames outside Dr. Dee's door) to a mystic island.

Here we discover the dynamics of the power points that make up the nodes of the etheric web that spans our planet. Acupuncture points, to coin a phrase, in the body of Gaia.

The imagery is in the form of a tower, but one that is a center of energies, of sound and of light, and of a range of inner energies as well.

By these means we may learn to identify and cooperate with actual power centers within the higher ethers of the Earth's physical structure. There are quite deep technicalities involved in all of this, to do with the tilt of the Earth's axis and the precession of equinoxes and polar stars. It would fill a large volume to go into all of it, but our building the imagery of a typical planetary chakra in this manner will enable us, on returning to it in meditation again and again, to learn for ourselves much of this lore.

JOURNEY 4: THE GUARDIAN OF THE MILL

We are seated in a small room. About us are shelves full of books, and upon tables and within cupboards an assortment of scientific and magical instruments: microscopes, telescopes, crystal balls, pendulums, flasks and retorts, rolled maps and charts, terrestrial and celestial globes. Before us there sits an old man, dressed in a medieval scholar's gown and close-fitting cap, with a long white beard. It seems that we are seeking wisdom from him.

He looks around the room and at all its objects with a quizzical and faintly amused air, and then produces from a high shelf a cubical box apparently made of some fragrant dark wood. He looks around, and so that we shall not be observed, pulls the curtains across the small and cluttered windows of the room. We sit in semidarkness, the room illuminated only by the chinks of light that pass through gaps in the curtains.

He carefully opens the box with a little silver key that hangs around his neck on a chain. From within the box he draws a quantity of fine, black silk cloth in which an object is concealed. He carefully unwraps it and we see that it is a little silver bell.

He bids us stand, and standing himself, crosses himself and makes a long personal prayer or invocation. Then, with a significant glance at us, and with an expression of great expectancy, he raises his hand and gently rings the little bell.

The silvery tinkle of its chime has hardly subsided, reaching into all corners of the room with its penetrating tone, when we hear a similar ring of some hidden bell in apparent answer to it. With great excitement our host rings his bell again in acknowledgment, and no sooner has the sound ceased to echo round the room, than one of the windows to the little room bursts open. Framed within the opening we see a fair-haired maiden wearing a blue cloak that is covered with stars, and she also has wings. We can see them arched behind her as she leans in at the window, smiling, and ringing her silver bell. Looking around at us, and apparently satisfied by what she sees, she beckons, and withdraws from the window.

The old man hastens to the doorway and throws it open and we pass through it to follow the maiden. We find that we are in a small ornamental garden that abuts a wide river. The winged maiden is advancing across the garden to the river, where a boat awaits. Urged on by the old man, we follow her, and embark upon the vessel.

It is an open craft, that would hold perhaps two dozen people and although it has rests for oars, it is propelled on this occasion by the wind. The winged maiden sits in the stern, at the tiller, and sets the single triangular sail so that we swiftly pass out into midstream.

It seems that we are going upriver. We pass through water meadows and occasional hamlets on either side of the wide, winding river until we see before us an island that divides the river in two. The boat glides up to a landing stage at the end of the island, but before we disembark, the maiden trails her hand in the water. All about us in the water we see fishes raising their heads above the surface. And also, at first beneath the surface of the stream, but then breaking the surface, other water creatures of another plane of being—nymphs and naiads and undines of all kinds associated with inland waters. One of them, who seems to be some kind of senior, or elemental king, rises up out of the water and hands her a large freshwater pearl.

She gives thanks to all the water beings, and then, holding the pearl before her, leads us off the boat and onto the island. The pearl seems to shine with its own light. Passing along a serpentine way through willow trees whose branches hang down all about us, we find we have come to the foot of a tower.

It is sealed with a stout and formidable looking door that seems not to have been opened for ages. The tower itself also looks dilapidated, made of clapboards that hang, blistered and peeling in disarray. All up the tower can be seen windows that appear dark and uninhabited, mere frameworks for hanging cobwebs within.

The winged maiden, however, holds up the pearl, which brightens considerably, and the door swings silently and smoothly open. She passes within. All is dark, and there is a musty smell. But she proceeds up a steep and winding stair, the way illuminated by the bright pearl. As we pass upward, we see by the light of the pearl that all is not dilapidated as it might have appeared from the outside. It seems that we are passing up the stairs of a mill, and all about us is the machinery, well-oiled and polished and which gleams as if meticulously maintained and ready to work at any time. From the corner of one's eye one might even glimpse some of the workers of the mill. They are very elusive to sight, however; little people with pointed caps and boots like elves or gnomes in fairy tales.

We press on up the tower behind the swiftly climbing maiden. It seems to be far higher than it appeared from the outside. We come eventually to a broad room near the top of the tower, that is well lit by broad windows at all four sides. Looking out we can see in all directions, the country stretching far beyond and beneath us.

At the center of the room is a table and upon the table a little golden stand. The maiden places the pearl in the center of the stand, and it seems as if it was made for it. As she does so there is a great rumbling and whirling, and we see through the windows about us the great sails of the windmill—for that is what we are in—beginning to turn. The rumbling we hear is of the machinery below us, and also, we realize, of the massive granite mill stones at its base that grind all that is fed into them into fineness.

The sails of the mill as they whirl past the windows seem multicolored with bright mosaic patterns. A great whirling Catherine wheel of color it must seem to anyone observing from afar. At the same time the pearl within the center glows ever brighter until it is virtually incandescent. It seems that the mill tower is also like some kind of light house. Then we realize that the sails of the mill are connected to a peal of bells that hangs high in the dome above us. And so we stand high in the center of this tower, conscious of the whirling light and sound of this mighty beacon.

The old man, who has accompanied us upon this journey, now tells us to look at the surface of the table upon which the pearl rests. It is like a map, and upon it we see a point of light that represents our own tower of sound and light, and various points mark other similar towers, linked to each other in a network of sound and light.

And below the table itself, we see a slowly turning terrestrial globe, its axis along the same line as our tower and axle of the mill wheels below. There we see more plainly still the web of light and sound and other subtle forces that sustain and protect and energize the world upon which we live.

The winged maiden directs our attention upward. Looking to the ceiling of the room, we see that it is domed, with a representation of the circumpolar stars upon it. The Great and Little Bear, the Dragon, and centrally in the midmost point, the North Star of our epoch, which we call Polaris. And looking from the windows, we see, not the familiar countryside we saw before, but snowy polar wastes. We realize that the tower in which we stand has somehow relocated itself and stands at the North Pole. At the same time we realize that all of the towers we have seen represented on the map or globe, can, in another dimension of being, locate themselves at the actual pole. This is a great mystery and a point of commonality between them all. By this same token, we could, if we felt so inclined, with the permission of those who rule the towers, descend our tower when it is attuned to the mutual polar point, and find ourselves in any of the other towers the wide world over, even the most central tower of them all, which exists on a subtle level of the physical ethers, somewhere in the Gobi Desert. (Other important foci also exist.) The old man from whose room we started our journey seems aware of all this, and has the secrets in a great book that rests in this room, and that he is currently leafing through.

But on this occasion such ventures are not for us. Our attention is retained looking out over the snowy wastes, and it is telepathically instructed by the old man as he turns the leaves of the book. We realize that at the global pole, familiar terrestrial directions distort; for in whatever direction we care to gaze, we can only look to the south, as our gaze is land and sea bound, bent to the curve of the Earth. But looking out with eye attuned to the cosmos we see the celestial directions that define the position of the Earth in space. These are marked by four bright stars, each at right angles to the next. Aldebaran, the eye of the bull, in the constellation Taurus; Fomalhaut, the mouth of the Southern Fish, which lies beneath Aquarius; Antares, the heart of the scorpion, in Scorpio; and Regulus, the little king, or heart of the lion, in Leo.

Holding these cosmic directions in our hearts, we are aware that the winged maiden is giving us her blessing. And as she does so we feel ourselves sinking and fading from this scene of cosmic dimensions, to that of our own conscious mentality, adapted to life in the world. Yet as we return to normal consciousness and awareness of our physical surroundings we retain something of the memory and awareness of these other modes of orientation and reality, the viewpoint of our Earth in space.

BRANCH FIVE

The Faery Queen and the Magic Mountain

The latter half of the twentieth century has seen a growing trend in what conventional religionists have called an "abandonment of faith," and conventional materialists a "flight from reason." It would seem that there is perhaps some great truth that is seeking reexpression that has been too long neglected, and which remains neglected by conventional attitudes to inner and outer worlds.

Variously defined and containing many subgroups, and discursive elements, from neopaganism to a revival of interest in Renaissance magical theories, this movement has given plenty of warning of its approach for those who can read the signs—rather like the underground rumblings or changes in the atmosphere prior to a volcanic eruption.

In the Rosicrucian ludibrium we have examined just one example of the course of this hidden flow that now seeks outward and surface expression. We could have chosen from a score of alternatives, such as Goethe's symbolic tale "The Green Snake and the Beautiful Lily" of 1795, or the Abbé Montfaucon de Villars' account of elemental contacts *Le Comte de Gabalis* of 1670; to say nothing of the nineteenth century interest in fairy stories, whether collections of traditional tales such as those of the Brothers Grimm, Perrault, or Andrew Lang, or intuitive originals such as those of Hans Christian Andersen, much of which contain mythopoeic material relating to the Goddess in the form of fairy godmothers and the like, forerunners of a genre of modern children's writing in this vein that extends from Tolkien to *Mary Poppins.*

Toward the close of the nineteenth century more overt approaches to the dynamics involved in this movement are to be found in the establishment of societies devoted to the study and systematic practice of occult metaphysics. The very title of one of the pioneering books of this wave is significant: *Isis Unveiled.* Published in New York in 1877, its author, Helena Petrovna Blavatsky, followed up in 1888 with a more systematic exposition of oriental mystical tradition adapted for Western consumption with *The Secret Doctrine.* Although it is more taken for granted than emphasized, the cosmology cited in the "Stanzas of Dzyan," on which the rest of the book is a commentary, assumes a divine feminine principle. "The Eternal Parent wrapped in *her* ever-invisible robes had slumbered again for seven Eternities" (our italics). Or, "The Mother swells, expanding from within without, like the bud of the lotus . . ."

A more occidental approach to recover the Western Mystery Tradition from its centuries of neglect and persecution was the Hermetic Order of the Golden Dawn, which despite the overtly masculine assumptions of the times, opened the door to a resurgence of the divine feminine principle as the very names of some of its temples suggest—Isis-Urania and Stella Matutina.

These were early days however, and in the subsequent hundred years, what began with small groups of secluded "initiates" or esoteric enclaves seeking spiritual self-development has burgeoned forth into a wide spectrum of publishing activity and a plethora of conferences, workshops, experiential journeys and the like. In short, it seems that the Mysteries have been democratized by the emergence of the feminine.

In all this rediscovery and recognition of the power of ancient symbolism it is quite easy to lose one's way. Two elements stand out, however, as fundamental dynamics. These we might typify as, a) the tradition of Faery Queen, and b) the tradition of the Magic Mountain. The two can indeed come together, for the domain of the Faery Queen is very much the interior of the Magic Mountain.

In secular circles the mention of the Faery Queen will most likely be associated with childrens' fairy stories and quips about what might be found dancing at the bottom of New Age gardens! The reality, however, is somewhat more powerful than juvenile fiction-writers' whimsy. The Faery Queen is an embodiment of the feminine principle as expressed in the powers of the inner earth, and her attendants are strong and terrible elemental powers, not the delicate fairies of never-never land.

The Faery Queen and her powers are deeply attached to the land. Hence their description by the poet and mystic W. B. Yeats, as the lordly ones, who dwell in the hollow hill. And the Magic Mountain is the archetype of all hollow hills—that is, of the inner earth—that can profoundly affect the consciousness of whoever wanders in. A different experience of time is but one of such effects, as hinted in the legends of those who went in and returned (if ever), only after many years, the equivalent of what seemed to them but a mere day within.

The detailed lore of all this is both rich and diverse, and so as not to wander completely guideless through a labyrinth of symbolic wealth, we will follow the journey of one contemporary man, who managed to discover the main dynamics in both a scholarly and experiential way, in areas as apparently unconnected as Celtic folklore, Tibetan Buddhism, and Native American traditions. This is the American anthropologist W. Y. Evans-Wentz.

In his early days he was honored by European universities for his investigation into Celtic studies and evidence of the fairy faith and second sight. He then spent the bulk of his life in the Far East, translating and editing for Western eyes important texts of Tibetan Buddhism. Finally he returned to the United States where he spent his last years concerned with the traditions and the importance of sacred mountains.

THE FAIRY FAITH

In this spiritual odyssey, his first work was *The Fairy Faith in Celtic Countries* published in 1911, and significantly dedicated to two members of the Hermetic Order of the Golden Dawn, the poets George Russell ("AE"), and W. B. Yeats. It seems slightly odd to read in the dedication of an academic text the tone of his thanks to George Russell, "whose unswerving loyalty to the fairy faith has inspired much that I have written," and to W. B. Yeats, "who brought to me . . . the first message from fairyland, and who afterwards . . . led me through the haunts of fairy kings and queens." It is also something of a surprise to find on the very first page a reference to the legendary lost continent of Atlantis. All this seems a nod and a wink as broad as that of Apuleius when he started out on the story of the Golden Ass. And his heart is on his sleeve when he describes the Celtic lands as subject to "subtle forces so strange and mysterious that to know them they must be felt."

In his intuitive sympathy for his material, and perhaps because of his own Celtic ancestry, Evans-Wentz certainly did seem to feel these strange and subtle forces as the evocative descriptions in his book amply demonstrate. And the locations he visited over a period of four years throughout Ireland, Scotland, the Isle of Man, Wales, Cornwall, and Britanny, reads much like an itinerary for a New Age magical mystery tour.

As well as collecting direct evidence of accounts of the fairy traditions he compared them with medieval and Renaissance theories based in turn upon the metaphysical beliefs of the ancient world. According to this line of thought, the denizens of the invisible worlds can be divided into four categories: angels, in character and function similar to the ancient gods; devils or demons, like the above but malefic in character; elementals or nature spirits, a more neutral commonwealth;

and souls of the dead, humans of the past, the ancestors. It is the third class that covers the fairy world and is in turn divisible into four branches: gnomes, who inhabit the earth, minerals, and rocks, who haunt mines and caves and underground places; sylphs, who are beautiful and graceful spirits of air, like the fairies in *A Midsummer Night's Dream;* undines, beings of water, who dwell in fountains, lakes and rivers as well as the seas; and salamanders, who are creatures of fire.

Evans-Wentz also turned to the literary records of ancient myth and legend. According to Irish romance and tradition, Ireland has two populations: the Celtic human one, and an invisible one—the people of the goddess Dana (the Tuatha de Danaan), or the Sidhe (pronounced shee), a fairy folk of eternal youth and never-ending joy. Their lady, the goddess Dana, was later known as the goddess Brigit (after whom the Celtic kingdom of Brigantia was named), Christianized into Saint Bridget or Saint Bride. She was a remarkable saint, associated with Kildare, whose prophetic gifts enabled her to witness the incarnation of Christ from afar.

The mythical history of these people is contained in old written collections of oral lore, such as *The Book of Leinster* and *The Book of the Dun Cow.* And as Evans-Wentz found on his travels, they are held to live to this day in secret places in the hollow hills or under lakes, and offerings of milk and the fruits of the earth may be made to them in return for the ripening of crops and the fruitfulness of cows. Sometimes they may appear as magpies or crows.

That they are taken seriously may be adjudged by the testimony of a Roman Catholic priest to Evans-Wentz. "My private opinion is that in certain places here in Ireland where pagan sacrifices were practiced, evil spirits through receiving homage gained control, and still hold control, unless driven out with exorcisms."

A somewhat less fearful or more liberal attitude was taken by a Protestant minister in Scotland, "When I was a boy I was a firm believer in fairies; and now as a Christian minister I believe in the possibility and also the reality of these spiritual orders, but I wish only to know those orders which belong to the realm of grace. It is very certain that they exist. I have been in a state of ecstasy, and have seen spiritual beings which form these orders."

The Scottish tradition was investigated and recorded early on by a Christian minister, the Reverend Robert Kirk of Aberfoyle, in his *Secret Commonwealth of Elves, Fauns and Fairies* of 1691. And so strong is it that he was believed not to have died but to have been translated into fairyland.

In the fairy geography, Ireland is divided into four provinces, Connacht, Ulster, Leinster, and Munster, sometimes with a central fifth province, Meath, added. Each province has a distinct quality attributed to it. In the version cited by the scholars Alwyn and Brinley Rees in their book *Celtic Heritage* these are:

North: Ulster—battle
East: Leinster—prosperity
South: Munster—music
West: Connacht —learning
Center: Meath—kingship

We may recognize this as a local expression of a universal pattern, to be found in the ancient Hindu *Rig-Veda,* in the fivefold cosmic Hall of Light of Chinese tradition, and a version of the Grail Castle has it built on an island, with on outer tower on each of four walls, and a central fifth. Evans-Wentz was later to discover a similar pattern in Tibetan Buddhism, and it is also to be found in the Native American medicine wheel.

In Welsh tradition the old gods and fairy folk became absorbed into Arthurian legend. At the time of the Saxon conquest of Celtic England the old stories were carried by refugees to Britanny where they influenced Breton storytellers, some of whom found work at the courts of the Norman lords who were in time to conquer England from the Danes and Saxons. Thus the tales formed the basis for a school of courtly French prose and poetic romance, and later, through translation and adaptation, the glory of early English literature in the works of Sir Thomas Malory, whose *Morte d'Arthur* was one of the first books published on Caxton's printing press in 1485.

Evans-Wentz was fascinated by links of the Arthurian legends with fairy tradition. Not least of these is a derivation of the name of Arthur's queen, Gwenhwyvar, from "white ghost" or "white phantom," a description that might well fit a fairy woman. Arthur's halfsister, Morgan le Fay, is also obviously a fairy woman by her very name. And Arthur himself gained his sword from, and was always watched over by, the Lady of the Lake.

This led Evans-Wentz to see Arthur as, in origin, a god, ruling over a fairy court, akin to the Dagda, the king of the Tuatha de Danaan; or to Osiris, the divine ruler of the Underworld in ancient Egypt and consort of the universal goddess, Isis. Arthur had a wondrous coming, through the magical arts of Merlin, and a wondrous going, on the barge with three mourning queens (an aspect of the threefold goddess and the ancient sisterhoods), who take him, not to death, but to the fairy land of Avalon, from whence he may return when he is needed.

This Celtic otherworld is not in some remote cosmic condition but here on our own Earth. Normally it can be entered by humans only in an after-death condition. If a mortal gains access to it while alive, they may well not be seen again, as in the alleged case of Robert Kirk; Or may disappear for some period of earthly time to return with strangely enhanced gifts, like prophecy, as in the story of Thomas the Rhymer

There is, however, a traditional passport or emblem of safe passage to the fairy realm. This is described as a silver branch bearing blossoms or fruit of the sacred apple tree, which the Queen of Faery gives to mortals she wishes to have as companions. In classical legend it may appear as a golden bough, as in Virgil's *Aeneid*. The sybil commands the hero to pluck it from a tree near the entrance to Avernus, the Underworld, for it is sacred to the lower Juno (that is, Proserpine—the queen of rebirth and regeneration). Until this token is produced, Charon, the ferryman, will not conduct Aeneas into the Underworld.

It is from the golden bough, or silver branch, that is derived the magic wand, the staff of the pilgrim, the scepter of kingship, the baton of military command, the symbol of power. In the Tibetan mysticism and yoga to which Evans-Wentz turned, this symbol is the dorje, or thunderbolt wand. In its esoteric sense it has a correspondence with the human spinal column, as the vehicle of the serpent power—or kundalini. Learn to wield that powerful wand and the inner worlds will open.

TIBETAN YOGA

Having distinguished himself in no uncertain way, it may come as a surprise that Evans-Wentz did not pursue his researches into Celtic studies. But he found a natural extension to them, in a complete and intellectually satisfying form, in the mystical traditions of Tibet. Thereafter he produced a series of translations of texts that pioneered the Western interest in Tibetan Mahayana Buddhism. These works are *The Tibetan Book of the Dead, Tibet's Great Yogi Milarepa, Tibetan Yoga and Secret Doctrines,* and *The Tibetan Book of the Great Liberation.*

The similarities between the Tibetan system and that of the Celts are quite remarkable. The circled cross as a structure of the soul and inner worlds is expounded in *The Tibetan Book of the Dead.*

The Tibetan Book of the Dead is meant for recitation to one who is dying, and its purpose is to direct the attention of the soul to key images that will open a pathway out of the recurrent cycle of rebirth and death. It is held that immediately at the moment of death there is a unique opportunity to escape this wheel by focusing attention to its center.

If this opportunity is lost, then another stage follows when attention to the spiritual images around the circumference in the four cardinal directions, can still be highly efficacious.

In these two stages we have a replica of the magic circle and equal armed cross. The images are, however, in oriental form. That is, of a buddha—or ideal man—visualized in a different color at each station, and with different symbolic attributes. Each buddha also has a feminine counterpart or companion, often in intimate embrace, thus giving a polar completeness to the whole imagery.

The central buddha is Bhagavan Vairechana. He represents the father and seed of all that is and he is embraced by the Divine Mother of Infinite Space, also called the Sovereign Lady of Heavenly Space (according to translation). She is known as Akasa Dhath Ishvari, and represents the feminine principle in the universe. From the heart of this buddha and his consort there radiates the blue light of heavenly wisdom.

In the east is the Realm of Preeminent Happiness and Bhagavan Vajra-Sattva Akshobhya, who is pictured in blue, seated on a throne supported by elephants, and holding a five-pronged dorje. The dorje is a Tibetan form of magic wand, also called the thunderbolt sceptre. This buddha is known as the Hero-minded One, or One of Indestructible Mind. In short, he is a veritable Heracles. He is embraced by Mamiki the Divine Mother, and from them radiates the white light of the principle of consciousness.

In the south, the Glorious Realm, is Bhagavan Ratna-Sambhava. He is called the Beautiful One Born of a Jewel, and bears a precious gem, seated on a throne supported by horses. He is embraced by another form of the divine mother, known as Sangyay-Chauma, She of the Buddha (or Enlightened) Eyes. From them there radiates a dazzling yellow radiance of the wisdom of equality.

In the west, the Realm of Happiness, Bhagavan Buddha Amitabha bears a lotus blossom, and is seated on a peacock throne. He is known as the One of the Boundless and Incomprehensible Light, or of Life Eternal, and is embraced by the Divine Mother Gokarmo—the White-robed One. From them emanates the red light of discriminating wisdom.

In the north, the Realm of the Successful Performance of the Possible Actions, is Bhagavan Buddha Amogha-Siddhi—the Almighty Conqueror—bearing crossed dorjes. This is the Tibetan image of supreme achievement and power, being in itself a form of the circled cross. He sits on a throne supported by harpies—or winged goddesses. His consort is the Divine Mother Talma, known as the feminine savior. From them emanates the green radiance of wisdom in action.

We therefore find that we have an Eastern form of our Western magic-circle symbolism. It is useful to ponder the related symbolism and to realize that different cultures will produce different versions of it in terms of symbolic instruments and colors, based upon the same geometric form. In figure 5 the similarity of Tibetan, Amerindian, and Celtic Irish systems is immediately apparent, with four modes of activity around a common ruling or synthesizing center. This pattern

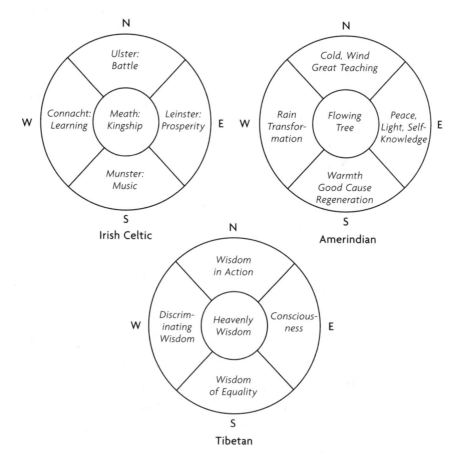

Figure 5

will also be familiar as the "quaternio" or "mandala" to all students of Jungian psychology.

A more comprehensive schema, which includes the "higher" formless worlds as well as the worlds of form, is the Mount Meru system. This, like Dante's *Divine Comedy,* assists the mind through the aid of pictorial imagery to comprehend something of the whole, and the interrelationship of parts in the inner worlds.

The image of Mount Meru (figure 6) is a complex glyph that comprehends within its symbolism all the worlds, from the deepest hells of hatred and delusion to the greatest formless heights of abounding grace and love. It is thus, par excellence, a model or three-dimensional solid map of the universe, inner and outer, formless and formed. It is depicted as a great four-sided mountain, ascending into the heights of

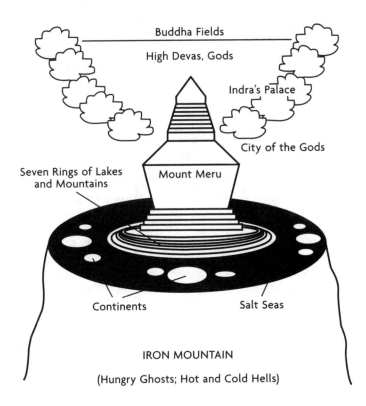

Figure 6

space, with the city of the gods at the summit, and the ordinary worlds of men at its base.

It stands at the top of a great iron mountain in the center of a sevenfold crater of clear sweet lakes and circular mountain ranges. Beyond these is a circular salt sea in which are four island continents, at each of the cardinal directions around the central island of Mount Meru. These four continents, a mere one of which represents the whole physical universe as we know it, represent different modes of human existence. The particular continent representing the current human condition is to the south of Mount Meru and is known as Jambu Island.

Deep within the iron landmass are the various hells of the evil doers. While they are perhaps not as comprehensive in their imagery as Dante's vision of hell, their various degrees of hotness and cold-ness and forms of torment fit the particular form of vice to which they are appropriate. We should state that all hellish punishment, in Western or Eastern esoteric systems, is self-inflicted and a result of a continued voluntary embracing of evil. It is not, as in popular ideas of medieval theology, a rigorous punishment from a vindictive and merciless deity. The point is that those who give themselves to hatred, greed, lust, or any of the moral vices, will, in time or out of time, find themselves surrounded by an objective state that corresponds to their interior condition. Strange as it may seem, we get what we desire. The court of Yama, Lord of the Dead, reigns supreme in a hall of justice over the system of hells. These are often classified into sixteen dif-ferent hells (eight hot and eight cold) each with sixteen appendices. The deepest hell is as far down in the iron mountain as the peak of Mount Meru rises above it.

Various entities share the worlds of men. They include the angelic and elemental oversouls or guardians of various parts of the Earth's surface: rivers, springs, woods, trees, hills, and so forth. These are con-ceived in the generic title of *nagas,* or *asuras,* or divine animals. They have at their highest level much in common with Western god-forms and archetypes. At the lowest level they are conceived as "hungry ghosts," wandering the earth, or just under its surface, tormented by unsatiated greed or desire. On reflection it will be realized that most ghosts are indeed hungry for something, and the adjective invariably accompanies the noun in Tibetan mysticism.

Mount Meru, rising foursquare out of the center of the sevenfold ring system of mountain peaks and cool clear lakes, is the abode of higher forms of consciousness. The four sides of the holy mountain are each of a specific jewel—emerald, crystal, lapis lazuli, and ruby. It stands between the Sun and Moon and its peak rises into the clouds and formless realms above the Sun and Moon.

The lower slopes of the holy mountain are known as the Heaven of the Four Great Kings. These are divine beings of a relatively minor order who regulate the form worlds. In the West they would correspond to orders of angels and archangels.

At the top of the holy mountain is the city of the gods, and within it Indra's Palace—a place of surpassing beauty and delight and which might be compared, in the West, with the New Jerusalem, or the uncorrupted Garden of Eden, the Earthly Paradise.

There are various levels of heavenly existence, however, just as there are in Dante's *Paradiso,* and all of them represent various modes of perfect expression in the worlds of form. However, beyond the topmost towers of the palace of the chief of all the gods, there extend, into and beyond the skies, the formless worlds. These are variously known as the Buddha Fields, the Mythic Lands, or the Pure Lands of the Buddhas. Their equivalent in Western systems of exegesis would be the Ain Soph beyond Kether on the Tree of Life; or the Divine Empyreum in which there floats the mystic rose in Dante's *Divine Comedy.*

There are various ways by which we can aspire to these higher realms, and these are represented by various spiritual disciplines and ways of meditation, ranging from the form discipline of yoga to the formless disciplines of mystical contemplation.

THE AMERINDIAN TRADITION

Evans-Wentz's work on Tibetan mysticism brought him consider-able fame but the outbreak of the Second World War took him back to California, and by a happy synchronicity, he inherited an exten-sive ranch that embraced an Indian sacred mountain, Mount Tecate, (known to the Indians as Cuchama), and this led him into a concern for the religion of the American Indians.

He came to realize the similarity of the shining beings of the red man with the Tibetan devas and dakinis and the fairy folk of the Celts. This occupied him until his death in his late eighties, in 1965, and culminated in the posthumous publication of his various notes on the subject in *Cuchama and Sacred Mountains* (Athens: Ohio University Press, 1981).

By this time Evans-Wentz was not so much a pioneer as part of a general wave of opinion about the importance of native traditions, par-ticularly in the Americas.

The Indian medicine wheel has come to be recognized as another expression of the familiar fourfold pattern based upon the cardinal directions. In an anthology of Indian writings, *Touch the Earth* (New York: Simon & Schuster, 1971), for example, Black Elk, of the Teton Dakota branch of the Sioux Indians, speaks of everything an Indian does being in a circle, for the reason that the "Power of the World" always works in circles. This gives rise to the image of a flowering tree in the center of a quartered circle. From the east, comes peace and light, from the south warmth, from the west rain, from the north the cold and wind that give strength and endurance.

In her Sunray Meditation Society, Dhyani Ywahoo has systematized this for a non-Indian audience in *Voices of our Ancestors* (Boston: Shambhala, 1987), a book intended "to strengthen individuals' relationships with their families, communities, nations, and the land, the Earth herself."

In her worldview, all things are related in the circle of life, with guardians at the different directions. The north is a place of great teaching, hiding place of the thunderbird and resting place of the sacred buffalo. Self-knowledge comes from the east, the place of all relationships. Good cause and regeneration is to be found in the south, the place of the dancing corn mothers, scattering the seed. And transformation lies in the west, the place of the sacred medicine and wisdom of the dancing bear. Here in the west lies the choice either to proceed off the circle to the "land of boundless light," (a parallel to Avalon, or the Hesperides), or to continue round the wheel of natural expression, or of birth and death in the oriental traditions.

So much for the fourfold pattern. There is also the powerful symbol of the sacred mountain, which is a major concern of Evans-Wentz's last book, and this has its parallel in the Mount Meru schema of oriental tradition, and in the hollow hills of the lordly ones in Celtic fairy lore—to say nothing of the alchemical tower of Rosicrucian symbolism.

Evans-Wentz discovered Cuchama to have been an initiation site for young men of the local tribes who were approaching manhood. There the young man made his pilgrimage, after preparation by the tribal elders, in search of a mystic dream, on the heights under the stars. Guided by the "shining beings" he came to a realization of his future lot and function in adult life.

This initiation, Evans-Wentz went so far as to say, was equivalent, and even superior, to a university graduation in modern society: ". . . the Red Man had good reason to maintain, as did the most illustrious of the Greeks and as do the sages of modern India and Tibet, that all real knowledge lies hidden within man, and that real education consists in the awakening of this hidden knowledge."

Any sacred hill, whether it be mighty mountain or humble tump or tumulus, is also reckoned to be hollow. In some cases this is a physical actuality, either through burial chambers, mine working, or underground watercourses, but beyond any physical actuality is the meaning that another level or plane of existence lies within, and the actual physical location happens to be a place where the veil between the two worlds is thin. For this reason any such contact is also frequently associated with wisdom and prophecy.

THE FAERY QUEEN

As a typical example, and one that has particular relevance to our theme of the Goddess, we may cite the ballad of the late thirteenth-century figure Thomas Learmont of Erceldoun, or Thomas the Rhymer, who is reckoned to have received the gift of prophecy from the Faery Queen, deep in the Eildon Hills on the Scottish borders. In reference to these prophetic powers he was called True Thomas.

In various sets of verses he is said to have foretold the Battle of Bannockburn that occurred shortly after his death, and also the union of the thrones of England and Scotland that occurred some three hundred years later:

> *When Tweed and Powsail meet at Merlin's grave*
> *Scotland and England one monarch shall have.*

In 1603 the Powsail burn burst its banks at Drumelzier, legendary site of the death of the Scottish Merlin, and joined the small watercourse with the River Tweed into which it still flows. This same year saw the accession of the son of Mary Queen of Scots to the thrones of England *and* Scotland, as James I and VI.

In the ballad that commemorates his meeting with the Faery Queen, Thomas is lying on a riverbank by a tree. A common feature of goddess contacts is a site near water (be it lake, fountain, river, well, or millpond) and a tree, particularly the fairy thorn.

> *True Thomas lay on Huntlie bank;*
> *A ferlie [strange thing] he spied with his 'ee;*
> *And there he saw a lady bright,*
> *Come riding down by the Eildon Tree.*

> *Her skirt was o' the grass-green silk,*
> *Her mantle o' the velvet fyne,*

And ilka tett [each lock]of her horse's mane
Hang fifty siller bells and nine.

This turns out to be the Faery Queen, although at first, being a good Catholic, he mistakes her for the Virgin Mary, but she soon puts him right on this score.

True Thomas he pull'd aff his cap,
And louted low down to his knee;
"All hail, thou mighty Queen of Heaven!
For thy peer on earth I never did see,"

"O no, O no, Thomas," she said,
"That name does not belang to me;
I am but the queen of fair Elfland,
That am hither come to visit thee."

He kisses the fairy lady, even though this may mean that the human world will never see him again, and they ride off to the parting of three ways—one that leads to heaven, one that leads to hell, and the middle way to Elfland, which in this location is via the interior of the Eildon Hills.

Here they pass through a magical garden where she plucks an apple and offers it to him, and which will confer the gift of prophecy. There is always danger and opportunity in magical fruit, depending upon the way that it is taken. If it is offered as a gift or reward it may confer benefits—though benefits that may entail high responsibilities or even suffering. If it is simply taken, without permission or by stealth or conceit, or in defiance of warnings, then it can be very much a poisoned fruit—as in the Garden of Eden story.

There is also a time lag between inner and outer worlds that can be catastrophic in the case, say, of Rip van Winkle, who disappeared for a hundred years. But Thomas returns after only seven human years to take up his destiny as prophet, attuned to the etheric network of his nation and the archetypes of the world soul.

He led a life containing much travel and concerns with intelligence work and the high politics of his time, as Merlin did long before him, and the Elizabethan magus Dr. Dee did long after. He also foretold his own end, which was heralded by the appearance of a magical totem animal, a white deer, on the occasion of which he cries:

> *My sand is run, my thread is spun,*
> *This sign regardeth me.*

And he is never seen again, apart from a much later story of his apparition leading a terrified vagrant into the interior of the Eildon Hills.

ARTHURIAN FAIRY LORE

The story of Thomas the Rhymer is but one instance of the power of the divine feminine as revealed in traditional lore. It permeates Arthurian legend too, which for the most part is ancient Celtic lore dressed up in medieval plate armor.

The tale of Sir Gareth in Malory's *Morte d'Arthur* is a quest in search of a fair lady, the Lady Lyonesse. On his journey he is tested by variously colored knights, each representing different archetypal powers. A black knight, as dweller on the threshold, guards the stream that divides the worlds. A green knight represents the elemental powers, and is summoned by blowing a horn hung upon a tree. A red knight, emblematic of aggressive power, guards a tower, a barrier on the way. And a blue knight dwells within and rules a city, representative of organizing powers. He is accompanied on all these adventures by a female guide, and initiatrix, the Lady Linet, who tests him in her own way.

Similarly, Sir Uwain in Chrétien de Troyes' *Yvain* has adventures that begin with meeting a wild man of the woods, the Lord of the

Animals, who directs him to a spectacular initiation, evoked by pouring water upon a sacred stone that brings about a magical storm. This is the start of his involvement with the Lady of the Fountain, and subsequent adventures, which include overcoming and having to take the place of her champion. Again we see the hero guided on his intiatory tests by an initiatrix, the Lady Lunette—a name similar to Gareth's Lady Linet, and by its spelling revealing a connection with moon magic.

And Sir Gawain in the Middle English ballad "The Weddynge of Sir Gawen and Dame Ragnell" is particularly apposite in our survey, wed to a loathly damsel, the Lady Ragnel, who turns out to be the most beautiful Lady of Nature, and sister to the brute nature force that is personified in the terrifying giant, the Green Knight. This apparently hideous damsel, the outer face of nature "red in tooth and claw" is transformed by his attitude to her predicament. She suffers under an evil enchantment but when he ceases to try to impose his will upon her, but allows her to choose her own mode of appearance, she is revealed in perpetual beauty.

And central to all these tales is the organizing genius behind the whole Round Table company, the magician Merlin, who also has his feminine consort, one of the companions of the Lady of the Lake. The story has been much misunderstood, seeing the lady as evil, or Merlin as besotted or enchanted. Powerful, beautiful, and enchanting a feminine figure though she may be, she is a cooperator with the magician, not an adversary. For his disappearance into a rock or hawthorn tower is not a banishment or perpetual prison, but a vantage point from which he can continue to exercise an influence upon the outer world and to guide it to its proper redemption and destiny.

In the imaginal working that follows we find symbolic images arising from various aspects of the wide-ranging field that we have just surveyed, and as in our previous journey, we commence with a specific physical location in mind, which helps to anchor or "earth" the dynamics involved.

This time we find ourselves in the heart of Snowdonia, the land around the great sacred mountain of Celtic tradition in Wales. The village of Beddgellert is the site for the legend of the faithful hound, Gellert, unjustly slain after fighting off a child-eating wolf. Gellert's Grave is now a popular tourist attraction but it has deeper dynamics as we shall see. The dog is a totem animal that has always represented a guardian and guide. Examples are to be found in the dog-headed god Anubis, the Opener of Ways, in ancient Egypt, or in Cerberus, the three-headed guardian of the Greek Underworld. The particular connection between dog and wolf, as in the Gellert legend, may also be found in the Tarot, where the trump card called the Moon shows a dog and a wolf guarding a path into an inner landscape beyond a stream. This card is sometimes called The Twilight, and signifies psychism and a doorway between inner and outer worlds. Interestingly, the French have an expression for the twilight, *entre chien et loup,* "between dog and wolf."

Our inner journey proceeds from the inner gateway of Gellert's Grave, over the river that runs through the Aberglasslyn Pass, and into the foothills of Snowdon and the site of an old copper mine. Here, inner symbolism increasingly takes over from outer as we proceed into the copper mountain. The figures we encounter include the Faery Queen, whom we have already described as being a very potent feminine power of the inner earth. We also find the magician Merlin and his consort Nimuë, who is another aspect of the feminine powers of the inner earth. They are to be found associated with a nearby peak, Dynas Emrys, which takes its name from a Welsh form of Merlin.

The rainbow bridge between the two peaks is a construction on the higher ethers, a veritable magical bridge, at the apex of which we may find the idealized form of the Planetary Being in a position to link consciously with the cosmic spiritual powers.

These cosmic powers can be left unformulated, and subject to intuitive aspirations alone, for they pertain to the formless worlds. Although if more detailed imagery is sought, one can consult either the crystalline spheres of Dante's *Paradiso* for a useful framework of medieval spiritual vision based upon pagan Greek roots, or the Mount Meru system of Tibetan Buddhism. As in all evocatory matters, however, the essentials are in the experience, which is obtained, not by intellectual speculation, but by becoming emotionally involved with the images.

JOURNEY 5: INTO THE MAGIC MOUNTAIN

We are standing in a green field. Behind us is a river and before us, at the end of the path that runs across the field, there is a copse of trees. A fairy creature appears in the air above our heads and invites us to follow her along the path. She flits along before us, a being who seems entirely at one with the butterflies of the meadow that wander from flower to flower in the rich grass.

We come to the grove of trees and we see that there is a stone in the center, with a little stone trough of water and a cup beside it. At a sign from the fairy, we enter the cool green shade of the trees, and taking the cup, sprinkle some drops of water from the trough onto the stone, which we see has a carving upon it in the form of a dog's or a wolf's head.

As the drops of water strike the stone the leaves and branches of the trees sway violently above our heads in a sudden breeze and drops of water fall upon us, as from a sudden shower, or from drops of water that have lain upon the leaves.

The wind drops as quickly as it sprang up, and turning our gaze back to the stone we see that there now stands beside it a great dog. At first it is phosphorescent and phantomlike, but as it moves between us it takes on the solid form and appearance of an ordinary dog, of the type used for herding sheep in the hills.

The dog trots quickly and with purpose back down the path whence we have come, and turning its head invites us to follow.

We hasten to do so, and it leads us back to the river. Here it plunges straight down the bank, and we follow, relieved to find that at this place the river is broad but shallow, running over variegated stones, and with large flat boulders close enough together for us to step upon. The dog leads us up the steep bank on the other side and through thick undergrowth and heathlike land. The going is quite rough but we feel well able to keep up the stiff pace. The land slowly rises as we proceed and we realize we are climbing out of the valley and toward the range of green mountains through which it runs.

After a time, as we ascend the foothills we turn a rise in the ground and find ourselves before a large flat space. Beyond it there rises an almost sheer cliff. We wonder if and how we are to climb such a forbidding obstacle but the dog turns to one side to a pond with an overhanging tree.

There the dog stops, and looking around at us, wags his tail with a mischievous gleam in his eye. Being assured that he has all the company safely about him, he raises his head and barks loudly three times. The barks echo, and then echo again round the walls of the rock face beyond us.

As we look up at the rock face, we notice, way up, a kind of ledge, with another tree upon it, similar to the one under which we stand. A figure appears beside it. It is of a beautiful woman dressed in white and sparkling finery, who holds a wand that appears to have a star at its tip. It seems as if she waves the wand in recognition of the dog's bark.

The dog immediately starts up, but before proceeding further, circles round the pool looking into it. We do the same, and see to our surprise that there are many artifacts that have been dropped into it. In particular there are tools associated with the mining trade, such as shovels and picks, and old lanterns; but strangely, all appear to have been transformed into gold. The dog barks warningly against our being tempted to try to reach into the pool to take any, and we are also dimly aware of ethereal golden beings that drift slowly in the pond, like ornamental fish. We see that the dog is hurrying off and we hasten to follow. He goes straight toward the foot of the cliff and we see that there is a small doorway in it, surrounded by piles of rocks and other excavating spoil.

The dog disappears into the dark entrance and we follow, noticing as we do so, the old wooden door that lies back on its hinges and seems to have been once inlaid, perhaps with copper. Upon it we can dimly see an ancient sign. It appears to be that of a bear.

The sounds of the dog scrambling up a steep path come clearly back to us down the narrow passageway, and we struggle to follow. The floor is rough and uneven under our feet, and the gray rock walls press closely either side as does the low roof over our heads. There is the dusty smell of powdered rock.

We realize that we are in some kind of mine, but that the passageways do not go down, as in an ordinary mine, but upward, for it is boring up and into the mountain.

As we progress so does the passage way become broader, and from time to time, we are amazed and delighted by sudden grottoes to either side that are studded with precious stones, or veins of different metals, all of which glow, giving a dim light to the whole of the workings so that we can see our way dimly as we go.

Eventually we come, at what must be halfway up the mountain, to a great internal cavern. Here there is a long and broad, clear flat stretch of water. At its center is an island formed out of the natural rock that has been built up by erosion or the dripping of mineral-bearing water into the form of a fairy palace. It is like looking upon a miniature magical landscape of a fairy lake, illuminated by crystals in the rock above as if by starlight. If we gaze upon the central island and its representation of a palace, we can almost see it come alive, with miniature folk in a complete, different world of their own.

A gentle bark from the dog however, prevents our getting too involved in this reverie. He indicates that we look upward. In so doing we see a chink of daylight far above us, that is apparently reachable by climbing up a wide but steep escarpment. As we gaze upward we see a figure standing within the opening, clearly to be seen against the blue sky behind. It is the figure of the woman whom we saw from the ground below. She is throwing something to us down the steep rock escarpment. We realize it to be a bundle of golden threads. One falls before each of us, and as we take hold of it we realize its incredible strength despite its seeming delicacy. Firmly holding on to it, we find ourselves being hauled up almost effortlessly toward the patch of sky at the top.

We come out into open air and find ourselves on a greensward high above the surrounding countryside that we have left. Looking out and around us we see that this is the first of a range of what eventually become ever higher mountains.

We are greeted by the lady, about whom the dog jumps and barks delightedly. We can now see that she is dressed in green and silver, with a golden jeweled circlet upon her head, and her wand is a truly magnificent thing—long and slender and of some pure silverlike metal with the most brilliant diamond star at its tip.

She smiles upon us and, brandishing her wand, points it in the direction of a nearby mountain top. It is of about the same level as our own, and similarly covered with grass and the occasional tree. There is indeed a mighty tree that stands at its summit and as we look we see that two figures come from beneath it. Without needing to be told, we realize that they are the magician Merlin and the fairy maiden Nimuë. They are aware of our presence, and we see that the magician raises a staff of his own in recognition of our presence.

Then, as if the result of the raised wands of our own Faery Queen and that of the magician Merlin, the air between the two mountaintops begins to sparkle, as if filled with millions of rainbow-colored motes of light, and as we watch, so an arc appears in the air between the two summit and forms a kind of rainbow bridge.

We do not venture upon it, for it is not for those of our condition or destined part in the scheme of things, but as we gaze we see that something is forming in the center. It is a tree, beside which is a pool and a fair maiden, formed from the subtle emanations of the earth and the trees and the plant and animal life of the mountains, conjured by the magician and the Faery Queen.

The nature being, representing the aspirations of the elemental Earth, sits under her tree by her magic pool and gazes into the sky, her hands held out part in supplication and part in wonder. And as she does so our vision is extended so that we see, forming in the skies about her, and seemingly going on and out into infinity, ring upon ring, and circle upon circle of beings radiating and receiving love and joy. Whether they be angelic or elemental or of kinds of beings unknown to us or to any human speculation is of no real concern to us. We simply feel the presence of that great choir of spiritual beings in communion with the nature maiden, conjured by the magician and the faery queen, at the summit of the rainbow.

Something of the heavenly powers she contacts can be felt flowing down the arc of the rainbow that ends before our feet, and we are conscious of it flowing into the Earth, and something of it also into ourselves.

We look around us from our mountaintop, and think of the world from which we have come, the human world all about us, at another level of being, and we aspire to channel something of this holy healing power into the dark valleys of the Earth. As we gaze into the distance so we become aware of our own earthly links, and as if on a beam of energy from the mountaintop we find ourselves gliding through the air and over the countryside that is familiar to us in our earthly lives, until we see the rooftop of our present habitation. We pass through it, and down into the room where our physical body awaits our return to normal consciousness and the resumption of our duties and destiny in the workaday world, bringing something of the knowledge we have gained of other worlds and the powers we have contacted.

BRANCH SIX

The Initiation of the Earth

We began this book with instruction on how to build a magic circle, and having built that circle, how to equilibrate the forces of the watchtowers of the elements so that the rose of the expressed spirit could grow at their interchange, in the center of the encircled cross. Through the center of the concourse of elemental forces the mighty spiritual forces of the divine feminine are expressed.

We now give a pattern for all who aspire to put into effect the expression of the feminine principle. Seldom is work of this nature given out, but the urgency is great and the issues profound. It needs all the active esoteric participants in the world today to take part in it.

The need is for those of esoteric ability, experience, breadth of vision, and goodwill to use their talents in a dynamic and positive way, to bridge the gap, the yawning gulf, that presently lies between the stars in the heavens and the stars within the Earth—between the crystals of the Inner Earth and the jewels of the Madonna that are set in the splendor of the heavens. One must realize that these are not terms of an overheated poetic fancy, but images of a reality more solid than our everyday world of dreams and illusions, unconscious projections, and wish-fulfilment fantasies.

This work requires another dimension of consciousness. This dimension can be reached through the active use of imagination. It is not the same as idle fancy. But through this God-like and God-given creative faculty, the creative imagination, an objective perception of a greater reality that complements the physical can be attained.

It requires also a breadth of vision and largeness of soul. Those who revere nature and the natural world, including its inner aspects, must strive toward a perception of those great spiritual forces that transcend nature. And those whose hearts are in the transcendental must reach in love toward the natural world and the deep powers that lie within it, the elementals, the archetypes, and the gods, man-made or otherwise.

The meeting point and fulcrum of this mighty axis between Deep Heaven and Deep Earth lies in the human heart. The human heart has, in potential, the capacity to contain all, however mean and miserable its capacity may seem to be as reflected in the state of the world, wherein man's inhumanity to man makes countless thousands mourn, to say nothing of the animal and other dependent creations at the mercy of human stewardship.

THE PLANETARY BEING

There is another archetypal feminine principle, that is particularly important to us in this day and age.

This is not as the Queen, Empress, or High Priestess of the high Cosmic Spaces or Deep Heaven—but the being of the planet Earth, representing the body of elemental consciousness that goes to make up the material sphere upon which we live and move and have our being. A more common way of describing her would be as Mother Nature, or in more esoteric terms as the Planetary Being (or in some works as the Planetary Entity).

There is a great deal to be gained from coming to some conscious awareness of the reality of this vast pool of elemental consciousness which we call the Planetary Being. Yet it is difficult to describe such a great being as a real thing, for it is not readily apparent to the human mind except in some forms of psychism or clairvoyance.

When there is a strong contact made with it by a human being, a tremendous fear can arise, a fear which is akin to the fear of open spaces. It is a very terrible thing, and some would call it a form of deep hysteria—or panic terror. But it does not matter what we may care to call this awful awareness, the fact is that it is a real thing, very real on its own plane and very real in the feeling it can give to a human being.

Nevertheless, as in the legends of Pan (and the forces of the Planetary Being are closely linked to the mythology of Pan), those who are truly attuned to the earth do not feel the fear. Those who feel fear are those not so attuned, who are frightened of natural things and who have no real love or need of nature, for underlying the Planetary Being is the great essence from which primeval nature bubbled up into the Earth itself and into the instinctual side of man. It is precisely this factor that lives with and in primitive man very strongly.

This primeval force is by no means evil—save when the minds of men make it so. It has, indeed, something of the reflection of God the Father within it. Thus is Pan conceived of as a male being. But there is equally a passive or feminine side to it as shown in the Tarot figure of the Empress and her Venus symbolism. In all great natural forces there is a "positive" and a "negative," a "male" and a "female" side.

The positivity of the male force is known through various terms such as the "libido," "hyle," "life force" and so on. The negative female force is perhaps less understood. It can be very terrible and strong—for it can hold itself open to bring through and to mold forces from far-off spheres. It is certainly by no means a timid, resigned, and inferior force as is sometimes so wrongly and indeed so ridiculously thought.

If we want to think of the Planetary Being in the best way, we must think of it as a holy being; and also as one which is, in a way, a parent to us, a father/mother type, whom it is our duty to cherish, to help, and to some extent guide, for new aspects of being have come to us in the course of our evolution through the development of mind. But the Planetary Being has no mind.

It is often very difficult for those who have no great deal of esoteric awareness or experience to visualize a mindless entity; and in this case a mindless entity with tremendous force—absolutely pure, good, and true on its own level, but from a rational point of view, ruthless, or even antagonistic. For it works through great will and instinct but not through mind or through any considerations of a mental nature.

The beings who are closer to it than man, the elementals, also work in this way. They are pure and blind forces too, for the most part, with no mind; absolutely holy, pure and good in their own law—which they do not seek to break. It is humankind who breaks the laws, who have been guilty of breaking laws throughout all our evolution. And indeed one could say it is part of the human type of development. We must play forever the rebel and be forever breaking laws, because only by breaking certain laws can we develop! This is, at one and the same time, the blessing and the curse of what we call mind.

But we are not here concerned with issues of moral philosophy. We are striving for an awareness of the real relationship that exists between the subtler forces of the Earth and ourselves. Really it is a feeling of love for the Earth that is necessary, an awareness of nearness and a sense of relationship—even for the most city bound of us. For in this sense of relationship and of love there will not be room for any fear—or any evil. It is only through fear that evil first came to the world, and still comes, to this very day.

Long ago it was said that at the time of the Crucifixion, a strange voice was heard calling out across the seas: "Great Pan is dead," and this was thought to mean that all the old gods and all their ways had been killed because the One True God had come. This is not quite accurate—though there is truth in it. Pan was not dead, but something connected with "death" did come to the Earth. It changed.

It changed through the tremendous energy which came to Earth two thousand years ago. It did actually change within itself, in its own nature. There was something in the Earth itself, after this great event, a little bit more approaching to spirituality than there had been before. After the Crucifixion, the spiritual factors which came from the Christ-force in connection with the Earth entered into the structure of the Earth, and the Earth began, very slowly and very subtly, to change, and to go upwards to a course where it shall become a fully developed planet—"when the Kingdom comes to Earth."

The Crucifixion was as a "pause" in a great cycle, like the "pause" one gets in any cycle when the nadir or zenith of an arc is rounded. On the lesser cycle of the year one finds these pauses at two points—at the summer and the winter solstice. And in the cycle of each day there can be detected by those who are sensitive, in the very early morning and between two and three in the afternoon, a very curious type of stillness. This curious feeling, this sense of rest, or silence, or stopping, is called appropriately enough, "the pause in nature." And so are there similar pauses in epochs and evolutions; and the coming of the Christ marked one of them—possibly the greatest in human experience.

Since that event, Great Pan is changed. He is not dead. Were he dead then the Earth itself would be dead, for the living Pan is an aspect of the Planetary Being, though the Planetary Being is by no means entirely described in the mythology and pagan conception of Pan. In many ways the various goddess or feminine mythological images are a more appropriate form.

There is, in the Planetary Being, a tremendous primeval urge for unity and reunion with its own children—and these children include humankind. Indeed, humankind can help the Planetary Being more than any other kind of terrestrial life can, for man has within himself all levels of being, from the primitive instinctual (which relates closest to the Planetary Being), to the spiritual (toward which, in its dim way, the Planetary Being aspires). Primitive humans were, and are, very close to the Planetary Being, as are the animal kingdoms—and a comparison of the grace and vitality of the animal and the primitive with that of the average sedentary urbanized man shows that there is much to be gained from retaining this link with the Planetary Being. It is a source of vitality and health and correct bodily functioning.

But the link is not made intellectually. One will never contact the Earth if one is always in a process of thought. One must feel and wish and will toward these things. It is not exactly prayer. Prayer is a lifting of the mind up to God. But here we are not concerned with lifting the mind up to God in Heaven, but with extending the heart toward and down to the Planetary Being—who is potentially God in Earth. And though the Planetary Being is greater than we are, it is less than we are also—and we can bring it far toward a spiritual growth.

Even as with the elementals, where, according to tradition, a person—if of the right esoteric stature—can educate an elemental being—so it is with that vast "generating elemental," the Planetary Being of Earth. Though in this case one person alone cannot help and educate the Planetary Being fully, but all people together can— and must. This is the true meaning of evolution. We ourselves grow, and contribute growth to that which first brought us forth.

This awareness of responsibility is particularly important for those who aspire to open up the deeper levels of themselves in esoteric or similar work. The more so since the growth of urban civilization and the development of the concrete mind have tended to atrophy the imaginative capacity, through which the divine intention function- ing through sensory life can be the easier perceived than by intellec- tual philosophizing. Thus humans no longer strive to apprehend the work of God and to adore the creator through the instincts and animal nature. Humankind cuts itself off from the deep parental love of the Earth Mother.

In this respect the "higher" nature of humanity has much to learn from the personality in the world. And many attracted to occult- ism or the enclosed orders of religion are not necessarily "advanced" souls—but souls who cannot bring themselves to accept and assimilate the experience of the instincts and lower emotions through life in the world. So while the worldly personality should all the time be listening in to the higher nature, whose promptings are usually called "the voice of conscience," the higher nature has also the task of adjusting itself to the ever-changing conditions of ordinary human life. If this were better understood, many tragedies could be avoided. For instance, a man may have such a strong link with his higher nature that the pressure of conscience is so strong that he feels his own line of action *must* be right—whatever the cost. Though this may often be lauded as heroism or sanctity it is more often than not fanaticism and bigotry and a travesty of real human values.

So while "spirituality" and "the voice of conscience" are very valuable things, there is a world of difference between a spiritual nature operating blindly and ruthlessly after the manner of Torquemada, the founder of the Spanish Inquisition, who tortured souls in order, as he thought, to "save" them, and spiritual values put into action in the world through the mediation of human love and compassion. So it is not merely a question of the purity or strength of the spiritual force which can be contacted by a soul, but also the means by which this force is applied—and this brings in considerations of relationship with others.

Considerations of relationship grow more important, not less, as evolutionary or spiritual growth is attained, and many experience much difficulty because of this. The personality may be a dedicated and willing instrument but the difficulties raised by a higher nature learning to function rightfully through human channels can be very great. It is a question of taking responsibility for one's effect upon others—and these others extend beyond the frontiers of the human kingdom. They extend to God in Heaven on the one hand—and on the other to his creation in Earth, the Planetary Being, and all the other lives, animal or elemental, that have the destiny to share the planet with us. It is up to us to endeavor to make that destiny, not a horror, but a blessing.

One way is, as we have tried to indicate in this book, by the equilibration of the elements within, and the cultivation of the civilizing influence of the eternal feminine at its many levels, from heights of Heaven to depths of Earth, with the mediation of human love between.

RITES OF COSMIC INTERCHANGE

In Part One we learned to build our magic circle. But now we seek to work in the three dimensions of space instead of on a ground plan that embraces only two. Our work must reach upward to the deeps of the heavens and downwards to the heart of the Earth.

Visualize your magic circle as described in the first section of this book, with its four elemental quarters and its central altar point.

Now remove it from its abstract setting. See it in relation to a sacred site of your choice. This may be one of the ancient megalithic circles that abound or be a modern place of worship. The pagan and the Christian, and indeed all other religions of humankind, are encompassed in this work. Any place that is, or has been, set aside for human contact with numinous realities, however inadequately expressed or conceived, is a power point, a center for a magic circle whose circumference, in potential, embraces the universe.

Ancient churches and abbeys, in that through time they have channeled the devotions and aspirations of our ancestors—back to the remotest times when the site may have been but a grove on a holy hill—are of particular value and importance for those who can work with them, even if some have been occluded by ancient or modern ignorance. The power of some of these old sites was diverted from spiritual and Inner Earth ends by ecclesiastical and political ambitions of some of our forebears. Hence the evidence we see of great splendors in stone falling into decay. Nonetheless the original pure source of power may be felt and seen shining through as the fountainheads are unblocked.

Build, then, your magic circle over a site of your choice. It is sufficient to have visited it, with some care and devotion. The contact will have been made by this physical pilgrimage and subsequent inner work can then be conducted from far away, or in your own home.

Having built the circle to embrace the ground plan of your selected site, see the circle, with its four cardinal points and its central altar, rise into the air, so that it takes its station high in the sky above the site. Define the circumference of the circle by visualizing free-standing pillars around it, of any manageable number, say seven between each quarter, but there is no need to be too precise or pedantic about it.

Be aware of the fourfold dynamic of the quarters, and at each quarter see a simple stone altar, with a small ritual fire upon it, standing between two of the pillars to form an elemental gate. See the central altar take the form of a glowing, flaming brazier or tripod. From the quarters see bands of light and power flow forth across the floor of the temple to meet at the central altar/brazier, so that a pattern of a rose cross is made, the central fire taking the place of the central rose upon the cross. Indeed, it may be conceived as a red rose of fire (see figure 7).

Now see the central fire/rose fill like a cup and overflow with red and with crystal-clear liquid, like wine and water, which at times, in its confluence, shimmers like liquid gold. See this liquid overflow from the heart of the temple into the four triangular-shaped spaces that are

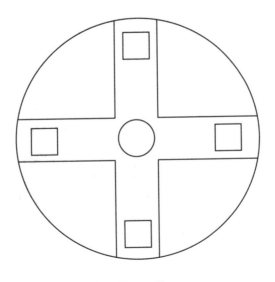

Figure 7

formed between the arms of the elemental cross. Then see these red, crystal clear, and shimmering gold streams flowing down from the floor of the temple toward the Earth in four great, gradually converging, roughly triangular columns. They penetrate the surface of the Earth, encompassing the sacred site as they pass.

At a hidden point within the Earth's core, below the site, they converge, and from the point of their convergence streams of force return that rise to meet the four ends of the arms of the cross in the temple overhead. From each of the four descending columns two upward rays ascend, one to each quarter point on either side of the original triangular space. Thus twice as much power ascends as descended. See now a cup of water appear on each of the four elemental altars beside the ritual fires.

A similar pattern of flow may be seen to build above the temple, with a convergence point high in the heavens. The whole sequence thus gives a geometric form that is similar to an elongated octahedron (see figure 8).

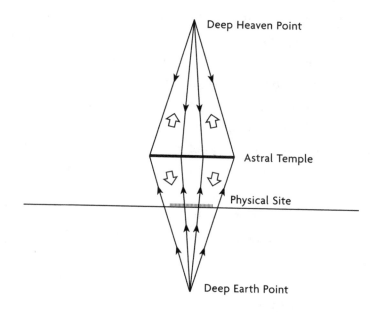

Figure 8

At the point of entry at the surface of the Earth around the physical sacred site you may see some of the liquid force flow outward in various directions toward other sites. These lines of force are orderly and straight. And from these secondary sites they flow on again, but now running like golden rivers instead of straight canals, or like veins or arteries, some large some small, fructifying the land and all who live on it with their spiritual and elemental force.

Realize now that the lower point of the octahedron is in fact a gateway to the Underworld forces of the Earth, and that it is as the opening to a cavern that leads ultimately to the secrets of the center of the Earth.

Be aware, within that hollow and hallowed place, of a feminine figure who represents the under-Earth forces of blood, land, sea, sap, the ancestors, the elemental generating powers, the form givers: Mother Earth herself. This may present itself in a variety of ways—from a fish or serpent-tailed woman to the sleeping Lady Venus of the Rosicrucian vault, from the white and green clad Faery Queen to one of the black madonnas associated with the crypts of certain cathedrals.

Similarly, realize the top of the upper point of the octahedron to be a gateway to the heavens. See a great shining cosmic feminine figure, who, like the figure below, may appear in one of a variety of forms. It could be as Dante's Beatrice stepping from the triumphal carriage; or Astraea, the Star Maiden of the heavens; or the Blessed Virgin crowned in glory. She is the polar complement and cosmic equivalent of the Lady within the Earth; Isis Urania in polar conjunction with Isis of Nature, the Queen of Heaven in relation to the Sorrowing Mother beneath the Cross.

As these figures form be aware of the power of the Lady of the Heavens flowing downward through the central point of the temple to meet with the upward flowing forces from the Lady beneath the Earth. These forces continue in their polar direction so that there is a complete blending of their currents. Then one is aware, as a climax to the working, that the figures have interchanged. The figure of the Earth

Maiden is triumphant in the Heavens, and that of the Star Maiden is radiant, deep within the Earth.

Hold this vision for as long as you will. Then see the figures slowly resume their former positions; although after this interchange you realize that nothing will ever be quite the same as it was before. A great cross-fertilization and sanctification has taken place.

The upper and lower gates slowly close. The upper and lower pyramids shrink to their former size, and then revert to the simple two-dimensional circular temple in the sky. Draw your consciousness back into your daily surroundings, and go about your daily round, content that you have helped to perform an act of high magic that will help the Earth to shine forth its ultimate cosmic deity.

A similar type of working can be effected inside a sacred building. In a typical structure this may best be conceived at the cross-point of transept with nave.

Here, however, simply visualize a golden circle with a rose cross at each quarter. The golden arms of these four equal-armed crosses can be visualized to reach one toward the other so that a circular band of golden light is formed. And then also their upper and lower arms similarly extend and meet at a central point overhead and beneath the floor in an interlocking three-ring system (see figure 9).

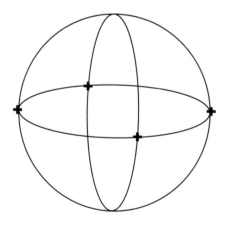

Figure 9

At the center of this golden network see a point of diamond and ruby light, with flashes of gold. It grows in size and power until it becomes a mighty gem. This jewel may grow to encompass the whole of the spherical figure, and then may be seen to pulsate, like a beating heart. At the same time it may transform from one type of Platonic solid to another—to and from octahedron and cube, dodecahedron and icosahedron, or as a continually reversing pair of tetrahedrons. However, the sense of spiritual and organic life is more important than the geometrics. The colors may also vary according to the site or time of year, month or day.

Once again, above and below this pulsing figure see the Star Maiden and the Earth Maiden in whatever forms you will or however they present themselves to your inner vision.

The justification for performing this type of working in churches and abbeys should perhaps be emphasized. In ancient, pre-Christian times, wise men understood how the stars and planets influenced the metals and crystals of Earth. Some Earth sites were indeed magnetized to a particular metal or crystalline stone, and by this means became a center for the dispersal of this influence or an adjunct to a larger site or center. Lines of travel for this influence ran between sites, linking with other centers, and not only with other centers upon Earth but also starwards.

At many of these centers churches or abbeys came to be built, they themselves receiving a living charge from the lines, and transmuting the influences according to the abilities and understanding of the churchmen. Some transmuted the influences well, so that they became great seats of learning and teaching. Others were blocked by lack of understanding, or became centers of power only, the power being contained at its source and not fed into the living Earth and its people.

It may be thought that the early church was unlikely to have had any sympathy with these ancient forces and that it would have cut off, stamped out, or buried "pagan" influences of this kind; but throughout the history of mankind, whether conquest be cultural or physical, local and national religions have been absorbed and incorporated rather than cut off completely.

At the beginning of Christianity's influence the churchmen were an integral part of the land. And their churches were at first no more than what we would call huts. They lived in a natural fashion in the earth, utilizing cave, rock, and tree for their first shelters, building their wattle and daub churches from growing tree and plain earth. They partook directly of Earth, understood it, and were very much part of it, though carrying a mighty spirit within them, and able to link their own spirit with the spirit of Christ and the Godhead.

They were spirit and earth in combination and their early churches were also thus. Their design is remembered for all time in the later great stone edifices filled with column and vaulting, like a great stone forest indeed. Vine or ivy leaves, and oak, and other references to the early shelters of Christians abound in church decoration.

Abbeys later also gave much time to the tilling and cultivation of the soil, to fishing, and other natural pursuits of man. As so often happens, however, the reason for this work on the land, that is, close contact with God's earth—a great gift—was forgotten and changed to the pursuit of wealth for the foundation itself, thus concentrating power at the source again.

As time proceeded, the knowledge and understanding of the holy use of these sacred lines of force deteriorated and personal motive overcame spiritual intention. Original lines were lost and overlaid, many churches even being built to *stop* the influence of these power lines rather than to transmute their energies.

Already some awareness of these things is being revived. Men and women of great hope and idealism have begun the release of the stopped or diverted streams. Mainly the power is simply redirected into the Earth again, for most people assume that these Earth lines belong solely to the Earth. Much is accomplished by those who direct the unstopped energies into the "grid" of lines. Better still, a very few are able to link the power lines to the physical heavens through star lore.

And there are yet others, even fewer, who try to link the lines with the Godhead and thus bring about the "spiritual" rebirth of the planet.

This is the real "craft lore" that is needed to help the travailing Earth. It is also the real "churchmanship" that is needed. God created the Earth as well as the Church and the two are not irreconcilable. The great divorce is only in the narrow minds and constricted hearts of men and women.

The wisdom of the heart is all important. For wisdom is unbalanced and distorted when held only at the intellectual level. The silver wisdom of the head must be changed to the golden wisdom of the heart by the warmth of human love.

Tend the fires of love and understanding most carefully, for without the glow of their light and warmth, there is not only no wisdom to be had, there is no point in having the wisdom at all. The greater vision of unity lies in the transformations of the Goddess, the dancer at the heart of the rose.

Reflect upon these deep things. And thus may the wisdom of the stars shine in your brow, the grail of love flow from your heart, the waters of life encompass your loins, and the stones of Earth support your feet. This is the image and function of redeemed humankind, the new Adam and new Eve, conjoined in the new Heaven and the new Earth, the new Avalon where the green apples have turned to gold.

Index

Aberglasslyn Pass, 184
Achernar, 68
Actaeon, 83
Aeneas, 171
Aeneid (Virgil), 123, 171
Aeschylus, 71
  The Phorkides, 58
Aigle, 69
Ain Soph, 60, 140, 177
Akasa Dhath Ishvari, 173
Akrisios, 52
alchemy, 65, 79, 94, 132, 136, 141, 149,
  150–52, 157, 158
Alkymia, 133
altar, 16, 20, 22–23, 26, 27–28, 32–33,
  103, 143, 144, 146, 151, 197–98
Amerindian tradition, *174,* 178–79
Andromeda, 49, 51, 66–67, 73, 102, 127
  meditation on, 74–78
angel(s), 25, 40, 45, 46, 109–11, 114, 122–
  23, 124, 126, 168, 176, 177
  in *The Chymical Marriage,* 137, 140, 146
Anna, 109
Anne, Saint, 113, 127
Annunciation, 110, 112, 113, 115, 123, 124
Anubis, 93, 184
Anxiety, 87
Apollo, 37, 62, 63–65, 71, 86

apples, 52, 68, 69, 72–73, 77, 118, 136,
  143, 171, 181, 204
Apuleius, Lucius, 79–81, 96, 106, 168
  Discourse on Magic, 79
  The Golden Ass, 79–102
Arabs, 113
Arcadia, 61, 68
archangels, 11, 13, 14, 16, 25, 46, 48, 115,
  123, 177
Arethousa, 69
Argos, 67
Ark of the Covenant, 119, 126
Armada, 158
Artemis, 61, 64–65
Arthurian legend, 55, 64, 158, 170–71,
  182–85
Asclepios, 89
Assumption of the Blessed Virgin, 112,
  115, 125
Asteria, 64–65
Asterope, 69
Astraea, 200
astral projection, 85
asuras, 176
Athena. *See* Pallas Athene
Atlantis, 66, 157, 168
Atlas, 72–73, 143, 147, 153, 157
Atropos, 72

aura, 13, 14, 18, 24, 42, 43, 44, 54, 55, 137
Aurora, 35
Avalon, 136, 158, 171, 179, 204
Avernus, 171. *See also* Underworld

Bacchanals, 90
Bacon, Francis, 153
Bailey, Alice, 122
Battle of Bannockburn, 180
Beatrice, 117–18, 123, 126, 200
Beddgellert, 184
Bellerophon, 69
Belos, 53
Benevolent, the, 71
Binah, 113–14, 140
birds, 70, 84, 136, 141, 150–52, 178
birth, 12, 28, 29, 53, 56, 61, 62, 64–65, 68,
    70, 72, 107, 108, 114, 127, 139, 179
Black Elk, 178
Black Isis, 81, 114
black madonnas, 114, 200
Blavatsky, Helena Petrovna, 166
Blessed Virgin. *See* Mary, Blessed Virgin
blood, 66, 70, 110, 143, 145, 148, 150, 151,
    152, 200
boar, 58, 76–77, 89
book, 143, 145, 151, 156, 163
Book of Leinster, The, 169
Book of the Dun Cow, The, 169
bread, 135, 136, 154
Bretons, 170
Bride, 33, 36, 108, 122, 125, 127, 143, 144,
    149, 169
Bridget, Saint, 169
Brigantia, 169
Brigit (goddess), 169
Britanny, 168, 170
British Museum, 158
Buddha Fields, 116, 123, 177
Buddhas of the Magic Circle, 172–74
Buddhism. *See* Mahayana Buddhism

buffalo, 179
Byzantium, 112, 113

candle, 23, 24, 25–26
candlesticks, 119, 143
Canis Major, 122
Canticles of Solomon, the, 108, 122
Cassiopeia, 15, 51, 66
Celtic Heritage (Rees), 170
Celtic tradition, 37, 58, 167, 168–70, 184
Cepheus, 15, 51
Cerberus, 68, 184
Ceres, 87, 98, 100
Cetus, 51, 66, 68
chakra, 55, 137, 159
Chalcedon, 112
Chariot, 38, 39, 121
Charitë, 85–86, 88–90, 91
Charites, 61, 71
Charles the Bald, 113
Charon, 171
childbirth, 114. *See also* birth
Chimaira, 69
Chinese Hall of Light, 170
Chi-Rho, 128
Christianity, 106–7, 203
Chrysaor, 66, 69, 70
Chrysothemis, 69
churches, 32, 112, 113, 197, 202–3. *See also*
    Shrines to Blessed Virgin Mary
*Chymical Marriage of Christian
    Rosencreutz, The,* 118, 133–58, 159
circled cross, 16, 17, 172, 174, 190
Clithon, 70
Cloud of Unknowing, The, 156
Connacht, 170
corn mothers, 179
Coronation of the Blessed Virgin, 125
cosmic interchange, 50, 197–204
Councils of the Church, 112
cross, 4, 8, 10, 12, 19, 32, 33–34, 41, 107,

126, 135, 154, 172, 199, 200. *See also*
  circled cross; rose cross
crucifix, 144, 149
Crucifixion, 193–94
Cuchama, 178, 179
Cuchama and Sacred Mountains (Evans-
  Wentz), 178
Cupid, 38, 42, 86–88, 92
  in *The Chymical Marriage,* 143, 144,
    147–48, 149, 152, 153
Cybele, 92
cycles, 3, 4, 27, 34–37, 43, 172, 194

Dagda, 171
dakinis, 118, 178
Dana, 169
Danäe, 52–54, 55, 65, 67
Danaos, 53
Danes, 170
Dante, 116–24, 145, 176
  Divine Comedy, 116–24, 175, 177
  Paradiso, 177, 185
da Vinci, Leonardo, 124
death, 27, 28, 30–31, 53, 65, 68, 70, 72, 85,
    87, 88, 90, 101, 107, 112, 116, 136,
    143, 148, 155, 172, 179, 193
Dee, Dr. John, 133, 158–59, 182
della Francesca, Piero, 124
Delos, 65
Delphine, 62–63
Demeter, 58, 64
demons, 24, 168
de Troyes, Chrétien, 182
devas, 78, 178
de Villars, Abbé Montfaucon, 165
devils, 113, 168
Dhyani Ywahoo, 178–79
Diana, 83, 100, 112
Diktys, 53, 67
Dionysus, 90, 102
Discourse on Magic (Apuleius), 79

dissolutio, 94
Dissolution of the Monasteries, 124
Divine Comedy (Dante), 116–24, 175, 177
Divine Empyreum, 177
Divine Mother of Infinite Space, 173
Djinn, 13
dog, 41, 91, 93
Dog Star. *See* Sirius
dolphin, 14, 68
door, 104, 120, 129, 142, 144, 146, 148,
    150, 160, 161, 186–87
dorje, 172, 173
Dostoevsky, Fyodor, 85
dove, 61, 84, 109, 110, 136, 140, 154
dragon, 13, 51, 60–63, 107, 163
Dubhe, 122
dweller on the threshold, 95, 140, 182
Dynas Emrys, 184

eagle, 4, 40, 88, 120, 140, 144, 146
Earth, vii, viii, ix, 3, 9, 12, 16, 18, 33,
    34–35, 36, 48, 52, 58, 62, 68, 71, 72,
    78, 125, 141, 143, 149, 153, 159, 163,
    164, 178, 189, 190–204
Earth lines, 203
Earthly Paradise, 116–18, 145, 177
Earth Maiden, 202
Earth Mother, 36, 58, 195
Easter, 107, 133
Echidna, 68–69
ectoplasm, 144
Eden, Garden of, 59, 107, 117, 136, 177, 181
egg, 40, 61, 150
Egypt, 18, 53, 80, 84, 85, 93, 100, 112,
    114, 141, 171, 184
Egyptian Book of the Dead, 139
Eildon Hills, 180, 181, 182
elders, 109, 119, 120, 121, 128–29, 143, 179
elemental creatures, viii, 9, 11, 13, 14, 16,
    45, 48, 78, 161, 165, 167, 168, 191,
    193, 195

Eleusis, 58, 98
Elfland, 181
Elisabeth of Schonau, 115
Elizabeth, Saint, 111
Ely Cathedral, 124
Empress, 38, 42, 191, 192
England, 115, 158, 170, 180
Ephesus, 98, 112
Eridanus, 68
Erinyes, 61, 71
Erytheia, 69
Esoteric Astrology (Bailey), 122
esoteric societies, 132
Etna, 62
Eumenides, 71. *See also* Erinyes
Euryale, 58
Eurynome, 61–62, 71
Evangelists, 4
Evans-Wentz, W. Y., 167–79
    Cuchama and Sacred Mountains, 178–79
    The Fairy Faith in Celtic Countries,
        168–69
Eve, 204
evil spirits, 169
evocation, 3, 18, 44, 46, 48, 97–102
Ezekiel, 4, 119, 146

Faery Queen, 50, 167–71, 180–82, 184,
    188, 189, 200
fairies, 10, 78, 96, 167, 168–72, 178, 181,
    182, 185
Fairy Faith in Celtic Countries, The
    (Evans-Wentz), 168–72
falcon, 140
Fall, 59
Fates, 60, 71–72, 110
Faverches, Richeldis de, 115
feminine Christ, 123
feminine principle, vii–viii, 2–6, 25, 37–
    39, 46, 48, 59, 67, 116–22, 125, 166,
    167, 173, 190, 191

and Christianity, 106–116, 122, 124,
    125–27, 132
in *The Chymical Marriage,* 133, 134–
    35, 140, 142
flame, 21, 23, 24–25, 26–27, 33, 145, 150,
    152
fleece, 88, 129, 142, 153, 156
flood, 66
flowers, 12, 23, 35, 42, 77, 105, 119, 123
Fortuna, 39, 43, 44
fountain, 55, 56, 68, 140, 142, 143, 150,
    151, 169, 180, 183
fruit, 13, 40, 72, 73, 123, 146, 147, 149,
    171, 181
Furies, 60, 61, 71

Gabriel, Archangel, 14, 115, 123
Gaia, vii, 61, 62–63, 64, 68, 69, 71, 159
Ganymede, 88
garden, 52, 104, 109, 140, 149, 160, 181
Garden of Eden. *See* Eden
Garden of the Hesperides. *See* Hesperides
Gareth, Sir, 182
Gawain, Sir, 60, 64, 183
Gellert, 184
Geryon, 69
Geryoneus, 69
Gethsemene, Garden of, 107
globe, 141, 143, 150, 151, 158, 159, 162, 163
gnomes, 16, 162, 169
Godiva of Coventry, Lady, 115
Gods of the Greeks, The (Kerenyi), 55,
    62–63, 68
Goethe, 165
Gokarmo, 173
gold, 52, 61, 65, 75, 105, 126, 134, 138, 142,
    143, 145, 151, 152, 154, 186, 198, 204
Golden Ass, The (Apuleius), 79–102
golden bough, 171–72
Gorgons, 52, 54, 56, 57–60, 65, 67, 74,
    76, 77

Graces, 55, 61, 71, 77
Graiae, 52, 56–57, 60, 70, 76, 77
grandmother, 127
Graves, Robert, 61, 79
Great Bear, 122
Great Mother, 59, 62, 82
green knight, 182, 183
"Green Snake and the Beautiful Lily, The,"
    165
Grief, 87
griffon, 121, 122, 140
Gwenhwyvar, 171

Hades, 68, 71, 80, 88
Harpies, 60, 70, 174
healing, 11, 21, 24, 44, 114, 189
heaven, 30, 33, 46, 62, 70, 72, 108, 115,
    116, 120, 125, 136, 143, 177, 181, 190,
    191, 199, 200, 204
Heavenly Spheres, 117
Heaven of the Four Great Kings, 177
Hecate, 64, 100
Helicon, Mount, 118
Helios, 72
hell, 100, 117, 181
    in Mount Meru system, 116, 175, 176
Henry VIII, 115, 124
Hephaistos, 62
Hera, 62–63, 68
Heracles (Hercules), 70, 72–73, 143, 173
Heraclius, Emperor, 113
Hermes, 54, 55, 57, 142
Hermetic Order of the Golden Dawn, 166,
    168
Hesiod, 61, 62, 68
Hesperia, 69
Hesperides, 52, 56, 57, 67, 69, 72, 73, 107,
    118, 136, 143, 179
Hieroglyphic Monad, 159
High Priestess, 38, 41
Holy Grail, 60, 67, 127

Holy Spirit, 60, 71, 136
House of the Sun, 144

Ignatius of Loyola, Saint, 114
illumination, 83
Immaculate Conception, 125, 127
incarnation, 27, 29–30, 31, 86
    of Christ, 127, 145, 169
Indra's Palace, 177
initiation, 31, 33, 68, 70, 80–81, 84–85,
    88, 91–92, 95, 96, 107, 116, 117, 134,
    135, 148, 155, 179, 183, 190–204
Inner Earth, 41, 44, 167, 184, 190, 197
inner world, 22, 28, 30, 35, 46, 48, 72, 94,
    142, 172, 175
intellect, 2, 17, 46, 59, 64, 101, 106, 116,
    117, 123, 156
invocation, 10–16, 18, 48, 97, 102, 112, 160
Io, 53, 64
Iris, 70
Isis, 50, 53, 64, 79, 81, 122, 123, 133, 171
    and Blessed Virgin Mary, 108, 110, 114
    in The Chymical Marriage, 133, 147,
        156, 157
    feasts of, 112
    in The Golden Ass, 81, 84, 89, 90, 91, 92,
        95, 96, 97, 100–1, 105, 118
    temples of, 112
Isis Unveiled (Blavatsky), 166
Isis Urania, 133, 159, 166, 200
island, 54, 65, 75–76, 148–50, 152, 159,
    161, 170, 176, 187
Isle of Apples, 136. See also Avalon

Jambu Island, 176
James, Book of, 108, 111, 127
Jerusalem, 109, 112, 123
Jesuit Order, 114
Jesus Christ, 89, 90, 107, 108, 111, 112,
    114, 115, 123, 145, 169, 194, 203
jewels, 87, 142, 144, 173, 177, 202

Joachim, 109
John of Patmos, Saint, 108
John of the Cross, Saint, 94
John the Baptist, Saint, 111
John VII, Pope, 113
Joseph, Saint, 110
Journey 1, 74–78
Journey 2, 102–5
Journey 3, 128–31
Journey 4, 159–64
Journey 5, 185–89
Judgment of Paris, 96–97
Judgment Hall of Osiris, 30, 139
Jung, C. G., 94, 125
Jungian psychology, 81, 175
Juno, 87, 93, 100, 171
Justice, 38, 43–44, 139. *See also* karma
    (divine justice)

Kabeiroi, 62
karma (divine justice), 71, 91, 139
Kedron, 107
Kerenyi, Carl, 55–56, 61–65, 68, 69, 71
Kether, 33, 140, 156, 177
Kildare, 169
king, 11, 13, 16, 51, 52, 53, 55, 67, 108, 123,
    140, 143, 144–45, 146, 149, 153–54,
    156, 161, 164, 168, 170, 171, 177
Kirk, Reverend Robert, 170, 171
Klotho, 72
Knights of the Golden Stone, 153, 154–55
Koios, 64
Kronos, 58, 61, 63
kundalini, 13, 55, 58, 172

Lachesis, 72
Ladon, 68, 69, 73
Lady of Nature, 183
Lady of the Fountain, 55, 183
Lady of Heaven, 117, 200
Lady of the Lake, 171, 183

Learmont, Thomas, 180
Le Comte de Gabalis (de Villars), 165
Leinster, 170
Le Morte d'Arthur (Malory), 171, 182
Lethe, 139
Leto, 64–65
Libra, 153
library, 80, 140, 141, 158
light, 6–7, 10, 12, 14, 23–26, 31, 40, 60,
    64, 81, 83, 98, 102, 103, 104, 112,
    117, 129, 131, 134, 137, 142, 147, 156,
    162–63, 173, 179, 202
lilies, 119, 123
Limbo, 117
Linet, Lady, 182
lion, 4, 40, 44, 69, 78, 120, 128, 137, 140,
    142, 146, 164
Lipara, 69
Livy, 94
Lord of the Animals, 182–83
Loretto, 124
lotus, 18, 119, 123, 137, 166, 173
Lovers, 38
Lucia, Saint, 117
Luke, Gospel of, 111
Luke, Saint, 114
Lunette, Lady, 183
Lyonesse, Lady, 182

Madonna della Misericord (Piero della
    Francesca), 124
magic circle, 3–46, 72, 102, 172–73, 174,
    190, 197–98
Magic Mountain, 50, 167, 185
magic wand, 172, 173
magnetization, 34, 202
Magnificat, 109
Mahayana Buddhism, 116, 123, 172. *See
    also* Tibetan Buddhism
maidens, 35, 37, 40, 44, 49–50, 51, 52, 55,
    70, 76, 77–78, 103, 109, 118, 121–22,

126, 129–30, 144–45, 150, 160–64, 188–89. *See also* Earth Maiden; Star Maiden

Malory, Sir Thomas, 171, 182

Mamiki, 173

man, 4, 8, 13, 55, 59, 61, 64, 101, 120, 122, 128, 130, 134, 146, 157, 192, 194–95

mandala, 3, 175

Mars, 84, 148, 149

Mary, Blessed Virgin, 108–15, 116, 117, 123–25, 181

  feasts of, 112–13

  modern cult of, 125–27

  shrines of, 112, 114, 115

  visions of, 115–16

Mary Magdalene, 127

masculine principle, 3, 5, 19, 59

matron, 36, 41, 43, 126, 149

Meath, 170

medicine wheel, 170, 178

meditation, 6–8, 17–18, 19, 24–25, 39–44

Medusa, 53, 54, 56, 57–58, 65–67, 69, 75

Merak, 122

Mercury, 10, 14, 148, 149

Merlin, 158, 171, 180, 182, 183, 184, 188

Meru, Mount, 116, 123, 175–77, 179, 185

Michael, Archangel, 13

Middle Earth, 45, 48, 50

Midsummer Night's Dream, A (Shakespeare), 96, 169

mill, 90, 94, 161–63

Mistress of the Magic Mountain, 50. *See also* Faery Queen

Montserrat, 114

Moon, 35, 38, 44

Morai, 71. *See also* Fates

Morgan le Fay, 171

Mortlake, 158–59

mother, 53–54, 58, 65, 67, 69, 71, 81, 107, 108, 113, 126, 127, 134–35, 166

Mother Nature, 154, 191

Mother of Form, 107

mountain, 54, 62, 86, 102, 105, 116, 175–79, 184, 185–89

Mount Tecate, 178

Munster, 170

Muses, 37, 118

Mythic Lands. *See* Buddha Fields

nagas, 176

Naiads, 52, 54–56, 60, 75, 78, 161

nature spirits, 168

Nereides, 54–55

New Jerusalem, 108, 125, 177

Nimuë, 158, 184, 188

Nirvana, 116, 156

Normans, 170

northern pole, 51, 163

Notre Dame at Chartres, 113

nymphs, 14, 54, 55, 65, 66, 67, 69, 72, 73, 74, 118, 148, 149, 161

Oceanos, 62

octahedron, 199–200

Odysseus, 73–74

Oedipus, 8, 69, 89

Office of Our Lady, 124

Okeanos, 67

Old Testament, 90, 120

Ophion, 61

Orestes, 71

Orion, 68

Orpheus, 102

Orthos, 69

Osiris, 84, 95, 101, 114, 171. *See also* Judgment Hall of Osiris

Otherworld, ix, 171

Ouranos, 58, 61, 62, 64, 71

Overworld, 41, 45, 48, 50, 56

ox, 92, 120, 146

page, 138, 140, 146–47

Pallas Athene, 53, 54, 57, 58, 62, 65, 67, 71, 73, 74, 75, 76, 85, 123
    temples of, 74, 77, 78, 112
Pan, 55, 87, 192, 193, 194
Paradiso (Dante), 177, 185
Parthenon, 112
pause in nature, 194
pearl, 144, 149, 161–62
Pegasus, 66, 69, 70, 71
Pelasgians, 60–61
Periegeta, Pausanias, 61–62
Persephone, 35, 70, 71, 85
Perseus, 49, 51–58, 65–67, 73
Peter, Saint, 114
phoenix, 140, 141, 148
Phoibe, 64
Phorkides, The (Aeschylus), 58
Phorkys, 68, 71
pillars, 18–22, 28, 29, 31, 33, 41, 65, 74, 103, 105, 129–30, 137, 198
pinecone, 104, 114
Planetary Being, vii, 48, 49, 73, 102, 127, 184, 191–96
planetary hierarchy, 122, 157
Pole Star, 15, 122
Polos, 64
Polydyktes, 53, 56
Poseidon, 53, 54, 66
power, ix, 3, 25, 30, 33, 38, 39, 43, 46, 48, 49, 51, 52, 56, 57, 58–59, 62, 63, 64, 65, 66, 67, 73, 80, 87, 90, 102, 106, 107, 117, 123–24, 137, 142, 159, 167, 178, 182, 184, 189, 191, 197, 199, 200, 202, 203
pregnancy, 66, 114
Prometheus, 25, 53, 72, 73
prophecy, 78, 86, 171, 179, 180, 181
Proserpine, 88, 98, 100, 101, 171
Protestants, 124, 132, 169
Proteus, 68, 72
Psyche, 50, 86–88, 102, 127

Pure Lands of the Buddhas, 177. *See also* Buddha Fields
Purgatory, Mount, 116, 117
Python, 63

Qabalah, 32, 57
quaternio, 175
queen, 36, 51, 62, 70, 96, 100, 126, 143, 144, 145, 149, 154, 171. *See also* Faery Queen
Queen of Heaven, 98, 108, 125, 200

Ragnel, Lady, 183
raven, 136, 154
Rees, Alwyn and Brinley, 170
Reformation, 124, 125, 132, 145
Resurrection, 107, 127, 133, 141
Revelation of John, 108, 119, 120
Rhea, 61
Rig-Veda, 170
Risus, 84
ritual year, 36–37
river, 65, 68, 88, 139, 159, 160–61, 169, 176, 180, 185–86
robe, 16, 42, 76, 77, 113, 138, 142. 153, 173
Roman Catholic Church, 106, 111–13, 116, 127, 132, 145, 169
rosary, 115, 125, 126
rose, 17, 18, 21, 76, 84, 85, 100, 122, 126, 135, 177, 190, 198, 204
rose cross, 17, 198, 201
Rosicrucians, 50, 80, 134, 135, 136, 141, 145, 153, 157, 158, 159, 165, 179, 200. *See also Chymical Marriage of Christian Rosencreutz*
Russell, George (AE), 168

sacrifice, 22, 52, 58, 71, 144, 146, 147, 150, 169
salamanders, 12, 169
salt, 135, 136

Sangyay-Chauma, 173

Saturn, 134, 148, 149

satyr, 55–56

savior, 89–90, 93, 107, 126, 174

Saxons, 170

scapular, 116

scarlet woman, 126

scepter, 156, 172

Scorpio, 4, 153, 164

scrotum, 65

Secret Commonwealth of Elves, Fauns, and Fairies (Kirk), 170

Secret Doctrine, The (Blavatsky), 166

Sergius I, Pope, 113

Serpent, 5, 13, 52, 58–59, 60–61, 62, 67, 68–69, 70, 73, 74–75, 78, 99, 104, 107, 143, 151, 172, 200

Set, 84, 85

sexuality, 55, 56, 59, 81, 85, 92, 114, 154–55

Shakespeare, William, 90

   A Midsummer Night's Dream, 96

Shamballah, 122

shoes, 100, 137. *See also* winged shoes

shrine, building of, 16–24

Shrines of the Blessed Virgin Mary, 112, 114, 115

Sidhe, 169

silver branch, 171–72

Simeon, 112

Sioux Indians, 178

Sirens, 14, 60, 70, 148

Sirius, 112, 122

skull, 143, 151

Snowdonia, 184

Socrates, 79, 82

Soissons, 112

Solomon, Canticles of, 108, 122

Solomon, Temple of, 112

solstice, 194

Sorrowing Mother, 200

Sovereign Lady of Heavenly Space, 173

Spanish Inquisition, 196

Sphinx, 69

staff, 11, 15, 104, 105, 110, 128, 129, 131, 172, 188

"Stanzas of Dyzan," 166

star, 10, 13, 14, 15, 19, 33, 46, 65, 68, 78, 122, 126, 141, 142, 159, 163–64, 190. *See also* Dog Star; Pole Star; Star Maiden

Star, the (Tarot trump), 38, 40, 44

Star Maiden, 44, 50, 200, 201, 202

Sthenno, 58

Stock, Simon, 115–16

Strength, 38

Styx, 88

sun, 10–11, 35, 36, 56, 105, 134, 142, 143, 148–49, 150, 177

Sunray Meditation Society, 178

swastika, 90

sylphs, 169

Talma, Divine Mother, 174

Tarot, 11, 12, 38–39, 40, 42, 44, 78, 79, 139, 184, 192

Temperance, 38, 44

Temple of Wisdom, 58

Theophilus, 113

Thetis, 62

Thomas, Gospel of, 108, 127

Thomas the Rhymer, 171, 180–82

Thrasyllus, 89

throne, 31, 41, 119, 120–21, 138, 143, 173, 174, 180

thunderbird, 178

Tibetan Book of the Dead, The, 70, 172

Tibetan Buddhism, 116, 118, 167, 170, 172–74, 177–78, 185

Tibetan mysticism, 172, 177–78

Titania, 96

Titans, 25, 58, 59–60, 61, 62, 63, 64, 72, 143

Tlepolemus, 86, 89, 90, 91

tokens, 136, 154, 156, 171

tomb, 28, 107, 141
Torquemada, 196
Touch the Earth (anthology), 178
tower, 41, 88, 126, 149, 157, 158, 159,
    161–63, 170, 177, 179, 182, 183
Tower of Olympus, 148, 149–53
Transformations of Lucius Apuleius of
    Madura, The. See Golden Ass, The
tree, 6, 9, 15, 40, 52, 55, 63, 65, 68, 73, 92,
    107, 109, 115–16, 127, 130–31, 135–36,
    146, 147–48, 171, 178, 180, 185, 188
Tree of Life, 19, 25, 32–33, 137, 140, 177
triangle, 19, 142
Tuatha de Danaan, 169, 171
Twilight, 184
Typhaon, 62–63, 69

Ulster, 170
Uncreate Empyreum, 117
Underworld, 41, 45, 48, 50, 53, 56, 58, 62,
    63, 67, 70, 71, 88, 107, 146, 171, 184,
    200
undines, 161, 169
Urania, 118. See also Isis Urania
Uriel, Archangel, 16
Ursa Major/Minor, 15
Uwain, Sir, 182

vault, 133, 146–48, 200
veil, 27, 28, 29, 30, 41, 110, 111, 123,
    129–30, 149, 179
veil of Isis, 105, 110, 133
Venus, 10, 14, 38, 42, 84, 86, 87, 98, 133,
    158, 192, 200
    in The Chymical Marriage, 146–49,
    152, 153, 154, 156
Vesuvius, 62
Virgil, 116–17, 119, 123, 126
    Aeneid, 171
Virgin at the Well, 50, 128–31

Virgin of Lights, 137–53
Virgin of the Rocks (da Vinci), 124
virgins, 25, 35, 52, 83, 89, 108, 109, 110,
    118, 123, 126, 137, 143, 144, 152
virtues, 113, 121, 154
Vision, A (Yeats), 35
Voices of our Ancestors (Dhyani), 178

Walsingham, 115, 124
watch, 143, 151
water, 4, 14, 15, 20, 42, 44, 54, 65, 75, 88,
    110, 129, 131, 135, 136, 142, 151, 161,
    180, 183, 185, 187, 199
waters of life, 40, 72, 127, 140, 204
weaving, 110–111, 129
"Weddynge of Sir Gawen and Dame
    Ragnell, The," 183
Welsh tradition, 170
Wheel of Fortune, 38, 39. See also Fortuna
wineskins, 84–85
winged horse, 39, 43, 66. See also Pegasus
winged shoes, 54, 56, 75, 77
wisdom, 15–16, 17, 20, 41, 42, 45, 57, 73,
    79, 82, 88, 118, 119, 126, 136, 140,
    141, 152, 154, 156, 173–74, 179, 204.
    See also Pallas Athene
witches, 82, 125
wolf, 41, 64, 184, 185
World, 38, 44, 78
wound, 82, 134, 148, 149

Yama, 176
Yeats, W. B., 35, 167, 168
    A Vision, 35
Yesod, 82, 137
yoga, 172, 177
Yvain (de Troyes), 182–83

Zeus, 52, 59, 61, 62, 63, 65, 67, 73, 88, 123
zodiac, 4, 101, 128, 153